Process and Pattern

Controlled Composition Practice for ESL Students

Of Related Interest:

Communication and Culture: A Reading-Writing Text

by Joan Young Gregg (New York City Technical College of the City University of New York)

For advanced-level ESL and basic writing classes: an integrated approach that develops writing, reading, listening, and speaking—with the emphasis on writing—and features college-level readings on cultural topics.

Science and Society: A Reading-Writing Text

by Joan Young Gregg and Joan Russell (both of New York City Technical College of the City University of New York)

For intermediate ESL students: an integrated-language approach that prepares students for academic/career coursework with readings and topics from academic disciplines.

Past, Present, and Future: A Reading-Writing Text

by Joan Young Gregg and Joan Russell (both of New York City Technical College of the City University of New York)

For low-intermediate, first college-level ESL courses: an integrated-language approach that emphasizes writing and features readings on cultural subjects from both American and cross-cultural perspectives.

Copy, Combine, and Compose: Controlling Composition

by Roseann Dueñas Gonzalez, Marycarmen E. Cruz, and Ann Barger (all of the University of Arizona)

For ESL and basic writing students: carefully paced, controlled composition practice that improves language skills and instills new self-confidence.

Communicating Effectively in English

by Patricia A. Porter and Margaret Grant (both of San Francisco University)

This innovative text is specially designed to teach ESL students important oral communication skills—including interviewing, small group discussion, and oral presentation.

Process and Pattern

Controlled Composition Practice for ESL Students

Charles Miguel Cobb

Wadsworth Publishing Company
Belmont, California
A Division of Wadsworth, Inc.

Wadsworth Publishing Company
A Division of Wadsworth, Inc.

Printed in the United States of America
10 9 8 7 6 5 4 3 2 —89 88 87 86 85

Library of Congress Cataloging in Publication Data

Cobb, Charles M.
  Process and pattern.

  Bibliography: p.
  Includes index.
  1. English language—Text-books for foreign speakers.
I. Title.
PE1128.C6664 1984   808'.042   84-7586
ISBN 0-534-03705-4

Subject Editor: Kevin J. Howat
Manuscript Editor: Stephan Bodian
Production: Stacey C. Sawyer, San Francisco
Text Design: Nancy Benedict
Cover Design: Nancy Benedict
Illustrations: John Foster and Charles M. Cobb
Typesetting: Thompson Type, San Diego

ISBN 0-534-03705-4

To Betty Woehrle
Who gave much more than she ever took,
Who was a greater inspiration than she ever knew.

Preface

Process and Pattern: Controlled Composition Practice for ESL Students is designed as a basic writing text for the high intermediate or advanced ESL student and for those native speakers of English who might have dialect interference. The terms *high intermediate* and *advanced* are general, and students may vary widely within a given class or between different institutions. For these reasons, the exercises in each section range from fairly easy to difficult. *Process and Pattern* is based on two concepts: First, students learn to write by writing, not by filling in blanks in exercise books; second, writing is a process that can be taught and learned. The book has three parts: The first part focuses on the paragraph as a unit; The second part shows the student how to combine paragraphs into longer compositions; The third part introduces the useful skills of summary writing and evaluation.

After introducing the paragraph and its structure, including the topic sentence and the outline, the book progresses from narration (usually the easiest) through description and exposition to argumentation. Each chapter builds on the skills of the previous lessons, and the Writing Practice exercises increase in difficulty. Because this book is designed for the student "in transition," all of the possible patterns of paragraph development are not given. The ones most commonly used are the ones taught. The emphasis throughout is on the kinds of writing a student will face in college and career. The examples are from all disciplines including business, science, and technology.

Each chapter—with the exception of Chapter Four, which introduces exposition—has a range of exercises increasing in difficulty and making use of the most widely used methods of teaching writing skills.

1. **Sentence combining.** Teaches variety in sentence patterns, use of phrases and clauses, elimination of redundancy, use of transitions and conjunctions.

2. **Sentence sequencing.** Teaches seriation, the following of steps in a process.

3. **Controlled writing.** Requires students to follow the pattern of a model paragraph while making minor changes, and to follow standard sentence and paragraph structure. Teaches effective use of phrases and clauses.

4. **Guided writing.** Allows students to use any pattern they wish, but presents a model paragraph as a source of ideas.

5. **Free writing.** Gives students suggested topics for each rhetorical mode to help them develop their own ideas and patterns.

This range of exercises allows the instructor to individualize lessons by assigning the more difficult ones to the more able students and the less difficult ones to students who need more controlled practice. There are enough Writing Practice exercises to allow the instructor to tailor the assignments to a particular class or student. Many exercises, especially in the early chapters, might be called "para-writing." They require the student to put pen to paper but do not call for original writing. However, there are also opportunities for the student to write eighty original paragraphs and fifteen longer papers (far too many for each student to do them all, but enough to allow the instructor to be selective). The division of the book into three parts makes it easy for an instructor to adapt the material to a particular course. For example, the section on paragraphs could be taught in one semester or quarter, and the sections on the longer composition, summary, and evaluation in the next.

The concepts taught are recursive; that is, they are presented several times in succeeding chapters in different contexts. For example, the difference between concrete examples and generalities is first emphasized in the chapter on definition and is highlighted throughout. There is emphasis on the fact that essays are rarely written in only one rhetorical mode. By the time the student has reached Chapter Six he or she is asked to write paragraphs from a list of information. This feature serves as an introduction to research: finding information and using it in an original paper.

The tone of the instructions and the subject matter of the model paragraphs and exercises change as the book progresses. The earlier exercises are oriented toward ESL students in the kinds of subject matter and types of exercises. By Chapter Ten there has been a gradual shift to the kinds of materials taught in a non-ESL class. Sentence structure and vocabulary (although still controlled) are identical to that of any pre-freshman English class. Students who work their way through all twelve chapters should be able to enter and do well in a regular English class.

Although certain grammatical and rhetorical elements have been woven into the text of each chapter, where they may be taught most effectively, this volume also includes a handbook that presents such material in a more orderly fashion. The handbook includes an outline of English grammar, a presentation of English sentence patterns and ways to combine them for infinite variety, and a guide to punctuation. Although not a complete grammar text, this outline stresses those elements most needed by ESL students and offers many exercises for practice and understanding. Key grammatical concepts are cross-referenced in the text. The appendices also include topics for composition, a guide to spelling, and standard correction symbols.

The vocabulary is controlled. It is based on the 5000 most-used words in English as given in *The New Horizon Ladder Dictionary of the English Language* (Signet, paperback). Words not in that dictionary are glossed in context. Most of the exercises and all of the concepts and patterns have been field-tested in intermediate and advanced ESL classes in the Los Angeles Community College District.

This is a text that needs a teacher. Students have questions and problems that are so varied (and interesting) that it would be impossible to design a book that could "out-guess" them. Each time a given lesson has been tried, different problems have arisen and different questions have been asked. Yet, in all classes, the process has worked successfully.

In closing, I would like to thank the following reviewers for their helpful suggestions: Jon Amastae, the University of Texas at El Paso; Richard Appelbaum, Broward Community College; Whitney Carpenter, Montgomery County Community College; Barbara Cohen, Wagner College; Dorothy Danielson, San Francisco State University; Mary Evans, Amarillo College; Charmaine Horvath, Kent State University; Lisa A. Mets, Vincennes University; John Ohst, Onondaga Community College; Kenton Sutherland, Canada College; and David Winsper, Springfield Technical Community College.

Charles M. Cobb

Contents

PART ONE
WRITING PARAGRAPHS

Chapter One

Introduction to the Paragraph

Definition

Kinds of Paragraphs

The Topic Sentence

The Controlling Idea

Outlining

Illustration 1.1

The smallest unit of meaningful communication when we speak is the word. It is possible to give much meaning to single words such as "Yes," "No," "Help!" or "Me?." However, when people speak, they usually use phrases and clauses to make their meaning clearer than it can be made with single words.

When people write, they usually write in complete sentences (main clauses). When you write for school or business, it is almost always a requirement that you use complete sentences. Composition teachers get very upset about what they call a *frag* (a fragmentary or incomplete sentence).

If you look at a book or a business letter, you will see that the next-largest unit of writing is the *paragraph*. The symbol in Illustration 1.1 (a kind of backward capital *P*) stands for the word *paragraph*. Many people believe that the paragraph is the basic unit of written communication. When we speak, we do not really speak in paragraphs; when we write, we almost always use paragraphs. After you learn to write good paragraphs, you will be able to combine them into longer papers, essays, even books!

Definition

A paragraph is a group of sentences about one idea. The paragraph tells the reader what the idea or topic is. It explains or describes the idea in some detail. If the idea is simple, the paragraph will be short. If the idea is complicated, the paragraph will be longer. Most paragraphs are from 50 to 300 words long.

 ## Model Paragraph

English is a strange language (1). It is very confusing to people who learned another language first and are trying to learn English (2). My friend Vinh Dao is confused about the difference between "the house burned up" and "the house burned down" (3). He wants to know if "the house burned up" means that the fire started at the bottom of the house and if "the house burned down" means the fire started on the roof (4). I explain that they both mean the same thing (5). He walks away, shakes his head, and says that English is not a logical language (6).

Analysis

This paragraph presents a single idea: "English is a strange language" (sentence 1). It limits the idea of strangeness to people who learned another language first (sentence 2). The reader knows that the paragraph is not going to tell about *all* of the ways English is strange but only about how it can confuse nonnative speakers. The third and fourth sentences give a specific example of the confusion. The fifth sentence makes it clear why the two phrases are confusing. The last sentence concludes by telling the main idea again in different words. This short paragraph, only 99 words, is a small but complete composition.

Note that the first line of the paragraph starts farther in than the rest of the lines. Starting the first line farther in is called *indenting*. Indenting the first line of each paragraph tells the reader that a new idea is going to be presented. It is a signal to the reader, like starting each sentence with a capital letter and ending it with a period, exclamation mark, or question mark. Illustration 1.2 shows how a paragraph looks on a standard sheet of 8½-inch by 11-inch notebook paper.

THIS IS HOW A PARAGRAPH LOOKS ON A SHEET OF STANDARD
8½" x 11" NOTEBOOK PAPER.
1. Write on every other line.
2. Do not write in the margin (left of the red line).
3. Do not write on the back; use another sheet.
4. Put name and date in upper right-hand corner.

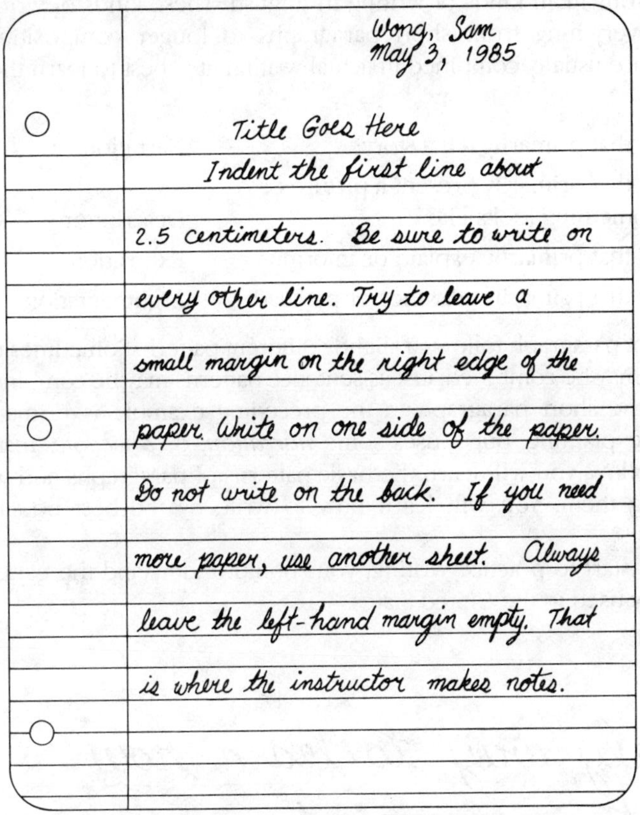

Wong, Sam
May 3, 1985

Title Goes Here

Indent the first line about

2.5 centimeters. Be sure to write on

every other line. Try to leave a

small margin on the right edge of the

paper. Write on one side of the paper.

Do not write on the back. If you need

more paper, use another sheet. Always

leave the left-hand margin empty. That

is where the instructor makes notes.

If you have made many changes and corrections on your paper, write it over neatly. A messy paragraph is hard to read.

Illustration 1.2

You will need to know how to write paragraphs because they are considered to be the basic units of written communication both in school and in business. Essays, essay examinations, reports, research papers, business articles, manuals, and stories are all written in paragraph form. Most of these kinds of writing are more than one paragraph long, but the way to start is to learn how to write the four main types of paragraphs. When you know how to do that, it will be easy to combine several paragraphs into a longer paper.

Kinds of Paragraphs

There are four main kinds of writing in English. These kinds of writing are used in everything from short paragraphs to longer compositions. Although they are usually combined in actual writing, it is best to learn them separately.

Paragraphs that primarily tell a story:	Narration
Paragraphs that primarily present a picture or tell what something looks like:	Description
Paragraphs that primarily explain or inform:	Exposition
Paragraphs that primarily convince or persuade:	Argumentation

Each kind of paragraph follows a slightly different pattern. Sometimes the different kinds may be combined, just as sentence patterns may be combined. For example, the short paragraph in the preceding example is primarily *exposition,* or explaining, but it uses some *narration,* or *anecdote.* In the chapters that follow, you will learn the basic patterns of paragraphs and will practice writing them. You will learn how to write by the best possible method: writing!

Before you start to practice writing, you should understand the pattern most commonly used in the United States.

The only way to learn how to write is by writing.

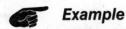 **Example**

Time Wasted

Enrolling and registering in college can be a long process (1). Last semester I had to wait in line for nearly an hour just to hand in my application for enrollment (2). At enrollment time, I had to spend another hour picking the classes I wanted and the correct times (3). Then I had to wait in another line for two hours to enroll (4). When I reached the front of the line, I found that two of my classes were "closed" (5). They were already filled (6). I had to find other classes at other times, stand in line again, try again (7). Finally, I was able to get four of the five classes I needed (8). It took almost the whole day, and I still do not have one of the classes that I need (9).

This paragraph is typical of the kind of direct writing expected by readers in the United States. It starts by telling clearly what the paragraph is going to be about. The first sentence gives the *topic:* "enrolling and registering in college." It also gives the *controlling idea:* "can be a long process." The rest of the paragraph (called the *body*) is brief and gives specific examples of how much time was spent at each part of the process. The last sentence tells the final result of the long process. Even the title helps to tell the reader what the paragraph is going to be about.

To people from other cultures, this pattern (often called *the American pattern*) may seem impolite. The American way of "getting right to the point" (see Illustration 1.3) may seem blunt. People who have been raised in the

Illustration 1.3
American Pattern

Near East use a different pattern (see Illustration 1.4). They tend to use several ideas that are similar to one another and to connect them with statements that are not directly part of the main purpose. People raised in an Asian culture tend to circle around the main idea before they finally state it (see Illustration 1.5). Even then, the main idea may not be as bluntly stated as it is in the American pattern.

Those who have learned to write in the Romance Language pattern (French, Italian, Spanish, Portuguese, Romanian) have a different way of presenting their ideas. They tend to skip to other related topics before they present the main idea (see Illustration 1.6). These other patterns are more polite than the

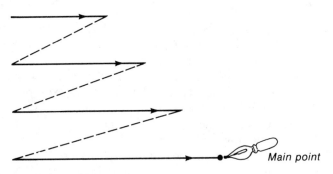

Main point

Illustration 1.4
Near Eastern Pattern

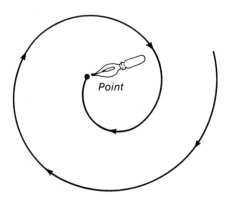

Point

Illustration 1.5
Asian Pattern

Illustration 1.6
Romance Language Pattern

American style of writing. Even when the main idea is reached, it is not often stated as bluntly as it is in the United States.

This direct pattern, in which the writer gets to the point immediately, is used frequently in *exposition* and *argumentation*. Most of the writing that you will do in college will be one of these two types.

The Topic Sentence

The pattern used in the United States and many other countries emphasizes the direct statement of the main idea at the beginning of the paragraph. This statement is called the *topic sentence*. It is usually the first or second sentence of the paragraph. Most often it is a single, declarative sentence that tells the reader exactly what the paragraph is going to be about. It is a promise that you, the writer, make to your reader. The topic sentence has two parts:

1. *The topic* (the subject matter, what it is about)
2. *The controlling idea* (feeling or belief about the topic)

The Topic

The topic must be selected very carefully. Many student writers pick a topic that is too general, too broad, to be written about in a single paragraph or short essay.

 ### Examples

Topics That Are Too General

1. Animals (It would be impossible to write about all of the animals in the world from the distant past until today.)
2. Animals of today (Still too general; there are thousands of different kinds.)
3. Animals that live with people (A little better, but is the paragraph going to include rats and mice?)
4. Domestic animals (More limited, but too broad—farm animals? pets?)
5. Cats (Well, much less general than "Animals," but still too broad.)

Topics That Could Be Written About

1. Feeding a cat
2. Training a cat (if possible)
3. The cats on my street
4. How to get a cat
5. How to get rid of a cat

It is possible to write a paragraph about these topics because they are *limited* enough. They do not promise the reader more than the writer can cover in a single paragraph. Sometimes it is necessary to limit a topic several times before you have one that can be clearly and completely written about.

 ### Example

Pollution → water pollution → water pollution in streams → nonchemical pollution in streams → the trash in the stream near my house (a possible topic)

 ### Limiting Practice

Directions: In each of the following groups of statements, decide which one is the most general or covers the broadest topic. Put the number 1 in front of it. Then decide which ones are less general (more specific). Put the numbers 2, 3, and 4 in front of them. Use number 4 for the statement that is the most limited.

 ### Example

0. __3__ a. Lan Sing goes fishing every week.

    __1__ b. Lan Sing enjoys being out of doors.

    __2__ c. Lan Sing prefers the mountains to the beach.

    __4__ d. Lan Sing caught a six-pound bass last Saturday.

The most general statement is *b*. "Out of doors" is very general. Write the number 1 in front of that statement. Statement *d* is the most specific. It is limited to one particular event: one day, one fish. Write the number 4 in front of that statement. Of the other two statements, which is more general, the one about the mountains or the one about fishing? Of course, fishing is more limited than going to the mountains. Statement *a* would be 3, and statement *c* would be 2.

1. __3__ a. The Ventura Freeway is crowded.

    __2__ b. Traffic is very bad today.

    __4__ c. Cars could go only 15 miles per hour today.

    __1__ d. Transportation in the city is difficult.

2. __3__ a. Prices are higher than last year.

    __4__ b. A loaf of bread now costs $1.45.

    __2__ c. Food is expensive.

    __1__ d. Each year it costs more to live.

3. __1__ a. Hamid is a sports fan.

    __3__ b. Hamid prefers team sports to individual sports.

    __4__ c. Hamid buys season tickets to soccer games.

    __2__ d. Hamid goes to many sports events.

4. __1__ a. I enjoy traveling.

    __2__ b. I prefer to drive on trips.

    __4__ c. I am planning a trip in my pickup truck.

    __3__ d. I like to travel on the ground, not in the air.

5. __1__ a. America has a major health problem.

    __2__ b. Many Americans are overweight.

    __3__ c. One person out of five is too fat.

    __4__ d. You need to lose 10 pounds.

Limiting Practice

Directions: Each of the following topics is too general to be the subject of a paragraph. Take each topic and make it more and more specific. The final topic must be limited enough to be written about in a paragraph. Use the exercise about pollution as an example. Write the topic as a complete declarative sentence on your own paper. Declarative sentences are explained on page 283.

1. Greetings   6. Education
2. Customs   7. Politics
3. Health   8. Television
4. Exercise   9. Automobiles
5. Families   10. Children

Except for narration, which tells a story, *every* paragraph needs a limited topic and a controlling idea. These two parts are usually written as a single sentence called the *topic sentence*. The next section will explain how to develop a *controlling idea* and give you some practice doing so.

The Controlling Idea

The controlling idea tells your reader exactly what part of the limited topic you are going to write about. It tells what you believe to be true about the topic. It may tell how you feel about the topic.

 ### Examples

Topic: loud rock music
Controlling idea: might make people deaf
Topic sentence: Listening too long to loud rock music can lead to hearing loss.

Topic: cats
Controlling idea: are good pets
Topic sentence: A cat can be a very good pet.

Topic: failure in college
Controlling idea: caused by not planning time wisely
Topic sentence: Many students fail in college because they do not plan their time wisely.

Topic: television comedies
Controlling idea: not really funny
Topic sentence: Most television "situation comedies" are not really funny.

Topic: large families
Controlling idea: not common now
Topic sentence: Large families with seven or eight children are not as common as they were 30 years ago.

Writing Practice

Directions: Complete each of the following limited topics with a controlling idea to make a topic sentence that could be used to develop a paragraph.

1. Studying psychology in college (benefits?)
2. Violence in television programs (effect on children, adults?)
3. Getting up early in the morning (good or bad?)
4. Living in a large city (good or bad points?)
5. Living in a small town (good or bad points?)

The topic sentence tells the reader the subject of the paragraph and makes a statement about that subject. It is the base for the rest of the paragraph. Every other sentence will support the topic sentence. The other sentences may give definitions, offer examples, present facts or opinions, but *in all cases* they must be about the topic sentence. For example, if your topic sentence states that many students fail in college because they do not use time wisely, you would not write about other causes for failure (laziness, family problems, or illness). To do so would break the promise you made to your reader in the topic sentence.

Writing Practice (Original Paragraph)

Directions: Choose one of the topic sentences you developed in the previous Writing Practice and write a paragraph of eight to ten sentences. Do not worry too much about making this paragraph "perfect," for it can be used to show you your strengths and weaknesses.

$T + CI = TS$

Topic + Controlling Idea = Topic Sentence

Outlining

The process of making and using an *outline* can be most useful for any kind of writing. An outline is a *brief* list of the main ideas a writer has decided to use when he or she develops a paragraph. The main purpose of outlining is to let you see, in a simple form, the overall plan of the ideas and examples you will use. It is possible to outline an entire essay on a single page. You can then arrange and rearrange the parts, add items, and take out whatever you do not like before you start to write. One good outline can save time and help you to organize your material in the best possible way.

There are many ways to organize an outline. This section will emphasize one that is widely used, *category order.* A *category* is a group of items that are similar to one another. Men, women, children, and babies are all members of the category called "people." Ants, flies, bees, butterflies, and cockroaches are all members of the category called "insects." Certainly, a bee and a butterfly are different, but they are more alike than a bee and a baby.

 Example

Here is a list of items a student found in his pockets:

house key	driver's license	$1 bill
$5 bill	library card	key to bicycle lock
two nickels	gum wrapper	credit card
car keys	student I.D.	social security card
one dime	matchbook	six pennies
key ring	wallet	cigarettes

It is possible to separate these items into several categories according to where they were found.

1. Things found in left front trousers pocket: keys and key ring.
2. Things found in right front trousers pocket: two nickels, one dime, six pennies.
3. Things found in right rear trousers pocket (in a wallet): $5 bill, $1 bill, credit card, driver's license, social security card, library card, student I.D.
4. Things found in left rear trousers pocket: gum wrapper.
5. Things found in shirt pocket: matchbook, cigarettes.

These items are put into categories on the basis of *where* they were found. This outline may be interesting, but it serves no useful purpose. When you make an outline, it should have some purpose. Look again at the list of items, and you will see that the contents of the pockets fall into four obvious groups:

I. Keys

II. Money

III. Cards

IV. Other items (matches, cigarettes, gum wrapper)

Of these groups, the first three contain useful items. Suppose you were going to make an outline for a paragraph about necessary things people carry in their pockets. You would start just as the previous list does. You might add some details.

I. Keys
  A. House key
  B. Car keys
  C. Bicycle lock key

II. Money
  A. Paper money
  B. Coins

III. Cards
  A. Credit card
  B. Social security card
  C. Library card
  D. Student I.D. card

This is a useful outline of the necessary contents of the student's pockets, with one exception. Is a social security card necessary? Probably it should be left out. Why include the wallet and key ring?

Note that there are three main divisions. Each main division has two or more subclasses. It would be possible to make even more divisions if you wanted to put *everything* in the outline. Take main class II, for example:

II. Money
  A. Paper money
    1. $5 bill
    2. $1 bill
  B. Coins
    1. Two nickels
    2. One dime
    3. Six pennies

It is usually not necessary to go into such great detail in an outline. The *outline* is supposed to tell the main parts; save the details for the paragraph.

The finished standard outline (actually used by a student to write a paragraph) looked like this:

Necessities of Life

Topic sentence: Most of the things a person carries around in his pockets (*topic*) are needed every day (*controlling idea*).

I. For buying things
   A. Money
   B. Credit cards

II. For security
   A. Keys for home
   B. Keys for transportation

III. For identification
   A. Driver's license
   B. Student I.D.
   C. Library card

Concluding sentence: It would be difficult to get through the day without all of the things I carry around with me.

The complete paragraph written from this outline was a little bit different. The student decided that those items he needed for buying things were less important than the keys he needed to get from home to stores. He decided to put security first. The finished paragraph showed why each category was necessary for a student to go through a day from home to school to work to shop and back home again. He added details and examples to the outline as he wrote.

The process of developing an outline is much the same for most types of writing.

1. Start with either a topic or a list of data.

2. Develop a topic sentence. What are you going to do with your data, or what kind of data do you need to explain your topic?

3. Investigation: Get all the information you can about the topic if you start with just a topic. Some information you will use when you write, some you will not. (For example, this student did not use the cigarettes, matches, or social security card when he decided on his final topic sentence. He did not think it important to state that he carried the keys on a ring or the cards and paper money in his wallet.)

4. Categorize your data or items. Put them into groups based on how they are alike. Do not be afraid to get rid of some items that do not fit your purpose.

5. Arrange your categories in the way you think will be most useful in explaining your topic sentence.

6. Decide if you need to change your topic sentence. Perhaps you might have more *useless* than useful items in your pockets or your purse.

7. Decide on an interesting concluding sentence.

8. Write a title that fits the paragraph.

Suggestion

Do not try to make a correct outline first. Take a piece of paper and write a "jot list" first. A "jot list" is a list of all of the ideas that enter your mind when you think about a topic. Just jot them down (that is, write them down briefly). Then cross out the ones you do not plan to use (see Illustration 1.7, page 18).

It is always possible that the information you gather might change your topic sentence. You might list the items in your pocket or purse and decide that the best topic sentence would be "Most of the things that people carry around with them are unimportant." You would have to change the topic sentence to agree with the information and the data. Otherwise, the paragraph would not be honest.

Writing Practice (Categorizing)

Directions: Look closely at the three lists of food. Divide them into three main classes. List the individual items under each of the main headings given.

Title: ___Various   kinds   of   food.___

   I. Food from animals

     A. From four-legged animals

       1. ___Pork___

       2. ___Beef___

       3. ___Hamburger.___

Topic: Movies

Star Wars   } any   ~~Gandhi~~
Return of Jedi   } more ?   ~~Annie~~
Empire Strikes Back   )   ~~Turning Point~~
~~Tootsie~~   ~~Flashdance~~
E.T.   Close Encounters
~~Jaws in 3D~~   Star Trek
Alien   ~~Halloween~~
~~Towering Inferno~~   ~~Friday 13th~~
Superman (II + III too)   ~~Poseidon Adv.~~

Topic: Kinds of popular movies
            Science Fiction
            Love Stories
            Horror Stories

Topic Sentence: Science Fiction movies are
                      popular entertainment

Check Newspaper !!   * Star Trek III
                                (maybe IV ?)

Illustration 1.7
Jot List

B. From other animals
    1. _Egg._
    2. _Fish_
    3. _chicken_

II. Food that is harvested

    A. From trees
        1. _Banana_
        2. _Oranges_
        3. _Apples_

    B. From the ground
        1. _Rice._
        2. _Peas._
        3. _Celery._

III. Food that must be prepared
    A. _Noodles_
    B. _Bread_
    C. _Soup_

List of Foods

bananas	chicken	apples
rice	fish	soup
pork	beef	hamburger
oranges	bread	eggs
noodles	ants	peas
lions	celery	bones

What is the topic?
What would be a good controlling idea?
Put a title on your outline.

Writing Practice (Categorizing)

Directions: Following are four lists of items. In each list there is one item that is more general than the rest; it will be the *topic*. Arrange the other items into groups according to similarities. In each list there will be some items that do not fit any category (like lions, ants, and bones in the previous Writing Practice); do not use them. Write the arrangement using the following form. The main divisions are not listed. You will have to develop your own.

Topic: _____ *Language* _____

I. _____ *English is the more common langue in the world.* _____

    math.

  A. _____ *ENGLISH* _____

  B. _____ *Spanish* _____

  C. _____ *FRENCH* _____

II. _____ *Three dimentional art* _____

    Two dimenction art.

  A. _____ *Smiling*   *Sculpting*   *Painting* _____

  B. _____ *Carving*   *sketching* _____

  C. _____ *Modeling*   *Drawing* _____

III. _____

  A. _____ *Countries.* _____

  B. _____ *California* _____

  C. _____ *Mexico* _____

List 1.

②geometry	①French	calendar
①English	②algebra	③geology
③physics	③chemistry	college classes
confusion	①Spanish	②calculus

List 2.

①painting	①fine arts *Sound*	sculpting
operas	symphonies	concerts
Music swimming	modeling	①drawing
sketching	smiling	carving

List 3.

⓪pigs	⓪cows	②eagles
⓪animals	⓪bears	dogs
①tigers	roses	sharks
②sparrows	②crows	①lions

List 4.

Mexico②	California	Iran③
Viet Nam②	Peru①	El Salvador①
Iraq③	China②	Chicago
Korea②	countries	Turkey③

UP TO

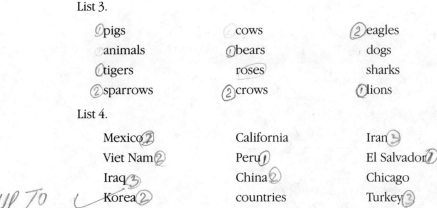

 ## Writing Practice (Guided Writing)

Directions: Look back at the outline developed from items in a student's pocket. Make a list of what you have in your pocket, purse, or wallet. Organize the list into groups based on the similarities of the items. Decide which three groups are the most important. Choose a topic and a controlling idea, and write an outline similar to the example. Select a title for your outline. Put the objects back into your purse, pockets, or wallet.

 ## Writing Practice (Alternate Assignment)

Directions: Following the same method, make your list from one of these other topics.

1. The kinds of books you have
2. The things in your bedroom
3. The items in the glove compartment of your car
4. The things you carry in your backpack

 ## Writing Practice (Using the Outline)

Directions: Now write a paragraph based on the outline you made.

Chapter Two

The Narrative Paragraph

Kinds of Narrative

Transitions

Narration is the kind of writing that tells a story or relates an event. The story may be very short to present a single incident. It may be longer to present a more detailed account of the event. It may be many pages long to tell about the life of a person or the history of a country.

Kinds of Narrative

Supposed to be true.

When a narration, or *narrative,* tells the true story of a person or a country, it is called *nonfiction.* When the story is not true but is "made up," it is called *fiction.* The ability to write narration will be useful when you need to explain something. (For example, the paragraph on page 4 that tells how English can be confusing uses an *anecdote* [a short bit of narration] about the writer's friend as an example of the confusion.) The purpose of writing fiction is to amuse, to entertain, or sometimes to teach a lesson.

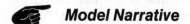 ### Model Narrative

The Easy Way

One afternoon last summer, I went for a walk along the beach as soon as I could leave work (1). My work had made me rush, rush, rush all week (2). I wanted to relax (3). Ahead of me on the beach I saw a man and a woman (4). She was sitting on a blanket on the sand, and he was fishing (5). He had a fishing pole at least 3 meters long (6). First, he put some bait on the hook (7). Then he threw the baited hook as far out into the ocean as he could (8). Next, he put the pole in a metal holder that kept it upright (9). Finally, when the pole was properly placed, he went over and sat down by the woman (10). She poured him a cup of coffee, and he relaxed on the blanket (11). When I walked up to them, he smiled and said to me, "Well, I have done my part. Now it is up to the fish to catch themselves" (12). As I walked on down the beach, I thought to myself, "Why must I rush so much?" (13) Perhaps in my work I could just let "the fish catch themselves" (14).

Analysis (Structure)

Introduction: The first three sentences tell *when, where,* and *why* the action takes place. Telling when and where is called the *scene,* or the *setting.* Sentence 4 introduces the *characters,* or the people in the story. Sentences 5 through 12 narrate the action that takes place. The action is presented in *chronological* (time) order. Sentence 12 brings the action to a close. Sentences 13 and 14 conclude the brief narration by giving the writer's reason for telling it. They also give the moral, or lesson, that the writer learned from the incident and explain why the narrative was written.

 ## Model Narrative

The Easy Way

One afternoon last summer, I *went* for a walk along the beach as soon as I could leave work (1). My work *had made* me rush, rush, rush all week (2). I *wanted* to relax (3). Ahead of me on the beach I *saw* a man and a woman (4). She *was sitting* on a blanket on the sand, and he *was fishing* (5). He *had* a fishing pole at least 3 meters long (6). First, he *put* some bait on the hook (7). Then he *threw* the baited hook as far out into the ocean as he could (8). Next, he *put* the pole in a metal holder that kept it upright (9). Finally, when the pole was properly placed, he *went* over and *sat* down by the woman (10). She *poured* him a cup of coffee, and he *relaxed* on the blanket (11). When I *walked* up to them, he *smiled* and *said* to me, "Well, I *have done* my part. Now it is up to the fish to catch themselves" (12). As I *walked* on down the beach, I *thought* to myself, "Why must I rush so much?" (13) Perhaps in my work I could just let "the fish catch themselves" (14).

Analysis (Grammar)

Most narratives are told in the past tense. See page 214 for kinds of past tense. They relate what has already happened. The simple past is used: *I went, I saw, he had, he put, he threw,* and so on. The past perfect is also used: *had made, have done.* Some use is also made of the past progressive: *was sitting, was fishing.* It would be possible to use the present or the present progressive tenses in a narrative, but that is rarely done. It would also be possible to retell this narrative using only the simple past tense, but the other tenses give it a variety of sentence patterns.

Model Narrative

The Easy Way

One afternoon last summer, I went for a walk along the beach as soon as I could leave work (1). My work had made me rush, rush, rush all week (2). I wanted to relax (3). Ahead of me on the beach I saw a man and a woman (4). She was sitting on a blanket on the sand, and he was fishing (5). He had a fishing pole at least 3 meters long (6). First, he put some bait on the hook (7). Then he threw the baited hook as far out into the ocean as he could (8). Next, he put the pole in a metal holder that kept it upright (9). Finally, when the pole was properly placed, he went over and sat down by the woman (10). She poured him a cup of coffee, and he relaxed on the blanket (11). When I walked up to them, he smiled and said to me, "Well, I have done my part. Now it is up to the fish to catch themselves" (12). As I walked on down the beach, I thought to myself, "Why must I rush so much?" (13) Perhaps in my work I could just let "the fish catch themselves" (14).

Analysis (Coherence)

This narrative has *coherence,* which means that it is tied together. It is not choppy or childish.

Choppy paragraph: The man put some bait on the hook. The man threw the baited hook as far out to sea as the man could. The man put the pole in a holder. When the pole was properly placed, the man went over and sat down by the woman. The woman poured the man a cup of coffee.

This writer has made the narrative flow smoothly by using three devices:

1. He repeats key words or phrases (*pole, hook*).
2. He uses pronouns instead of repeating nouns.
3. He uses transition words.

Transitions

Transitions are words used to join the ideas in a sentence. The root of the word *transition* means "to carry over." Transitions carry over the idea from one sentence to the next. They may be single words, phrases, or clauses. The writer of this brief narrative uses simple adverbs to show the time relationship between the ideas in this paragraph (*once, first, then, next, finally, now, when*). There are other adverbs that are especially useful for narrative writing:

Transition words·

accordingly	first, second, third, etc.	likewise
also	finally	meanwhile
always	furthermore	next
anyhow	hence	still
besides	last	then
consequently	later	therefore

Other adverbs and how they work in sentences are explained on pages 242–243. Sometimes *phrases* are used to tie sentences together (*after all, at the same time, by the way, for example*).

Subordinators (subordinate conjunctions) are commonly used as transitions. Whenever you use one of these words as a transition, be sure to remember that grammatically they make the clause *subordinate*; it is neither a main clause nor a complete sentence. For more information on subordinators, see pages 253–254.

Subordinator	Meaning	Example
after	later in time	I arrived *after* they left.
as	during that time	*As* I drove home, it began to snow.
before	earlier in time	*Before* you fish, bait the hook.
once	as soon as	*Once* you have baited it, throw it into the water.
since	from a former time to now	I have not caught a fish *since* last year.
until	up to a certain time but no longer	I will stay here *until* I catch a fish.
when	at that time	I will stop fishing *when* I catch one.
whenever	every time	*Whenever* I go fishing, my feet get wet.
while	during that time	*While* I was not looking, a giant fish ate my bait.

Writing Practice (Sentence Combining)

Directions: Sentence combining is a helpful way to practice making mature sentences out of shorter, choppy ones. Combine each of the following groups of simple sentences into one longer sentence. Make either compound, complex, or compound-complex sentences. (See page 265.) The transitions or conjunctions in parentheses are suggestions. You may use others if you wish.

 ## Example

   1. a. My father was a tall man. (*first idea*)

      b. My father was a strong man. (*second idea*)

      c. My father had a large mustache. (*third idea*)

   1. My father was a tall, strong man with a large mustache. (*All three ideas combined into one sentence.*)

 ## Example

   2. a. The children shaved off the cat's hair. (*since*)

      b. They were sent to bed.

      c. They were bad.

      d. They had no dinner. (*without*)

   2. Since the bad children shaved off the cat's hair, they were sent to bed without dinner.

   2. Since the children were bad and shaved off the cat's hair, they were sent to bed without dinner.

There is no one correct way to combine sentences; there may be more than one acceptable result.

 ## Suggestion

Look at the sentences to be combined. Cross out the parts that are repeated in each sentence. Then combine what is left into one sentence.

 ## Example

   3. a. Early travelers rode horses.

      b. ~~The horses were~~ shaggy.

c. ~~Early travellers used~~ sailboats.

d. ~~The sailboats were~~ small.

e. ~~Early travellers~~ walked. (*and*)

f. ~~They walked~~ from place to place.

g. ~~They walked~~ often.

3. Early travelers rode shaggy horses, used small sailboats, and often walked from place to place.

Read the following sentences. They are from an *anecdotal record* used in a psychology class. First combine each group into a larger sentence. Then combine them into a paragraph.

1. a. Sally and Sarah are twins.
   b. ~~Sally and Sarah are~~ identical.
   c. ~~Sally and Sarah are~~ twelve years old.

2. a. They wear similar clothes.
   b. ~~They have~~ similar hairstyles.
   c. ~~They wear~~ identical necklaces.

3. a. ~~They look alike.~~
   b. ~~They look~~ very much alike.
   c. They talk alike.
   d. They walk alike.

4. a. Teachers cannot tell one from the other.
   b. Strangers cannot tell one from the other.
   c. Their mother has trouble. (*even*)
   d. She has trouble sometimes.

5. a. Sally likes to read. (*however*)
   b. Sarah likes to play games. (*while*)
   c. Sally likes to study math.
   d. Sarah likes sports.

6. a. Sally likes boys.
   b. Sarah likes boys.
   c. Sally is shy with boys. (*but*)
   d. Sarah is not shy with boys.

7. a. They look alike.
   b. They dress alike.
   c. They do not act alike. (*yet*)
   d. Sally is an individual.
   e. Sarah is an individual.

Check: Refer to pages 233–237 to make sure that subjects and verbs agree in number. See pages 214–231 to make sure that you have used the right tense of the verbs. Your narrative should be seven sentences long.

 ### Writing Practice (Selecting the Correct Order)

Directions: Read the following sentences. Then arrange them in the correct time order. Look for clues, such as dates or transitions like *first, later,* or *finally.* Look also for logical arrangement. A person would not go to college before he or she had finished high school.

Example

2 1. Since he was a good soldier, he rose rapidly in rank. (*Military ranks in order of seniority are private, corporal, sergeant, lieutenant, captain, major, colonel, and general.*)

4 2. Later, because of his skill and leadership as a captain, he was made a major.

1 3. Alfred Corgie was born in Boston in the winter of 1776.

7 4. Finally, he reached the high point of his career by being made a general.

5. Not much is known about his life between 1776 and 1792.

6. However, it is known that he enlisted in the army in 1793.

3 7. First he became a sergeant and then a captain.

Which sentence tells when he was born? Are any other dates given as clues? Can you use his military rank as a clue? Which sentence is clearly the last one? Before you look at the finished paragraph, try to write this brief biography in the correct order on your own paper.

Correct Order (written in paragraph form)

The Rewards of Skill

Alfred Corgie was born in Boston in the winter of 1776. Not much is known about his life between 1776 and 1792. However, it is known that he enlisted in the army in 1793. Since he was a good soldier, he rose rapidly in rank. First he became a sergeant and then a captain. Later, because of his skill and leadership as a captain, he was made a major. Finally, he reached the high point of his career by being made a general.

Writing Practice (Correct Order)

Directions: Read the following sentences about the life of Jonathan Swift. Write the sentences in paragraph form in their proper chronological (time) order. Give this true (nonfiction) biography a title.

3 1. After grammar school he went to Trinity College in Dublin.

1 2. Jonathan Swift was born in 1667 in Dublin, Ireland.

9 3. He died in Dublin in 1745 at the age of 78.

8 4. This book tells of the amazing adventures of a ship's doctor.

2 5. His family was poor, so he had to depend on the help of his relatives to go to grammar school.

7 6. He wrote his most famous book, *Gulliver's Travels,* in 1726.

4 7. After graduating from college he went to work for Sir William Temple.

6 8. When living in Ireland, he had much time to write.

5 9. In 1694 Swift left Sir William's home and went back to Ireland.

 ## Writing Practice (Controlled Writing)

Directions: *Controlled writing*—writing that follows a model—will give you practice in putting your own ideas into standard sentence patterns (explained on pages 279–287). Read the model paragraph. Then write a paragraph of your own following the sentence patterns of the model. You do not have to follow the original exactly, but keep as close to it as you can.

 ## Model Paragraph

The Summer

It was early in the evening on a summer day. My father had spread a large cloth on the ground in the back yard. We were all sitting on it. My mother and father, my sister, and myself. It was warm, and there was a soft breeze blowing from the mountains.

Changing the time of year:

The Winter

It was early in the morning on a winter day. My father had spread a blanket on the ground in the back yard. We were all sitting on it. My mother and father, my sister, and myself. It was cold, and there was a chilly breeze blowing from the mountains.

Changing the place and the characters:

The Mountains

It was early in the morning in the winter. I had spread my sleeping bag on the ground under a tall tree. I was sitting on my sleeping bag eating a plate of cold beans. It was cold, and the snow was starting to fall.

You could change the people (make them friends or other relatives; be alone), the place (the beach, the desert), the time of day (noon, afternoon, early morning), the season (spring, fall, winter). There is no one "correct" change.

Directions: Using the preceding model paragraph, write a similar paragraph on your own paper. Give your paragraph a title. Be sure to check for verb tense; the past tense is best for narratives.

Writing Practice (Controlled Writing)

Directions: The following model paragraph tells about the early life of the American inventor Thomas Alva Edison. Following the sentence patterns as closely as possible, write a similar paragraph about someone you know or even about yourself.

Model Paragraph

The Dull Student

Thomas Edison was born in Ohio, the seventh and youngest child of Samuel and Nancy Edison. Even as a small child he was curious about everything. He always asked questions like, "Why is the sky blue?" or "What makes it rain?" When he was sent to school at age seven, he asked so many questions that the schoolteacher beat him with a leather strap and said that Tom was "dull." When Tom told his mother, she took him out of school and taught him herself. His total education in public school lasted three months. Because of his curiosity to find out what made things happen, he developed an interest in electricity and experimented constantly. Eventually, his experiments led to many inventions including the phonograph, the electric light, and motion pictures.

Analysis

The first simple sentence tells of his birth. The second notes his main characteristic. The third gives examples. The fourth, a compound sentence, tells the result of asking too many questions in school. The fifth, also compound, explains his mother's reaction. The sixth simply states the length of his formal schooling. The seventh, a compound sentence, again states another result of his curiosity. The last sentence gives some examples of his experimenting.

Writing Practice (Guided Writing)

Directions: *Guided writing* does not ask you to follow a model exactly. Instead, it presents the ideas that are to be written about in each sentence. You pick the best pattern and structure for each sentence. The model paragraph is part of a student's essay telling how she came to the United States.

Model Paragraph

Leaving Iran

We had to leave Iran because my father was a supporter of the Shah (1). Early in the afternoon, we gathered together what we could carry and managed to get a train to Basra (2). In Basra part of our luggage was lost, but we could not wait for it (3). We had to hurry to catch the last plane leaving for Lisboa in Portugal (4). In Lisboa we waited for three weeks for visas and other papers (5). My father had some money in London, but we could not get any that we had left in Iran (6). Finally we were allowed to get a plane to Brazil (7). We waited in Brazil for four months before we could enter the United States (8). It was a good feeling to get off the plane in Los Angeles and see my cousins waiting for us (9). It took us nearly half a year to travel from Iran to our new home in the United States (10).

Analysis

Each sentence serves a purpose. The first tells the reason for the journey, and the second explains the conditions. Sentence 3 presents a problem faced by the writer (often called the *narrator*) and his family. The fourth and fifth move the story ahead and describe another problem. The next two sentences continue with more movement and another problem. The last two sentences bring the narration to a close and tell the writer's feelings.

Notice that chronological (time) order is necessary to keep the events in the proper sequence. There is also a second kind of order in this paragraph, called *order of climax*. The most important thing to the narrator is that she finally arrived safely in the United States and met her cousins.

Directions: Write a paragraph following the idea patterns given.

1. Tell your reader the location and the people in the story.
2. Tell the reader what kind of action is going to take place. *what*
3. Tell the reader what happened. (This part may be several sentences long *what* and may present the problem to be solved.)
4. Tell the conclusion, the result of the action, the climax.

It might be easier to write a true narrative about what happened to you or to someone you know, but you may invent a fiction story.

Suggested Topics

A trip on a ship or airplane

An interesting event on the way to school

Going from one country to another

A storm you were in

A problem you solved

An incident in traffic

An experience that made you happy (sad, frightened)

Writing Practice (Free Writing)

Directions: *Free writing* allows you to present your own ideas in your own way. Only the general topic is given. Read the following fable.

Model Paragraph

The Lion and the Mouse

Once, when a lion was sleeping, a little mouse began to run up and down on his back. This soon awakened the lion, who placed his huge paw on the mouse and opened his big jaws to eat him. "Please, Lion," cried the mouse, "do not eat me. I am so small that I would be only a mouthful for you. If you will let me go, perhaps I can do something good for you one day." The lion laughed at the thought of a tiny mouse helping him, but he let the mouse go free. Some time later, the lion was caught in a strong net placed by some hunters. He roared and struggled but could not get free. The tiny mouse heard the roars and ran to see what had happened. When he saw the lion, he set to work with his sharp little teeth and soon gnawed the ropes apart. The lion sprang free and thanked the mouse kindly.

Moral: One good turn deserves another.

A fable is a short narrative that is supposed to amuse and to teach a lesson. In many fables, animals talk and act like people. Writing a fable will give you practice in telling a short narrative to illustrate a point. All countries have fables. Some are about animals; others are about people. Here is an old fable from China.

 ## Model Paragraph

Two Tigers

One day Kwan Chuang Tze was walking in the forest. Suddenly a large tiger jumped on him and knocked him down. The tiger was going to eat him. The tiger opened his jaws when another tiger leaped out of the forest. The two tigers both wanted to eat Kwan Chuang Tze, so they began to fight to see which one would get him. Kwan Chuang Tze crawled away and pulled out his sword. He was about to kill one of the tigers when his friend Lansing Yu happened by. "Stop!" cried Lansing Yu. "Do not kill one of the tigers. Let them fight each other. Soon one will kill the other and will be wounded and tired. Wait and you will have to kill only one tiger." Kwan Chuang Tze took his friend's advice, and, sure enough, soon one tiger was dead. The other one was wounded and tired. Kwan Chuang Tze killed the second tiger easily and went home safe and happy.

Moral: Let your enemies fight among themselves.

Home work.

Directions: Write a narrative paragraph in which you tell a fable that you know. It may be one you read in a book or one you remember from when you were young. Be sure there is a point or a purpose to the fable you write.

Write — Moral

Chapter Three

The Descriptive Paragraph

Definition

Uses of Description

Description is the kind of writing that tries to put a picture in the reader's mind. Description tells how something looks or sounds or tastes or smells or feels.

Definition

A good way for you to learn how to write a descriptive paragraph is to start with a *definition*. A definition is really a brief description in answer to the question, "What do you mean?" It is shared experience.

 Model Definition

Unicorn (yoo'-ni-korn) *n* 1. a fabled creature usually represented as a horse with a single horn growing from its forehead and often with a goat's beard and a lion's tail. [From Latin *unicornus: uni,* one + *cornu,* horn.]

Webster's Dictionary

35

Analysis

There are several methods of defining. The one most commonly used is called *classification*. It follows the pattern shown in the definition of the unicorn.

1. Give the largest possible group or class: **fabled creature**.
2. Tell how the "thing-to-be-defined" differs from other members of the large class: **like a horse**.
3. Show specific details: **single horn, goat's beard, lion's tail**.

Many dictionaries have illustrations to help make the meaning clear, but writers rarely draw pictures when they are writing. This pattern, classification, which moves from a large, or *general,* class to a smaller, or more *specific* class, is useful in many kinds of writing.

Largest Class	*Smaller Class*	*Specifics*
fabled creature	horselike	single horn
		goat's beard
		lion's tail

Definition Practice

Directions: Define the word *king.*

Largest Class	*Smaller Class*	*Specifics*
Human being	Rules country	Inheriting his position
		Powerful
		Rules alone

The definition, written as a sentence, might be "A king (*thing-to-be-defined*) is a male human being (*largest class*) who rules a country (*smaller class*) by inheriting his position, usually is powerful, and rules alone (*differences from other rulers*)."

Examples

A circle is a geometric shape consisting of a plane curve that is everywhere the same distance from a point called the center.

An island is a body of land surrounded on all sides by water.

A classroom is a place for removing ignorance in groups.

When you define a word to help a reader understand what you have written, always be aware that words have several meanings in English. The word *grain,* for example, means "a crop like wheat, corn, or barley" to a farmer. It means "a unit of weight equal to 64.79 milligrams" to a person who sells gold or silver. And it means "the growth pattern on a piece of wood" to a carpenter or wood carver. All of these definitions are correct. You must be especially careful if you are still using an English–foreign language dictionary. A student was writing a fable about a deer that had beautiful antlers. She did not know the word *antler,* so she looked up the word she did know, *horn,* in her English-Arabic dictionary. *Horn* was defined as "trumpet." A perfectly correct definition, but not the one needed (see Illustration 3.1).

There are other methods of definition that are not as widely used as classification. One is rather straightforward—simply show an example of the

Illustration 3.1
A deer with a beautiful set of horns.

thing-to-be-defined. If it is impossible to show an example, use a drawing or a photograph. (You can show a picture of an animal more easily than you can describe it in detail.)

 ## Example

A tetrahedron is a polyhedron (*general class*) with only four sides (*specific difference from other polyhedrons*). [Can you tell what a tetrahedron is just from the written definition?]

The drawing in Illustration 3.2 makes the meaning much clearer. This method is limited to things that can be pointed to or shown. It cannot work with abstract ideas like love, beauty, or democracy.

Another method often used is to provide a *synonym*, or word that means almost the same thing.

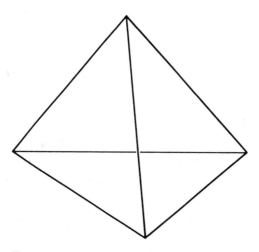

Illustration 3.2
Tetrahedron

 ## Example

A *tetrahedron* is a *pyramid.*

A *tankard* is a *cup* or a *mug* used for drinking.

A *dalmatian* is a *type of dog.*

Note

When you use the classification method to define something, you should be careful to meet the following three requirements.

1. Do not use the term-to-be-defined in its own definition.

   Bad: Glue means *to glue* things together.

   Good: Glue is a sticky substance.

2. Be sure that you use the part of speech in the definition that is the same as the thing-to-be-defined.

   Bad: Capitalism is when everybody can make money (*noun ≠ adverb clause*).

   Good: Capitalism is an economic system (*noun = modifier + noun*).

The two parts, thing-to-be-defined and definition, should be the same parts of speech (see pages 193–194 for parts of speech), or they should be *parallel* (have *parallel structure*).

3. Make sure that your definition is as complete as it needs to be to cover all of the important elements.

   Bad: A mermaid is a fabled creature (*general class*) of the sea (*limitation*) that is half fish and half woman (*specific details*) (see Illustration 3.3).

   Good: A mermaid is a fabled creature of the sea with the head and upper body of a woman and the tail of a fish (see Illustration 3.4).

Illustration 3.3

Illustration 3.4

Writing Practice

Define at least three of the following terms. The most general class is given in parentheses. Using parallel structure, show how each term is different from other items in the same general class.

1. Education (a process)
2. Recreation (an activity)
3. Parent (an animal)
4. Love (an emotional condition)
5. Square (a geometric shape)
6. Communism (an economic system)

Uses of Description

Description is a useful skill for writing many kinds of paragraphs and longer papers. Descriptive passages are widely used for explaining (*exposition*) and for convincing (*argumentation*). Although a completely descriptive paper is rare, descriptive paragraphs are very common.

There are four main patterns for descriptive paragraphs.

1. From *general* to *specific* (exactly like classification)
2. From *specific* to *general* (just the opposite)
3. *Space order* (top to bottom, near to far)
4. *Dominant impression* (especially for describing people)

4 Time order eg History

You will learn to write these patterns separately, but in the process of writing you will often combine more than one in a single paragraph.

General to Specific Order

The general to specific pattern for a paragraph is the same as the pattern for classification. The first sentence makes a general statement. ("There were children everywhere" in the following model paragraph. The rest of the paragraph gives *specific* examples of where the children were.)

Model Paragraph (General to Specific)

The Schoolyard

There were children everywhere.
Children ran out of the buildings to the yard.
Children played on the slides, on the swings, on the courts.
Children tossed balls, played their own strange games, or just ran back and forth.
Across the yard they sat in the lunch area or stood along the fence.
I have never seen so many children under the age of twelve all in one place before.

Analysis

This student is writing a school visit report for an education class. He describes the schoolyard by emphasizing the great number of children. He uses space order by going from the buildings to the playground to the yard to the lunch area to the far side of the yard. He limits his paragraph to the children. He does not describe the swings, the slides, or the buildings. He gives the paper coherence by repeating *children* five times and using the pronoun *they.* Notice that he uses active verbs like *ran, played, tossed, sat,* and *stood,* instead of saying "There *were* children. . . ."

 ## Writing Practice (Sentence Combining)

Directions: See pages 27 and 28 for general directions about sentence combining. Combine the following groups of sentences into a *general to specific* paragraph. The words in parentheses are suggestions; you may use others. Some other words often used as transitions in descriptive writing are listed here. Their main function is to show *additional* material. (The sentences are on the next page.)

additionally	another	just as
again	as well as	likewise
along with	besides	moreover
also	further(more)	similarly
and	in addition	too

Sentences

1. a. It was about noon.
   b. The snow began to fall. (*when*)

2. a. It came down slowly. (*at first*)
   b. ~~It came down~~ in flakes.
   c. The flakes were tiny.
   d. ~~The flakes were~~ white.

3. a. The wind was gentle.
   b. ~~The wind~~ became stronger.
   c. ~~The wind became~~ stronger. (*and*)

4. a. The snow was in the air.
   b. ~~The snow became~~ thicker.
   c. ~~The snow became~~ thicker. (*and*)

5. a. It was impossible to see.
   b. ~~It was impossible to see~~ more than a few meters.
   c. ~~It was impossible to see~~ in any direction.

6. a. The snow swirled around the trees.
   b. ~~The snow swirled around the~~ bushes.

7. a. ~~It was blown~~ into cracks.
   b. ~~The cracks~~ were in old houses.
   c. The wind blew the snow.

8. a. It began to cover the road. (*in addition*)
   b. It began to pile up.
   c. ~~It piled up~~ on the edges of the road.

9. a. The wind blew.
   b. ~~The wind blew~~ even stronger.
   c. The snow increased. (*and*)

10. a. The sun went down. (*finally as*)
    b. The world was covered.
    c. The cover was white.

Refer to pages 214–231 and 233–237 to check that you have used the proper verb tenses and that you have correct subject-verb agreement where you have combined more than one element. Make sure that each sentence is as short as possible without leaving out any part of the description.

Poor: The wind blew, and ~~the wind~~ became stronger.

Better: The wind blew stronger.

For an even better paragraph, you might decide to combine some of the sentences you have written. For example, sentences 3 and 4 could be combined into a compound sentence using *as*.

Specific to General Order

Sometimes a writer may want to change the regular order of a paragraph. In a descriptive paragraph he or she would place the most general statement at the end. The reason for this change would be either to *emphasize* the main idea or to keep the reader *curious* about the main topic.

 ## Model Paragraph (Specific to General)

Abandoned

The fading, rust-colored old building sits like a ghost in the middle of the busy Taipei traffic.

The heavy wooden doors with iron spikes on top are sealed shut.

The high wall around the building is dirty and crumbling.

There is no flag on the flagpole.

Now rough boards are nailed on the sign that once read:

EMBASSY OF THE UNITED STATES OF AMERICA.

 ## Analysis

This writer wants to make the reader wonder what this old building is. The writer also wants to make the main point that the United States, one of the most powerful countries in the world, has a fading, crumbling building in Taipei, Taiwan.

 ## Writing Practice (Selecting Correct Order)

Directions: Read the following sentences about human behavior. On your own paper, write them in order from the most *specific* to the most *general*.

6 1. Copying adult behavior is a perfectly natural action for the young.

5 2. One of the ways children learn how to behave in the world is to copy the actions of older people. (*Continued on next page.*)

3 3. Often it is possible to see boys and girls pretending that they are doctors, police officers, or parents.

4 4. Many children like to pretend that they are already grown up.

1 5. Today, Tanya, Alicia, and Keiko put on their mothers' clothes.

2 6. The little girls like to pretend that they are adults.

7 7. Almost all young animals copy the actions of adults; it is one way that they learn how to behave when they are grown.

Space Order

One of the best ways to make your description clear to your reader is to use space order. As you describe something, guide the reader from the top to the bottom, from the bottom to the top, from one side to the other, from near to far, or from far to near.

Model Paragraph (Space Order)

The Lost City

The lost city had been built by some king long ago on a little hill. A great roofless palace topped the hill, and the marble of the courtyards and the fountains was split and stained with red and green; the stones of the courtyard where the king's elephants had lived were pushed up and apart by grasses and young trees. Down the hill from the palace were rows and rows of empty houses that had made up the city. In the square where four roads had met there was a shapeless block of stone that had once been an idol. Farther out was the shattered roof of a temple with wild trees growing on its side. The great wall that had surrounded the city was tumbled down, and bits of wood hung from the rusted hinges of the ruined gates.

Analysis

The first sentence introduces the subject of the paragraph, a lost city, and tells the general location, on a hill. The rest of the paragraph gives concrete (specific) details that describe the lost city. The writer moves from the top of the hill down to the empty houses, farther down to the idol and the ruined temple, and finally to the walls that had surrounded the city. The writer, Rudyard Kipling, who used this paragraph in *The Jungle Book,* could have started with the walls and moved up the hill to the palace at the top. Either method would have worked as well. Notice that the reader is guided by prepositions of place and by adverbs (*above, below, beside, outside, farther down*).

Writing Practice (Controlled Writing)

Directions: Using as a model either the paragraph about the lost city or the paragraph that follows, change the scene being described.

1. Change the location to another place. (Describe a statue or a building.)
2. Change the details. (Make the house beautiful or the city modern and full of people).
3. Change the tense from past to present or from present to past. (See pages 214–216.)
4. Follow the sentence patterns as closely as possible, but you may make some changes.
5. Be sure that the introductory (first) sentence tells your reader what you are going to describe.

Model Paragraph

The House

There is a strange house on my street. It is set back farther than the other houses, but there is no grass in front. Instead, there is sand where the other houses have a lawn. Here and there in the sand are strange desert plants: cactus and bushes with thorns. The front door of the house is carved with unusual flowers and vines. The windows have glass that is not clear so that no one can see in. The front of the house is not wood but is made of rough stones of many sizes. Strangest of all is the roof. It is curved up like a Chinese temple and is painted a bright blue.

Writing Practice (Sentence Combining and Guided Writing)

Directions: Pictured in Illustration 3.5 on the next page is the Leaning Tower of Pisa. Following is some information about this unusual building. Use the information to write a descriptive paragraph about the tower. Combine both time and space order. Start at the top of the building and move down, or start at the bottom and move up. There is no "correct" way to write this paragraph. You may combine the information any way you wish. You do not have to use all of the information.

1 1. A *campanile* is usually part of a church.

9 2. The tower was built in the city of Pisa, Italy.

6 3. The bottom story has 15 marble pillars, or columns.

3 4. It is 54 meters tall.

4 5. The top story holds bells that ring on special occasions.

5 6. The six middle stories have 20 smaller columns each.

2 7. It was started in the year 1174.

10 8. This kind of tower is called a *campanile*, or bell tower.

7 9. The tower is world-famous because it leans 5 meters out of line.

8 10. It is built so that it does not fall over.

11 11. It was not finished until 1350, 176 years later.

Illustration 3.5
The Leaning Tower of Pisa

Dominant Impression

Describing people requires a slightly different method than describing places or things. In addition to space order (like starting at the head and describing a person down to his or her toes) or general to specific order (like giving the general description and then adding details), many writers use the *dominant impression* method to describe human beings. The dominant impression is the main effect the person has on your feelings or senses. In the description of a basketball player, special attention might be given to his height. It is difficult to describe anything completely; it may be impossible. If you try to picture only the face of a person, there is so much to tell. The hair, the shape of the face, the eyes, their color and shape, the nose, the mouth, details like the eyebrows, eyelashes, the coloring of each part—it would take pages and pages. What do many writers do? They pick the most important feature and emphasize it, or they give their dominant impression of the person.

 ## Model Paragraph

The Lady

Her hands were crossed one over the other, her charming face held slightly to one side. There was warmth but little color in her cheeks; her large dark eyes were soft. But it was her lips—asking a question, giving an answer, with that little smile—that people looked at. They were sensitive lips, shapely and sweet, and from them seemed to come warmth and perfume like the warmth and perfume of a flower.

Analysis

This writer, John Galsworthy, gives us very little information about "The Lady." We do not know the color of her hair or eyes, although he does tell us that her eyes were "dark." He emphasizes what impressed him most, what gave him a dominant impression, which were her lips.

 ## Writing Practice (Guided Writing)

Guided writing does not give you a specific paragraph pattern to follow. Instead, you are given general directions and suggestions about how you might write a paragraph. You are free to develop your own sentence patterns and details.

Directions: Look closely at one of your classmates (or your instructor). What is the dominant impression? Is the person tall, short, fat, thin? Do the eyes, the hair, the mouth, impress you the most? Or is it the expression— usually happy, sad, frowning?

1. The first sentence should be a general statement. (*Bao Vu is a tall, slender young man.*)
2. The next sentence should narrow down (limit) the part to be described in the paragraph. (*His smiling face is smooth and unlined.*)
3. The next several sentences might tell some other details. (*He has brown eyes and wears glasses.*)
4. The final sentence should present the most striking feature or the dominant impression. (*His black hair is cut short and sticks out in all directions; it will not stay combed.*)

It would also be possible to *start* with the dominant impression. (*The first thing I noticed about Bao Vu was his black hair sticking out in all directions.*)

 ## Writing Practice (Guided Writing)

Alternate Assignments: If you do not want to describe a classmate or the teacher, describe yourself! Or you may describe the picture of the sixteenth president of the United States in Illustration 3.6. *Suggestions:* Note the large nose and ears and the expression on the face (calm? sad?). Is there a slight smile?

Illustration 3.6

Suggestion

You probably have noticed that descriptive paragraphs sometimes combine different types of order. The selection about the schoolyard, although *primarily* general to specific, also uses space order and gives one dominant impression. The selection about the lady is primarily dominant impression but also moves from a general view to the specific example of her lips. The lost city paragraph clearly uses space order, but it also presents the dominant impression of ruin. This mixing of more than one kind of order is common to all writing. What you, as a writer, must do is to pick the *main order* of your paragraph or longer essay. Within that basic plan, feel free to include other elements of order as you need them to make your writing clearer.

Writing Practice (Free Writing)

Directions: Free writing allows you to complete the assignment any way you wish. Choose one kind of order, or several different kinds. The suggestions are given to help you; they are not requirements.

1. Write a description of the room where you live or study. *Suggestion:* Start with a general impression, such as "My bedroom is always messy," and give examples. Space order would be good here, as would general to specific.

2. Write a descriptive paragraph about another student's manner of dressing. *Suggestion:* Select a student with an unusual style of dressing. Either space order or dominant impression would work here.

3. Describe a scene you can actually see. *Suggestion:* The room you are in now, a view out the window, the school parking lot.

4. Describe the sketch of the face of a man who is shouting (Illustration 3.7). *Suggestion:* Decide whether he is frightened, excited, angry, in pain;

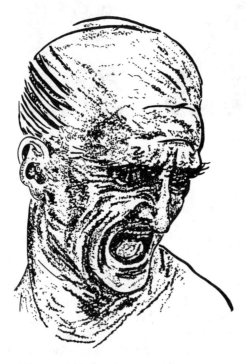

Illustration 3.7
(Adapted from a drawing by Leonardo da Vinci.)

let that be the dominant impression, and support it with details about his features.

✔ **Check**   your work to see that you have used the correct verb tenses throughout. (Refer to pages 214–231.)

✔ **Check**   to see that you have followed one main order.

✔ **Check**   to see that you have not left out any important details and that you have not included anything that is not important.

Chapter Four

The Expository Paragraph

Paragraph Review

Kinds of Exposition

Exposition is the kind of writing that explains or informs. The term *exposition* comes from the word *expose,* which means "to uncover, to make known, to reveal." *Expository* writing will reveal what you know, what you have discovered, what you believe. It is the most common kind of writing you will do in school and in business. You will write exposition to answer essay examinations, to present reports, to write term papers, to compose letters, to do most of your day-to-day writing. It is a most important form of writing to learn.

Paragraph Review

You will use the skills you have practiced in narration and description when you write expository paragraphs. These skills will be woven into your explanations and become part of the larger pattern of exposition.

1. *The topic sentence:* With very few exceptions, each expository paragraph must have a clear topic sentence—a single sentence with which your reader can either agree or disagree. The topic sentence not only tells your reader what the paragraph will be about but also helps you write better and stick to the topic.

2. *The outline:* A working outline may not be absolutely necessary, but it certainly makes writing easier. You can see at a glance the pattern and structure of the paragraph; you can tell quickly what needs to be left out or what additional material needs to be added to complete the promise of the topic sentence.

3. *Narration:* Narrative skills are useful in explaining. In some types of exposition you will use *chronological,* or time, order. In others you might use the order of climax. You may use brief anecdotes or narratives to make your explanations clearer and more interesting. Because paragraphs and longer papers need coherence, you will need transitions as well.

eg or story. 53

4. *Description* (including *definition*): In some exposition it will be necessary to define words that the reader might not know or words that have a special meaning in your paragraph. It may also be necessary to describe people or things to make your writing effective. You will find that moving from the general to the specific is one of the most common ways to give order to exposition. Moving from the specific to the general is also used, but not as often. Space order is also widely used in explaining or informing.

Kinds of Exposition

The skills you have been practicing are the tools you will use to construct expository paragraphs. In addition, you will learn new ways to organize the kind of writing that explains. There are several patterns, but you should practice and learn the four that are most useful.

1. Explain by the use of examples (*example and illustration*).
2. Explain by showing how things are alike (*comparison*) or how they are different (*contrast*).
3. Explain by showing what caused a certain event to happen (*cause*) or what was the result of a certain event (*effect*).
4. Explain by showing how something is done or how something works (*analysis*).

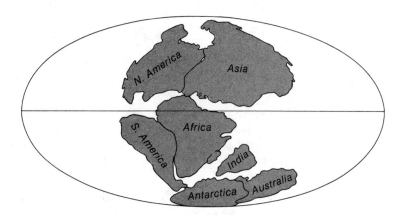

Illustration 4.1
Pangea

Model Composition

Earthquakes

From earliest times to this very day, people have been frightened, shaken, even killed by sudden earthquakes (1). The cause of earthquakes may now be explained by new scientific discoveries (2). As early as 1620, maps were so accurate that an Englishman, Sir Francis Bacon, noticed that the shoreline of South America could almost fit into the shoreline of Africa (3). Later, in the 1800s, the German scientist Alexander von Humboldt wrote in his book *Cosmos* that Africa and South America could fit together like a giant puzzle (4). Finally, another German scientist, Alfred Wegener, developed the idea that millions of years ago Africa and South America had actually been joined together (5). He explained his idea in 1915 in a textbook called *The Origin of Continents and Oceans* (6). He believed that all of the continents had once been joined together in one huge land mass he called *Pangea* (from the Greek *pan,* "all," and *geo,* "earth" (7) (see Illustration 4.1). Wegener thought that the continents floated over the *magma,* or hot melted rock that makes up the core of the earth (8). Although Wegener worked on his theory until his death in 1930, other scientists just laughed at him and forgot his work (9).

Analysis

The first sentence is an *introduction* used to get the attention and interest of the reader. The second sentence states the topic (*earthquakes*) and the limitation (*their cause*) and presents the controlling idea (*explained by new discoveries*). The next six sentences tell about the early development of a theory about earth movement. The general order is chronological (time). The main expository pattern is a series of *examples* of scientists. The last sentence tells what happened to these ideas by 1930. Notice that several words like *Pangea* and *magma* are defined for the reader.

 ## Model Composition (Continued)

It was not until after World War II that new instruments and improved old ones made it possible to examine the ocean floor carefully (1). Scientists from Columbia University discovered a great chain of mountains extending over 40,000 miles along the ocean floor like the seam on a baseball (2). Running along the top of these mountains is a *rift,* or thin, deep valley (3). The new instruments showed that hot material is pushing up from the earth's interior all along the rift (4). These new instruments also showed that the pattern of earthquakes in the ocean follows the mountain chain *exactly* (5). As this new material is forced to the surface, it pushes the continents apart (6). It seems that Alfred Wegener was right (7).

Analysis (Continued)

Sentence 1 presents the topic sentence (*new instruments + careful examination*). Sentence 2 tells what the examination revealed, and sentences 3, 4, 5, and 6 show the results of the careful examination in greater detail. The last sentence ties the second paragraph to the first. The author uses definition (*rift*) and repetition of key terms (*new instruments*). The basic pattern is general (*new instruments and careful examination*) to specific (*exactly what the examination showed*).

Model Paragraph (Concluded)

The results of these new discoveries are now widely accepted by scientists (1). Textbooks are being rewritten (2). New information shows that the continents and oceans are attached to great *plates* that move slowly around the earth like icebergs (3). When they meet and push together, they cause earthquakes and volcanoes (4). The movement is still going on (5). The Atlantic Ocean is widening at the rate of two inches a year; other rifts may widen at twice that rate (6). The San Andreas Fault in California is part of the Pacific Rift and is moving Los Angeles northward (7). After many earthquakes, Los Angeles will meet San Francisco in about 10 million years (8).

Analysis (Concluded)

In the last paragraph the author gives a topic sentence and explains what happens as the results are accepted. He ties this paragraph to the first one by pointing out that the cause of earthquakes is now known. He concludes with the interesting statement that Los Angeles will meet with San Francisco in the distant future.

A working outline of this three-paragraph essay might look like this:

Title: Earthquakes
(*no quotation marks, no underline*)

Introduction: From the earliest times to this very day, people have been frightened, shaken, and even killed by sudden earthquakes.

   I. New discoveries may explain cause of earthquakes.
      A. Early theories of land movement
         1. Bacon
         2. Humboldt
      B. Wegener's modern theory
         1. Pangea
         2. Floating continents
         3. Rejected

II. New instruments lead to new discoveries.
  A. Mountain chain
  B. Rift
  C. Continents pushed apart

III. New discoveries are accepted.
  A. Textbooks rewritten
  B. Plate theory accepted
    1. Atlantic Plate
    2. Pacific Plate

Conclusion: After many earthquakes, Los Angeles will meet San Francisco in about 10 million years.

This brief outline shows the structure of the essay. It does not include all of the details. A working outline may be as simple or as detailed as you, the writer, need it to be.

The next four chapters will show you how to develop paragraphs of *example and illustration, comparison and contrast, cause and effect,* and *analysis.* When you have mastered those forms, you will be shown how to use them in a paragraph to convince or persuade (called *argument*). The last section of the book will show you how to use all of these skills in writing a longer essay, like the one above, of three to five (or more) paragraphs.

Chapter Five

Explaining by Illustration and Example

The Purpose of Example

The first method of developing exposition uses *example*. *Example* means "to use specific, concrete events, occurrences, facts, or conditions to explain a topic." Start with a clear, well-limited topic sentence and support it with one example. Many writers use anecdotes or opinions as well as definitions or descriptions. The purpose of example is *to make clear* what you are writing about. When we speak, we often say, "Well, for example . . ." or, "For instance . . ." and then offer an example to clarify our statement. When we write, we do exactly the same thing.

 Model Paragraph

The Rainmaker

Although most people believe that formal schooling is required for scientific success, a college degree is not always necessary (1). An excellent example of a man who won fame as a scientist without academic training is Vincent J. Schaefer (2). His formal education ended after two years of high school when he had to go to work in an untrained job at General Electric (3). Because of his inventive mind and his skill as a model maker, he was soon allowed to try his own experiments in the company laboratory (4). His natural curiosity made him wonder about clouds (5). He developed, after many tries, a method of making clouds rain when they would not normally do so (6). This method, called *seeding,* has been very helpful to farmers, and it won him much fame (7). In 1961 he became director and leading professor of the Atmospheric Sciences Research Center of the University of New York (8).

In 1981 this professor, who had never gone to college, published a highly respected book, *A Field Guide to the Atmosphere* (9). Schaefer approves of a college education; but he believes that, for people who can work on their own, who learn by doing, who read books, who make friends with worthwhile people, and who, most of all, are interested in the world and everything in it, a college degree is unnecessary (10).

Analysis

The first sentence states the topic, "scientific achievement," and the controlling idea, "does not always require a college degree." The next eight sentences give an excellent example of a man who became a respected scientist without formal education. The last sentence explains what kind of people, according to Vincent J. Schaefer, do not need a college degree. The concluding sentence puts a further limitation on the topic sentence. Obviously, not everyone is the kind of person that Schaefer describes.

 ### Writing Practice (Sentence Combining)

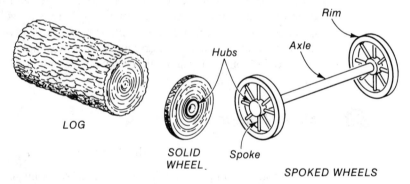

Illustration 5.1
Wheels

Directions: Combine each group of statements into a single sentence. Write the combined sentences in paragraph form on your own paper. The completed paragraph will use one example, the growth of the wheel, to illustrate that most inventions are developed slowly. Useful transitions could be *for example, for instance, namely, next,* and *then.*

Special Instructions: The topic sentence limits the paragraph to the steps in the growth of the wheel. (See Illustration 5.1.) Three sentences in the list *do not* illustrate the topic. Do not use them in your paragraph.

1. a. Most inventions have developed. *(been)*
   b. ~~The development has been slow.~~ (*slowly*)
   c. ~~The development has been~~ *in* a series of steps.

2. a. The common wheel has changed. (*for example*)
   b. ~~The change~~ was gradual.
   c. ~~The change~~ took years. (*over, during*)
   d. ~~There were~~ many years.

3. a. The first wheel-like devices were logs.
   b. ~~The logs were~~ rough and uneven. (*first*)
   c. ~~The logs were~~ smoothed. (*then*)
   d. Smoothed logs rolled more easily.

4. a. There was a next step.
   b. A solid wheel was cut.
   c. ~~It was cut~~ from a tree trunk.

5. a. The solid wheel is still used.
   b. ~~It is used~~ in Mexico.
   c. ~~It is used~~ on a wagon called a *carreta*.
   d. ~~The~~ *carreta* is pulled by an ox.

6. a. The spoked wheel was developed. (*later, finally*)
   b. ~~The development~~ took centuries. (*but*) *it*
   c. The spoked wheel was much lighter.
   d. It turned faster. (*and*)

7. a. The wheels still wore out.
   b. Someone had an idea. (*then*)
   c. The idea was simple. (*:*)
   d. Use metal on the rims. *as ties*
   e. ~~Use metal~~ as "tires."

8. a. The Incas and Aztecs had no wheels.
   b. They used animals.
   c. ~~The animals~~ carried loads.
   d. ~~The animals~~ pulled sleds.

9. a. The wheel with metal hub and axle was used.
   b. It was used for a long time.
   c. It is still used today.

10. a. North American Indians never discovered the wheel.
    b. They dragged two poles on the ground.
    c. They put their loads on the poles.
    d. The women pulled the poles.

✔ **Check:**   Have you used a past tense throughout? (Check page 216.) Have you combined as closely as possible? Did you leave out the sentences that do not illustrate the topic sentence?

Unity

Every effective paragraph has a quality of *oneness,* or unity. Each sentence in the paragraph has something to do with the topic sentence. You already know some of the ways to make a paragraph "stick together," to give it *coherence.* The next quality of paragraphs is *unity.* In the Writing Practice just given, sentences 5, 8, and 10 are about the use of the solid wooden wheel in Mexico and the fact that Native American Indians did not use the wheel. These sentences do not illustrate the gradual development of the wheel. If you were to use them in your paragraph, you would destroy the unity. These sentences are "off the topic."

Writing Practice (Selecting the Correct Order)

Directions: Arrange the following sentences in the correct order. Look for clues in the meaning of the sentences and in the transitions. Pronouns such as *it, this, he,* and *them* always refer to a noun already mentioned.

Special Instructions: The topic sentence for this paragraph states that the paragraph will illustrate two things about little animals: that they are interesting to us and that they are harmful to the farmer. A good way to organize this paragraph would be to find all of the interesting facts and all of the harmful facts. Arrange each subgroup (interesting facts and harmful facts) into sentences. Then write the sentences in a paragraph. Three of the sentences are off the topic. Do not use them!

Topic sentence: Many of the little animals we see along a country road may be interesting to us, but to a farmer they are often harmful.

1. A farmer trying to grow hay to feed his cattle does not care about this superstition.

2. Ten of them can eat five tons of hay in a single summer.

3. One example of such a little animal is the groundhog, or woodchuck.

4. If it sees its shadow then, it goes back into the burrow, for there will be six more weeks of winter.

5. The farmer's hay (called *alfalfa*) is good food for animals, rich in vitamins, minerals, and protein.

6. He cares about the very large appetite of the woodchuck.

3 7. This particular little animal is interesting because of the superstition that it can predict the weather.

4 8. When we learn that there can be twenty-four of them in 4,000 square meters (1 acre), we can see why they are harmful to the farmer.

6 5 3 9. On Groundhog Day (February 2) it is supposed to come out of its burrow and look around.

7 8 10. Winter officially ends on March 21 in the Northern Hemisphere.

2 11. A single woodchuck will eat half a ton of hay in one summer.

8 12. Woodchucks do not make good pets, and they are not used for food.

Illustration

Another way to explain your topic is to use several illustrations instead of just one example. Usually *illustrations* are shorter and less detailed than *examples*. An example, such as the woodchuck, represents a whole class of similar things. It would be equally effective to use several illustrations of little animals that the farmer considers harmful: mice, gophers, voles, prairie dogs, moles, muskrats, and rats.

 ### Model Paragraph (Several Illustrations)

Names

A great many names in European countries came from the job or occupation people had. For example, the name *Tailor* (a person who makes clothes) is common and is sometimes spelled *Taylor* or *Tailleur*. The German word for the same job is *Schneider*. Other names from occupations are *Glover* (glove maker), *Butcher* (meat cutter), *Fletcher* (arrow maker), and *Cooper* (barrel maker). There are thousands of *Smiths*, a name from the trade of metal worker. Some names even come from religious occupations, such as *Priest, Priestly,* and *Clerk* or *Clark*.

Analysis

This writer uses nine illustrations to explain the topic that European names can come from occupations. He gives the paragraph coherence by repeating the word *names,* and by using such transitions as *for example* and *other*. The paragraph has unity. He does not tell about names that come from places (*Hall, Wood, Hill,* or *Stone*). He keeps unity by following his limitation of European names. He does not bring in off-the-topic examples of non-European names like *Han, Wong,* or *Pundutit.*

Writing Practice (Controlled Writing)

Directions: Read the following student paragraph. Following the sentence patterns as closely as possible, change the student's name to your own. You may wish to change *surprised* to another past participle. (See page 232.)

Model Paragraph

My Name

I was really surprised to find out that everybody's name meant something. I had never thought about it before. I discovered that my first name, *Juan,* comes from Hebrew and means "God is gracious." My middle name, *Jorge,* comes from Greek and means "a farmer." My last name, *Martinez,* has two meanings. *Martin* comes from the Latin word *Mars* and means "warlike." The *-ez* on the end means "the son of." If I had been born in the United States instead of in Peru, my name would be John George Martinson.

Writing Practice (Guided Writing)

Directions: Following the basic idea of "The Rainmaker" (see page 59), develop an expository paragraph in which you use one brief biographical example to make the topic clear. The following topics are suggestions; you may choose your own.

1. One does not have to be rich to be happy.
2. Some students get good grades but never seem to study.
3. Some students study hard but never seem to get good grades.
4. Real beauty is more than just a pretty (handsome) face.
5. Great leaders must often be cruel.

Writing Practice (Free Writing)

Directions: Illustration 5.2 shows a mother and father playing a game of cards with their son and daughter. The are smiling and seem to be having fun. Write a paragraph in which you use *illustration* as the basic pattern of development. You may use either one example or several illustrations. The general topic is "Some families play together." You will need to think of your own controlling idea.

Illustration 5.2

Suggestions:

1. Playing together is beneficial.
2. Playing together may be bad.
3. More families should play together. (Why?)
4. Gambling teaches children about the real world.
5. There is too little family life in the United States.

Chapter Six

Explaining by Showing Similarities and Differences

Comparison

Contrast

Comparing and Contrasting

Whenever we have to make a choice between two or more things, we usually think about how they are alike or different. The process of showing likenesses or similarities is called *comparison*. The process of showing differences is called *contrast*. Think how often students will *compare* and *contrast* two teachers. (Teachers also often compare and contrast students.) If you have thought about buying a car, you have probably compared and contrasted two (or more) very carefully. The topic sentence must be carefully limited in compare-contrast paragraphs. Both items must be in the same general class. The first rule is to make sure that the things to be compared have something in common. The second rule is to limit the qualities compared or contrasted. For example, if you were to compare two friends, you would limit the discussion to how they are alike as students, or how they show their friendship, or how they are similar in what they like to do. It would take thousands of words to show how any two people are alike in *all* things.

Comparison

In his book *Civilization,* Kenneth Clark discusses two pieces of sculpture (see Illustrations 6.1 and 6.2). If he had written a paragraph of *comparison*, it might have looked like this.

Model Paragraph (Pattern 1)

Two Messengers

Once when I was looking at an African mask belonging to a friend of mine, I thought that all societies produce great works of art. I could not help

Illustration 6.1
The Apollo of Belvedere (head)

Illustration 6.2
African Spirit Mask

comparing it to the famous Greek sculpture of the head of the god Apollo. Both are supposed to be from the spirit world. Apollo is from Mount Olympus, and the mask from the forest world. Both are abstractions of the human face. Apollo is not an actual person, and neither is the mask. Both are greatly admired. The Apollo of Belvedere was the most admired piece of sculpture in the world for 400 years after it was found. The African mask is admired by many people, especially artists. Both are clearly great works of art.

Analysis

This paragraph uses one of the two patterns for writing a comparison (see Illustration 6.3). Using an outline is a good way to analyze the pattern.

Title: Two Messengers

Topic sentence: Comparing two sculptures shows that all societies can produce great works of art.

I. Both sculptures represent spirits.
  A. Apollo from Mt. Olympus
  B. Mask from forest world

II. Both are abstractions.
  A. Apollo not real
  B. Mask not a real person

III. Both are greatly admired.
  A. Apollo admired for 400 years
  B. Mask admired by artists

Conclusion: Both are clearly great works of art.

The writer selects three qualities that the two sculptures have in common: (I) both are spirits; (II) both are abstract; (III) both are admired. He then shows how each mask, in turn, shows these qualities. The paragraph is unified in that the writer does not introduce any ways in which the two sculptures are different, and he does not introduce any other works of art. It is given coherence by the use of *both* and by the repetition of the key words *Apollo* and *mask*.

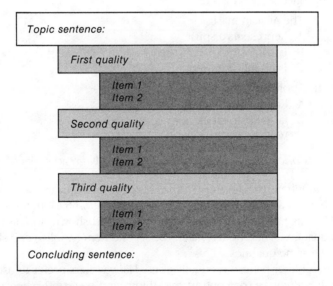

Illustration 6.3
Comparing or Contrasting: Pattern 1

Model Paragraph (Pattern 2)

Two Messengers

Once when I was looking at an African mask belonging to a friend of mine, I thought that all societies can produce great works of art. I could not help comparing the mask to the famous Greek sculpture of the head of the god Apollo. The African mask represents someone from the spirit world of the forest. It is an abstraction; it is not a real person. It has been admired by many people, especially modern artists. The Apollo of Belvedere, likewise, is from the spirit world of Mount Olympus. Similarly, it is an abstraction; it is not a real person. Also, it was the most admired piece of sculpture in the world for 400 years after it was found. Both are clearly great works of art.

Analysis

The outline for this paragraph shows the difference in structure.

Title: Two Messengers

Topic sentence: Comparing two sculptures shows that all societies can produce great works of art.

  I. The African mask
     A. Represents a spirit
     B. Is an abstraction, not real
     C. Is greatly admired
 II. Apollo of Belvedere
     A. Represents a spirit
     B. Is an abstraction, not real
     C. Was greatly admired

Concluding sentence: Both are clearly great works of art.

When using pattern 2, the writer has used exactly the same information but has arranged it differently (see Illustration 6.4). In the second paragraph he has taken the first item (the mask) and shown how it has three specific qualities. Then he has taken the second item (Apollo) and shown how it has the same qualities.

Either pattern is equally good. Many writers prefer to use pattern 1 when they compare or contrast two things and pattern 2 when they compare or contrast three or more things.

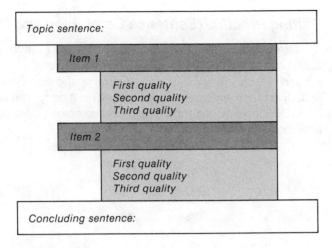

Illustration 6.4
Comparing or Contrasting: Pattern 2

 ## Note

When you are writing paragraphs or longer papers of comparison, you are trying to show how two or more things are the same. Do not include any ways in which they differ. Be careful to use items that are the same or similar. Choose the items carefully; it is difficult if not impossible to compare such totally different things as a dog with a house or things from different categories, such as a geometric shape with a natural process (see pages 36–40 for helpful hints).

Note also the words and phrases used in these two model paragraphs. In addition to the standard methods of using pronouns and repeating key terms, the author uses transition words like these:

again	just as
and	likewise
both	similarly
in the same way	too

Sometimes it is helpful in a comparison paragraph to tell what the things being compared are *not*. Then such correlative conjunctions as *neither/nor* are useful. See page 253 for other correlatives.

Writing Practice (Sentence Combining and Correct Order)

Directions: Illustration 6.5 shows sketches of two containers. One is a coffee cup or a teacup; the other is a measuring cup. The list of sentences is not arranged in any special order. Rearrange the sentences, combining them or adding other sentences of your own. Write a paragraph *comparing* the two cups. Develop a strong topic sentence. Remember, comparison is limited to how the objects are alike.

Coffee cup

Measuring cup

Illustration 6.5

1. A coffee cup holds 8 ounces (0.236 liter).
2. A measuring cup is usually made of glass.
3. A measuring cup has marks on the side to show amounts.
4. A coffee cup can hold other liquid than coffee.
5. A measuring cup holds 0.236 liter (8 ounces).
6. Coffee cups are made from glass or ceramic.
7. Measuring cups can hold any kinds of liquids or solids.
8. A coffee cup always has a handle.
9. There are many sizes of coffee cups.
10. Measuring cups have a handle for easy use.

11. Measuring cups usually are made in two sizes.

12. A measuring cup has a spout on one side for easy pouring.

Suggestion: Pick either pattern 1 or pattern 2. Arrange the sentences you plan to use into groups (for example, coffee cup versus measuring cup; or size, materials, function, and use). Then arrange the sentences in each group in the same order. Finally, write the topic sentence. The rest of the paragraph will almost "write itself."

 ### *Writing Practice (Additional Practice)*

Directions: Following the directions for the previous assignment, try to write a paragraph comparing the three vegetables shown in Illustration 6.6.

Suggestions: Vegetables can be compared by their color, the way they are prepared, the way they are grown, or their food value. Pattern 2 might be more effective than pattern 1 when you must compare three or more objects.

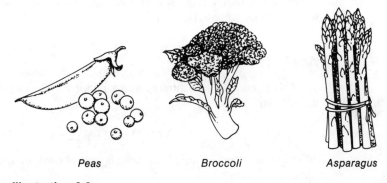

      Peas   *Broccoli*   *Asparagus*

Illustration 6.6

Contrast

The opposite of comparison (how things are alike) is *contrast* (how things are different). A paragraph of contrast follows exactly the same pattern as a paragraph of comparison. Either pattern 1 or pattern 2 will work to show differences. Suppose, for example, Kenneth Clark had decided to contrast the head of Apollo and the African mask. His paragraph might have looked like this.

 ## *Model Paragraph*

Two Messengers

It seems that the religious beliefs of different societies are shown in their art, both in how the art is made and in what the art means. Take, for example, the famous Apollo of Belvedere and a typical African spirit mask. The Apollo is carved from white marble, carefully finished and polished. The African mask is crudely carved from the wood of some African tree and has bone teeth and a brass ring in the nose. The Apollo is realistic; it might be an actual person. The mask, in contrast, is not at all realistic; clearly it does not represent a real person. Apollo represents light. He comes down from Mount Olympus and brings humankind joy and reason. The African mask, in contrast, comes from the dark world of the forest. A spirit to be feared, it brings punishment and destruction. Apollo shows the Greek belief that the gods were just like humans, but superior and helpful; the African spirits, instead, were ugly and were to be feared.

Analysis

This paragraph of contrast follows pattern 1. The outline will let you see the pattern clearly.

Title: Two Messengers

Topic sentence: Religious beliefs are shown in the art of different societies.

- I. Different materials
    - A. Apollo of marble
    - B. African mask of wood, bone, brass
- II. Difference in realism
    - A. Apollo could be real
    - B. Mask is clearly unreal.
- III. Different meanings
    - A. Apollo represents light and reason.
    - B. Mask represents darkness and fear.

Concluding sentence: Greek gods were helpful to humans, but African spirits punished them.

The writer follows the promise made in his topic sentence and limits the paragraph to telling how the two items differ in materials, construction, and meaning. Within the pattern for contrast there is also an order of climax. The most important idea is clarified in the concluding sentence. The paragraph uses different transitions than a comparison would.

Some Transitions Used in Contrasting

although	instead
but	neither
despite	on the other hand
except	rather
in contrast	unlike
in spite of	while
	yet

Writing Practice (Controlled Writing)

Directions: Read the model paragraph, and then write a paragraph of contrast following the pattern of the model. Change the person telling the story, or change the location—make it two different countries. You might contrast living in the mountains or the desert with living in a city. You might contrast two kinds of work you have done.

Model Paragraph (Contrast)

Changes

People in towns and cities are certainly different (1). When I was young, I lived in a small town (2). Everyone was friendly (3). In the evening, people would sit on their front porches and talk (4). They would smile and wave to others walking by (5). The front doors were open, and you could hear those inside talking and laughing (6). I knew the names of everyone in the neighborhood (7). Now I live in the city (8). People do not seem to be as friendly here (9). Instead of sitting out front, they go in their back yards behind walls (10). The front doors are shut and locked (11). Even the curtains in the windows are closed (12). I do not even know the name of my neighbor next door (13). Have people changed, or have I? (14)

This paragraph follows pattern 2. Sentence 1 states the topic. Sentences 2 through 7 describe small town people. Sentence 8 serves as a transition sentence introducing the city. Sentences 8 through 13 describe city people. Sentence 14 concludes the paragraph with a question. You might use the following model as a guide.

1. _____ and _____ are certainly different.

2. When I was young, I _____.

3. Everyone (everything) was _____.

4. In the evening (morning, afternoon) _____.

5. They would _____ and _____ .

6. The _____ were _____.

7. I knew _____.

8. Now I _____.

9. People do not seem _____.

10. Instead of _____, they _____.

11. The _____ are _____.

12. Even the _____ are _____.

13. I do not _____.

14. (*You may ask a question or write your own concluding sentence.*)

 ## Writing Practice (Guided Writing)

Directions: Write a paragraph of contrast in which you tell the difference between regular glasses and contact lenses. Use the following list of qualities as a source of information. You do not have to use all of the items. Be sure to write a clear topic sentence first so that you will know how to develop the topic, and your reader will know what to expect.

Regular Glasses

1. Frames can block vision.
2. May get blurry or foggy in steam or dampness.
3. May pinch ears or nose.
4. Good for nearsighted people.
5. Only average for deformed corneas.
6. Easy to take on and off.
7. Usually not too expensive.

Contact Lenses

1. No frames to block vision.
2. Cannot blur or fog up.
3. Do not pinch.

4. Excellent for nearsighted people.

5. Necessary for deformed corneas.

6. May be painful or difficult to wear.

7. Cost two or three times as much as regular glasses.

Suggestions:

1. Develop the topic sentence to show which you think is better.

2. Divide the paragraph into three sections:
   a. Differences in form and shape
   b. Differences in usefulness
   c. Difference in price

3. Or divide the paragraph into two sections:
   a. Good and bad points of regular glasses
   b. Good and bad points of contact lenses

4. Check to make sure that you have tied together the ideas in the paragraph with transitions. Make sure that your paragraph is unified; do not get off the topic.

5. Make a working outline of the paragraph before you start to write.

Comparing and Contrasting

Sometimes you will want to use both comparison and contrast to make your explanation perfectly clear. Naturally, the paragraph using both methods will be longer than the paragraph using just one method. In fact, when you start to write longer essays, you may choose to have one paragraph to compare and another one to contrast.

 ### Model Paragraph (Comparison and Contrast, Pattern 1)

The Elderly

Although old people in the United States and in my country, Japan, are treated the same in some ways, in other ways they are treated differently. In both countries the elderly are shown respect. Young people will give them a seat on a bus or train or will open a door for them. In both countries older people may ride the bus or go to a show for less money than the young have to pay. Nevertheless, in Japan the elderly have the highest respect. Grandparents live with their families all their lives. They help to raise the grandchildren. If anyone needs advice, the first person to be asked is the grandfather, because he is the wisest. In the United States, the grandparents live with other old people in "senior citizen" places. They see their grandchildren only on holidays or special times. I think it is better for families to live together in companionship.

Analysis

This paragraph by a Japanese student begins with a clear topic sentence. The *topic* is "treatment of the elderly"; the *controlling idea* is "both similar and different in two countries." The student gives three examples of similar treatment (giving the elderly seats, opening doors, charging them less money). Then she shifts (using *nevertheless*) to the main difference (living with the family, not in senior citizen homes). She concludes the paragraph with her personal opinion. Notice that she uses three illustrations for comparison and one example for contrast.

Title: The Elderly

Topic sentence: Old people are treated similarly and differently in Japan and the United States.

I. Similarities
- A. Given seats on buses, trains
- B. Doors opened
- C. Lower costs
  1. Transportation
  2. Entertainment

II. Differences
- A. Japanese elderly live with family.
  1. Help raise children
  2. Get more respect
- B. United States elderly live with other elderly.

Conclusion: Japanese treatment is better.

As you can see, this pattern for both comparing and contrasting is very much like pattern 2 (see Illustration 6.7).

It would also be possible to use a pattern similar to pattern 2. The paragraph would look like this.

Model Paragraph (Comparison and Contrast, Pattern 2)

The Elderly

Although old people in the United States and in my country, Japan, are treated the same in some ways, in other ways they are treated differently. In

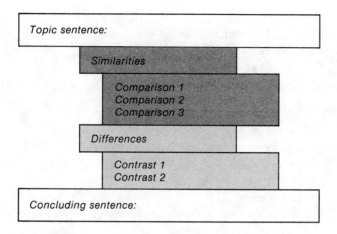

Illustration 6.7
Comparing and Contrasting in One Paragraph:
Pattern 1

Japan the young people will give an older person a seat on a bus or train. The young open doors for the old. The elderly get lower prices on buses and tickets to shows. In Japan the grandparents live with the family. They help to raise the grandchildren. If anyone needs advice, the first person to be asked is the grandfather, because he is the wisest. In the United States the young will also offer their seat on a bus or train to an older person. They will open doors for the elderly, too. Older people in the United States also get lower costs for transportation and entertainment. However, in the United States older people rarely live with their families. They do not help to raise the grandchildren or give advice. They live with other older people in "senior citizen" places. I think that it is better for families to live all together in companionship.

Title: The Elderly

Topic sentence: Old people are treated similarly and differently in Japan and the United States.

   I. Treatment in Japan
      A. Similarities
         1. Given seats on buses and trains
         2. Doors opened
         3. Lower costs
            a. Transportation
            b. Entertainment

B. Differences
  1. Live with the family
  2. Help raise grandchildren
  3. Give advice
II. Treatment in the United States
  A. Similarities
    1. Given seats on buses and trains
    2. Doors opened
    3. Lower costs
      a. Transportation
      b. Entertainment
  B. Differences
    1. Do not help raise grandchildren
    2. Do not give advice
    3. Live with other elderly people

Concluding sentence: I think living with the family is better.

This pattern is very similar to pattern 1 in paragraphs that either compare or contrast (see Illustration 6.8).

Either pattern can be used. Pattern 1 emphasizes the differences by putting them last in a kind of climax order. Pattern 2 seems to be repetitious. It states the same thing twice, once for each country. Which pattern you decide to use will depend on your topic and your purpose in writing. In general, the simplest pattern is the best; it is usually easier for you to write and easier for your readers to understand.

 ### Writing Practice (Guided Writing)

Directions: Using one of the patterns for both comparing and contrasting, show the similarities and differences between one custom or way of acting in another country and a corresponding custom or way of acting in the United States.

Suggestions

Higher education (after high school)
  Requirements for getting into college
  Selection of classes to take
  How instructors treat students
  How students treat instructors

Holidays
  Main religious holidays (how celebrated)
  National holidays (reasons for them)

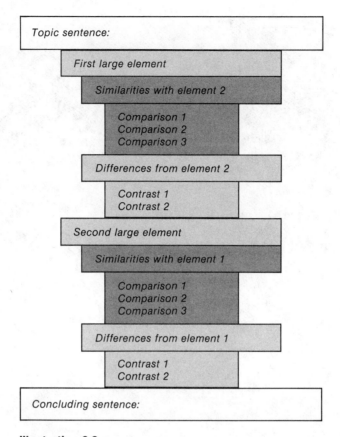

Illustration 6.8
Comparing and Contrasting in One Paragraph:
Pattern 2

Local holidays (reasons, how celebrated)
Special holidays (for parents, children, animals, ancestors)

Writing Practice (Free Writing)

Directions: Illustrations 6.9 and 6.10 represent the passing of time. The first, from the fourteenth century, is called "The Grim Reaper." The second is modern and is called "Father Time." Read the list of their characteristics. Then write a paragraph in which you compare the two, contrast the two, or both compare and contrast the two.

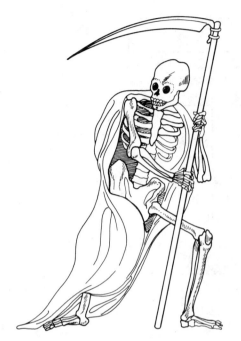

Illustration 6.9
The Grim Reaper

Illustration 6.10
Father Time

Characteristics

1. Similarities
   a. Each carries a tool called a *scythe*; it is used to cut grain, such as wheat, rye, or barley.
   b. Each wears a garment called a *cloak*.
   c. Each shows old age.
   d. Neither wears shoes.

2. The *Grim Reaper* (*Grim* means "shocking, frightful." A *reaper* is someone who cuts the grain. In this case the "grain" he cuts down, or kills, is people.)
   a. The Grim Reaper is shown as a living skeleton.
   b. He has a frightening look on his skeleton face.

c. It was said that he came for all men when it was time for them to die. No one could escape him.

d. He is the symbol for death.

3. *Father Time*
   a. Father Time is shown as an old man.
   b. He has a white beard.
   c. He has a happy look on his face.
   d. He carries an hourglass (an old device for measuring time).
   e. He is the symbol for the year that is just ending (on New Year's Eve).
   f. He is not the symbol for the death of people.

 ### Writing Practice (Free Writing)

Directions: Following is a list of characteristics that people are supposed to have, depending on whether they were born first, second, or third in their family. It is not necessarily the truth but is a theory of a German doctor named Karl Konig.

1. First-born children
   a. Hard-working
   b. Ambitious
   c. Serious
   d. Eager to please parents or boss
   e. Believers in tradition

2. Second-born children
   a. Charming
   b. Happy, enjoy playing
   c. Peacemakers in family arguments
   d. Angered when things do not go their way
   e. Casual about doing things on time
   f. Not much affected by punishment from parents or boss

3. Third-born children
   a. Very shy and sensitive
   b. Artistic
   c. Religious or spiritual
   d. Nontraditional in beliefs

4. Only children (a combination of first-born and third-born)

5. Fourth-born children (the same as first born)

Write a paragraph contrasting the characteristics of these *three* kinds of people. It might be interesting to use yourself or your brothers or sisters as examples of this theory.

Suggestion: Comparing and contrasting often makes use of adjectives. Review page 240 for the comparative and superlative forms of adjectives. Careful use of these forms will make your comparison-contrast paragraphs more effective.

Chapter Seven

Explaining by Showing Cause and Effect

Single Cause and Single Effect

Single Cause and Several Effects

Several Causes and Single Effect

Cause Then Effect That Becomes a Cause

Cause-and-effect thinking is used all of the time by most of us. A child runs home crying. The parent asks, "Why are you crying?" The child answers, "I fell down." You miss class one day. Your teacher asks you why. You answer, "I was absent because I was sick."

CAUSE	EFFECT
falling down	child crying
sickness	absence from class

Cause-and-effect paragraphs are an especially useful type of exposition for students to learn. Many questions on examinations, reports, or laboratory experiments will ask, "What were the results of ..." or, "Trace the causes of ..." or, "Explain the reasons for ..." or, "Show why ... happened." Such questions are best answered by the cause-and-effect paragraph. A *cause* is the thing, person, or event that produces a result or makes something happen. The *effect* is what follows or is produced by a cause.

Single Cause and Single Effect

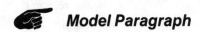 **Model Paragraph**

The Eclipse

An *eclipse* of the sun is the apparent darkening of the sun. It is caused when the moon comes between the sun and an observer on the earth. (See Illustration 7.1.) The shadow of the moon, as it moves across the earth, will

Illustration 7.1
Solar Eclipse

appear to completely cover the sun. To the observer, the effect will be a gradual darkening of the sun until it seems like night. As the moon continues to move along its path, the shadow will become smaller until it is full daylight again. A total eclipse of the sun never lasts for more than seven and one-half minutes.

Analysis

The topic sentence uses definition to introduce the subject of the paragraph. The next sentence states the cause. The next three sentences tell details about the effect of an eclipse to an observer on earth. The concluding sentence gives one last detail or fact. (The basic cause-and-effect pattern is given in Illustration 7.2.)

Illustration 7.2
Basic Pattern of Cause and Effect

Transitional words and phrases useful in cause-and-effect paragraphs include the following:

as	due to	therefore
as a result	for	the reason is
because	in order	the first cause (effect)
by	since	the second cause (effect)
consequently	so	(*and so on*)

Cause-and-effect paragraphs often give several specific details to explain either the cause or the effect.

Example

Cause:

Cocaine has become an increasingly popular "recreational drug" in the United States.

Effect:

The effect is both immediate and long lasting.

Specific details:

The user feels powerful right away.
The user feels great self-confidence.
After four hours the user is depressed.
Then the user is angry and nervous.
The user may even become mentally ill.

Concluding sentence:

The dangerous long-term effects are more important than the immediate good feelings.

 ## Writing Practice (Sentence Combining/Correct Order)

Directions: Arrange the following sentences into a cause-and-effect paragraph. You may start with either the cause or the effect. Give the paragraph coherence by using transitions or pronouns or by repeating key words. Make sure that the paragraph has unity; do not get off the topic. Since this paragraph was used as a case history in a health class, some of the sentences may be off the topic; do not use them.

1. Luciano loves the taste of fattening food. (*cause*)
2. Luciano can never seem to lose weight. (*effect*)
3. He enjoys rich Italian food. (*example*)
4. He likes spaghetti. (*specific detail*)
5. Luciano enjoys the taste of lasagna and pizza. (*specific detail*)
6. Luciano adores the taste of chocolate. (*example*)
7. He likes chocolate ice cream. (*specific detail*)
8. He likes chocolate cakes and cookies. (*specific detail*)
9. He loves chocolate candy. (*specific detail*)
10. Luciano also drinks much coffee. (*example*)
11. Just looking at rich desserts makes him hungry. (*example*)

Single Cause and Several Effects

Sometimes cause-and-effect paragraphs can be complicated. For example, in the following paragraph Charles Darwin tells about the effects of an earthquake on the South American town of Valdavia.

 ### Model Paragraph

February 20, 1835

This has been a terrible day in the town of Valdavia, for there was the most terrible earthquake ever known. The earthquake destroyed seventy nearby villages; large buildings were shaken down. The earthquake caused a great wave that washed away whole buildings. I soon saw proofs—the whole coast was covered with pieces of wood and furniture as if a thousand ships had been wrecked. Besides chairs, tables, bookshelves, there were several roofs of houses scattered about. The storehouse had been burst open, and great bags of cotton and other valuables were spread on the shore.

Analysis

Darwin has one cause (the earthquake) and several effects (destroyed villages, shaken buildings, a great wave). He also uses specific details (furniture, roofs, bags of cotton). Later on in his narrative he wonders what might have caused the earthquake. Was it a volcano? If it was a volcano, what caused the volcano to explode or erupt? Reasoning backward from effect to cause can be tricky. How far back is it best to go? You will have to decide when to stop; it will depend on your purpose in writing. Generally it is enough to focus on the immediate cause of an effect. Do not try to go back to the beginning of time! (The pattern consisting of a single cause and multiple effects is given in Illustration 7.3.)

Several Causes and Single Effect

There is still another pattern used to write cause-and-effect paragraphs: one effect may have several causes.

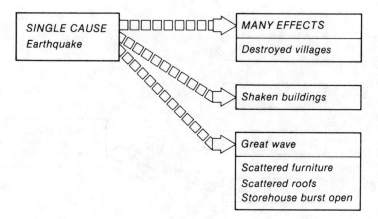

Illustration 7.3

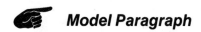   **Model Paragraph**

Failure

There are usually several reasons why students do not do well in college. One cause is poor study habits. Many students do not know how to study effectively. They will just glance at their books instead of reading them carefully. They do not know how to take notes that will help them to learn. Other students seem to be going to college only to have fun. They do not take their classes seriously. In my case, I almost failed my first year because I did not know how to use my time carefully. Given a twenty-five–page history assignment to read, two pages of French to translate, and a paragraph to write for English, I did not know where to begin. Often I never finished all of my homework. It took me that whole year to learn to budget my time. There may be other causes that students cannot help, such as health problems, money problems, or family problems, but not using time wisely is certainly a major cause of failure.

Analysis

This student tells what she is going to write about in her topic sentence (several reasons for failure in college). Then she lists several reasons. Next, she tells an extended example from her own experience. The concluding sentence contrasts reasons for failure that a student cannot control with her

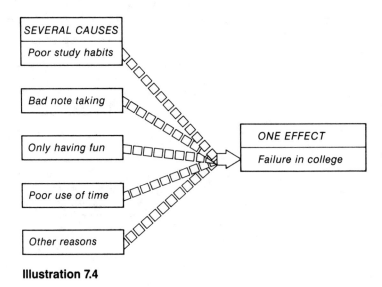

Illustration 7.4

own specific example. This paragraph gives several causes and one effect. (The pattern consisting of several causes and a single effect is presented in Illustration 7.4.)

Cause Then Effect That Becomes a Cause

Sometimes a single cause will lead to an effect that, in turn, will cause another effect. The following paragraph shows the cause-effect-cause-effect pattern (see Illustration 7.5).

 **Model Paragraph**

Let's Trade

During the recession of the 1970s, an unemployed electrician offered to do some electrical work for a doctor in exchange for medical services. Within a few months many people were trading services for services and goods for goods. This trading or *bartering* soon became widespread enough to cause the organization of a "trading exchange" where people could find out what goods or services they could exchange without using

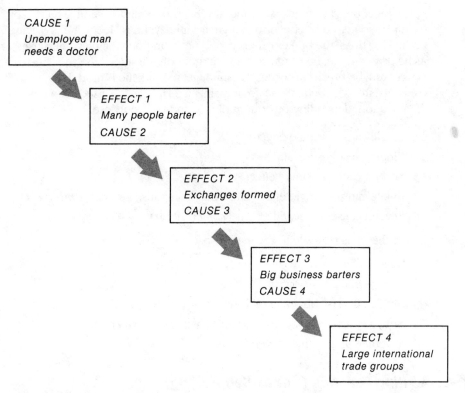

CAUSE 1
Unemployed man
needs a doctor

EFFECT 1
Many people barter
CAUSE 2

EFFECT 2
Exchanges formed
CAUSE 3

EFFECT 3
Big business barters
CAUSE 4

EFFECT 4
Large international
trade groups

Illustration 7.5

any money. The success of this first organization led to the formation of over 400 such exchanges all over the country (like the Michigan Trade Exchange with over 3,000 members). With the growth of such groups of individuals, big industries began to think about bartering. General Motors, for example, set up Motors Trading Corporation. In 1984 GM traded the government of Jamaica automobiles worth about $40 million for 400 tons of aluminum ore. Such trades led, in turn, to the development of international trading groups such as Metro Trading Association of Michigan. The final step in this chain of events was the joining of many trade associations into a large group, the International Association of Trade Exchanges. Its president, Joseph Weiss, says that trade associations do nearly $600 billion worth of business a year. That amount is nearly 30% of the world's business! And it all started because unemployed people with no money needed goods and services.

A longer essay might combine several causes and several effects. For example, someone has been working hard all day; he is sleepy; he is driving home very tired; the brakes on his car do not work too well (several causes). As he drives home, he is not alert; his car goes off the side of the road; the car is wrecked; he breaks his nose; he cannot get to work; he is fired from his job (several effects). Each of the four main patterns can be used alone or in combination, depending on your audience and your purpose.

1. Single cause—single effect
2. Single cause—several effects
3. Several causes—single effect
4. Single cause—single effect; effect becomes cause—effect (*and so on*)
5. Several causes—several effects (*combination*)

Remember, it is possible to reverse the pattern, if you wish.

1. Single effect—single cause
2. Several effects—show single cause
3. Single effect—show several causes
4. Single effect—show cause that was an effect (*and so on*)
5. Several effects—their several causes

Writing Practice (Controlled Writing)

Directions: Read the following model paragraph.

Model Paragraph

Traffic

Many people do not know that there were traffic problems in ancient Rome. There was too much noise from the clatter of the horses' hoofs and the banging of chariot wheels on the stone roads. The air was thick with dust and swarms of insects. The market place was so crowded that people could not move around freely. When Julius Caesar ruled Rome, he decided to do something about the problem. He allowed no chariots on the streets during the busy hours of the day. He made some streets "one-way" streets. He made it illegal to park a chariot in the downtown area of Rome. He required all horses and chariots to move "at a moderate pace" in Rome.

Write a cause-and-effect paragraph following the model paragraph. You may change the setting to the present day (the city where you live now, a city where you used to live). You may change the causes of the problem (noise, crowded streets, air pollution) to those of today. You might describe some of the effects today of too much traffic. You might present another problem, such as unemployment or high taxes, and show how a leader or a government tried to solve it. For example:

cause: the problem caused by too much traffic

effect: Caesar's new laws and rules

Writing Practice (Guided Writing)

Directions: Write a paragraph of at least five sentences on one of the following topics. Develop the topic sentence first. You may use any of the possible patterns. A working outline will make writing the paragraph easier.

1. Causes for cheating in college

2. Reasons why you need a new car (or motorcycle)

3. Reasons why motorcycles are dangerous

4. Reasons why you dropped a class

5. The main reason(s) why you are going to school

Writing Practice (Creative Free Writing)

Directions: Look at the picture in Illustration 7.6. It shows an old gentleman who has fallen down on the sidewalk. His hat is off; his glasses are hanging loose; his umbrella is crunched. Reasoning backward from the effect, give the possible causes for his fall.

Illustration 7.6

Suggestions: The sidewalk was slippery; he had too much wine with dinner; someone pushed him; he was trying to get out of the way of something. Use your imagination when writing this paragraph.

Writing Practice (Free Writing)

Directions: Much humor is based on cause and effect. Look at the cartoon in Illustration 7.7. A man from the City Pound (an organization that catches dogs that are running around the city) has just put his net over a large, mean dog. He says, "Now what?" Write a brief paragraph in which you tell what might be some of the effects of the capture of the dog.

Look at the next cartoon (Illustration 7.8). The father is entering the house. The mother says that she has given the baby away. Write a paragraph telling what you think caused her to give the baby away.

"Now what?"

Illustration 7.7

"I gave him away!"

Illustration 7.8

Writing Practice (Free Writing)

Directions: The cartoonists who drew the cartoons in Illustrations 7.7 and 7.8 picked just one brief moment in time. They expect you to reason forward or backward to the cause or the effect. Do you think either of these cartoons is funny? Write a paragraph telling whether you do or not (the effect) and why (the cause).

Chapter Eight

Analysis: Explaining by Looking at the Parts or Steps

How to Do Something (Process Analysis)

How Something Is Done (Process Analysis)

The Natural Process

The fourth main type of expository writing is called *analysis. Analysis* means to take something apart and look at the parts to see how they make up the whole. It is possible to *analyze* objects, ideas, people, organizations, or events. You are already familiar with grammatical analysis: taking a sentence apart and seeing how the parts work together to make meaning. You are also familiar with the analysis of the paragraphs used as models in this book. You will find that writing an *analytical* paragraph is useful in all of the sciences and engineering. Literary analysis is similar to the brief paragraph analysis you studied earlier, except that it looks at the parts of stories or poems to see how the author achieved his or her purpose.

The analytical process, then, serves two purposes. First, it is a method that you can use to understand something by examining the parts. Second, it is a method of organizing your writing so that others can understand you. Every time you make an outline, you are actually going through the process of analysis. You are able to see the parts of what you outline, and you are able to understand how they work together to form the whole paragraph or essay. Analytical paragraphs generally are used to answer three kinds of questions:

1. How is it made or done? (*process analysis*)
2. How does it work? (*functional analysis*)
3. How is it put together? (*technical analysis*)

These three kinds of analysis are sometimes combined. Many kinds of order are possible in the analytical paragraph, but usually time or space order is the most effective. You will make use of all of the kinds of writing you have studied so far. Your paragraph may use definition, some description, cause and effect (sometimes called causal analysis), even brief narrative.

How to Do Something (Process Analysis)

Probably the most familiar type of analysis is the recipe—instructions on how to prepare food.

 ## Model Recipe

Kara-age

It is easy to prepare the Japanese dish of kara-age; you will need six ingredients.

$\frac{1}{2}$ cup of soy sauce

$\frac{1}{4}$ cup of white wine

2 tablespoons of sugar

12 large shrimp, cleaned and cut into bite-size pieces

$\frac{1}{2}$ cup of corn starch

2 tablespoons of peanut oil

First, mix together soy sauce, wine, and sugar. Pour this mixture over the shrimp and let it sit for one hour in the refrigerator. Drain well on paper towels. Place corn starch in a bag, and shake the shrimp in the bag until the shrimp is evenly coated with the corn starch. Add the oil to your wok. When the oil is hot, cook the shrimp. Turn it until each piece is golden brown. Serve hot or warm. This recipe will make four to six main dishes or many appetizers.

Analysis

The first part serves as a topic sentence: Kara-age (*topic*) is easy to prepare (*controlling idea*). The next part lists the ingredients or materials needed. The following part gives the steps in time order. The last part concludes by telling how many people the recipe will serve.

In every bookstore and newsstand there are dozens of books and articles telling people how to do something. They range from cookbooks to "self-help" articles on how to lose or gain weight, how to build a fence or a gate, how to fix a broken door, how to get a job—in short, how to do almost anything. Each follows the same pattern that is used in a recipe. The total process is broken down into parts. The parts are each explained. The process is given step by step. The process analysis is also known as the "how-to" paper. The "how-to" paragraph should follow these guidelines:

1. Write in simple, direct sentences.
2. List the information the reader must know; check each item as you write it.
3. If ingredients or materials are needed, list them.
4. Give directions in the order to be followed.
5. Tell the importance of each step, if necessary.
6. Define any terms that are new or difficult.
7. Test the instructions by following them yourself. If you cannot do it, neither can your reader.

Writing Practice (Sentence Combining and Correct Order)

Directions: Rearrange the following sentences. Look for clues like *first, next, before,* and *after.* When you have the correct arrangement, write them in paragraph form on your own paper. You may decide to combine some of the sentences into longer ones for sentence variety.

1. The last exercise is called jumping jacks.
2. To do a knee-bend, stand; place hands on hips; squat down as far as possible.
3. After the upper body is relaxed, stretch the legs.
4. The proper clothing is not too tight.
5. More and more people find that jogging is a healthy exercise.
6. Repeat the jumping jacks at least fifteen times.
7. Knee-bends start the blood in your legs flowing.
8. Stretch the legs by sitting on the floor and reaching out to touch the toes with each hand.
9. Finally, you are warmed up and ready to go jogging.
10. When the legs are stretched, do a dozen knee-bends.
11. First, stretch the upper body by bending from front to back and from side to side several times.
12. Jogging can be a healthy exercise, but you must prepare yourself to avoid injury.
13. The clothing may fit snugly (not tightly) at the wrists and ankles.
14. After you have the proper clothing, warm up by stretching your muscles.
15. To do a jumping jack, stand up; place feet together; jump and spread feet as far apart as you comfortably can; jump again and bring feet together.
16. Before you start to warm up, get some comfortable clothing. *That may fit snugly at the wrists & ankles.*

Suggestions: Sentences 5 and 12 can be combined into a good topic sentence. Sentences 4, 13, and 16 are all about clothing. They could be combined into one sentence. If you wrote them as they are now, your paragraph would be choppy because the word *clothing* is repeated too often.

 ## Model Paragraph

Cleaning Up

When someone builds a wall or a barbecue of brick, he often finds that there is dirt, cement, or mortar left on the bricks. The careful worker will clean the bricks; hydrochloric acid will usually do the job. This powerful acid is sold under the name of "muriatic acid." It works by actually dissolving a thin layer of mortar or the brick or stone to be treated. To use, mix one part of acid to ten parts of water in a glass or plastic container. If a metal container is used, the acid will dissolve it. ALWAYS add the acid to water! Pouring water into the acid may cause it to boil and spatter. Wear rubber gloves. Using a stiff brush, scrub the surface. Take care not to get any acid on the skin or garments. It will eat holes in both. When the surface is clean, wash it with clear water.

Analysis

Note that this paragraph about building technology is specific about what *not* to do as well as about what to do. Sometimes "how to" directions must warn about possible dangers.

 ## Writing Practice (Controlled Writing)

Directions: Following the sentence patterns in either the recipe, the jogging paragraph (a series of steps in time order), or the "Cleaning Up" paragraph (what not to do), write an analysis paragraph in which you explain how to do something. Some suggestions:

1. How to play a game
2. How to cook something
3. How to build something
4. How to perform some sport
5. How to do some simple act (change a tire, put on makeup)

How Something Is Done (Process Analysis)

Another kind of analysis paragraph tells how something is done rather than telling someone how to do something.

 ## Model Paragraph

Keeping Clean

The process of keeping the streets of Shanghai free from litter takes an enormous amount of work. One reason is that the job is mainly done by hand. At last count there were 2,341 men and women who sweep the streets daily. They are helped by 48 additional groups who wash the streets in the main public places. Special "gangs" are also used for special clean-up operations after public events. If they stop doing these chores for even one day, the amount of trash and litter becomes huge. There is so much waste that many parts of the city are swept twice a day. There are even a few crews who have to clean the very dirty business areas four or five times a day.

Analysis

This paragraph explains how something is done. It starts with a clear topic sentence and uses seven specific examples of the enormous amount of work. Notice the use of synonyms to give the paragraph coherence and to add variety. Instead of repeating the word *work* four times, the writer uses *job, chores,* and *operations.* He also uses *crews,* "*gangs,*" and *groups* to avoid too much repetition. Use of synonyms serves the same purpose as the repetition of *key* terms but is better style (see Illustration 8.1).

 ## Writing Practice (Controlled Writing)

Directions: Following the basic pattern of the paragraph "Keeping Clean" as closely as possible, change the location. Tell, for example, how your room, your house, or your automobile is kept clean.

Suggested Pattern

1. "The process of cleaning my _____ is _____."
2. Tell how the work is done (tools used?).

3. Tell who does it.

4. Tell who (if anyone) helps.

5. Mention any special chores not done daily.

6. What happens if you do not clean it?

7. How often is it cleaned?

8. Make your own concluding sentence.

Illustration 8.1
Do not repeat yourself.

✔ **Check:**   How often did you use the word *clean* in your paragraph? Try using some synonyms to add interest and variety. Here are some synonyms and special words to substitute for *clean*.

cleanse	rinse	wipe	brush
sweep	whisk	mop	tidy
scour	vacuum	wash	scrub

The Natural Process

Another kind of analysis is one in which no one is doing anything. Instead, it explains how a natural process occurs.

 ## Model Paragraph

Rain

People used to think that rain was caused by the god of storms, but it is a perfectly natural process. Rain begins when moisture is drawn into the sky by the heat of the sun. Most of this process, called *evaporation,* happens over the warm oceans of the world. The tiny droplets of water vapor are carried upward by the wind. As the water vapor is carried higher, it gets colder. Then it forms the water-filled air we see as fog or clouds. When the water-filled air is cool enough, the droplets join together until they are big and heavy enough to fall. These falling drops are rain.

Analysis

The topic sentence is a compound sentence (see page 287) with the actual topic stated in the second part. The rest of the paragraph tells the sequence or time order of the forming of rain as the drops of water evaporate, get colder, join together, and finally fall.

 ### Writing Practice (Guided Writing)

Directions: Following the general pattern of the paragraph on rain, explain some process that does not need a human being. Some possible topics are listed here, but they are only suggestions. You may select your own topic.

1. Formation of snow
2. How ocean waves are formed
3. Growth of a plant
4. Development of a chicken in the egg
5. Lightning

Suggestions: When you have decided on your topic sentence, write an introductory clause like the one in "Rain." Many writers put an interesting introductory sentence *first* in their paragraphs. Then they put the topic sentence second. The purpose of using a separate introductory sentence is to catch the reader's interest. There are several kinds of sentences that can be used to introduce paragraphs. Here are some that might have been used in the paragraph on rain. First the *type* of sentence is given and then an *example*.

1. Use of statistics (facts or data)
   Enough rain falls each day to provide every person on earth with 22,000 gallons of pure water.
2. Narrative or personal experience
   During the heavy rains of last year I wondered where all that water came from.
3. Quotation
   Children kept indoors because of the rain often sing, "Rain, rain, go away. Come again some other day."
4. Question
   Do you ever wonder what makes it rain?
5. Striking contrast
   Rain is usually necessary to make plants grow, but last year it was so heavy that it caused floods and landslides.
6. Historical reference
   The Greek writer Plutarch believed that rain was caused by the gods to clean the air and earth after a battle.
7. Definition
   Rain is water vapor in the air that falls to earth in drops.

So that you will not have to write your paragraph several times, make a working outline first to see the parts and their relation to your whole paragraph. It is easier to make changes on the outline than to rewrite everything.

 ## Writing Practice (Free Writing)

Directions: Write a paragraph of analysis. Make an outline first. After you have decided on your topic sentence, write an introductory statement to interest your reader. The following are suggested topics.

How to play a card game	How to test equipment
How to take notes	How to make an outline
How a rainbow is formed	The aging process
Preparing to ski	Buying clothes
Driving in traffic	A chemical reaction

Writing Practice (Exercises for Exposition)

Directions: The following three-paragraph composition will give you some information about the topic of astrology. First read it. Then do the writing practices assigned to you by your instructor. The writing exercises will cover all of the kinds of expository writing you have learned in this chapter. After you have made your working outline for the general order and pattern of your paragraph, write the first draft, or copy. Then check it for effective use of transitions. Have you repeated key terms, made use of synonyms, and included an interesting introductory sentence? Is your paper free from mechanical and grammatical errors? Do you have an effective concluding sentence?

Model Composition

Astrology

Astrology is an ancient, worldwide belief in the power of the stars and planets to influence people on earth. The word *astrology* comes from the Greek meaning "star study." It is not the same as the science of *astronomy*, which comes from the Greek for "star laws." Astronomy is a science that tries to find out the exact positions and movements of the stars and planets. It also searches the skies for new heavenly bodies. However, the purpose of astrology is quite different. Astrology is the belief that the stars and planets have an influence on what happens to people on earth. Astrologers believe that the position of planets in the sky at the time of birth will determine the type of person one will become. They also believe that it is possible to tell what will happen in the future by studying the heavenly bodies.

There are two kinds of astrology; both are thousands of years old. About 5,000 years ago, near the Persian Gulf, people believed that the stars and planets moved around the earth in a regular path. They called this path or belt the *zodiac*. They divided it into twelve equal parts and gave each part a name, a sign, and a symbol (see Illustration 8.2). The signs are animals, different kinds of people, and a balance, or scale. The symbols are supposed to represent the signs. These people thought that the signs of the Western zodiac changed about every thirty days.

Halfway around the world, in ancient China, a different kind of astrology was beginning at the same time. Again, people looked up at the lights in the sky, the stars and planets, and decided that these bodies had an influence on what happened here on earth. They too divided the zodiac into twelve parts and gave each part a name, a sign, and a symbol (see Illustration 8.3). The signs are all animals (including a dragon), and the symbols are the Chinese characters for the animals' names. Unlike the West-

Illustration 8.2
Western Zodiac

ern zodiac, the Eastern zodiac changes once each year. After twelve years this zodiac repeats itself. Although both of these belief systems started long ago in different parts of the world, they are still believed by millions of people today.

Analysis

The best way to analyze a longer paper is to make an outline. Then see what each part of the essay does.

Illustration 8.3
Eastern Zodiac

Title: Astrology

Main idea, or *thesis* (the same as the topic sentence in a paragraph): Astrology is an ancient, worldwide belief in power of stars and planets to influence people on earth.

I. Differs from astronomy
   A. Astronomy: a science
      1. Exact positions of stars, planets
      2. Predict movements
      3. Discover new bodies
   B. Astrology: a belief
      1. Planets influence people
      2. Determine character at birth
      3. Predict future events

II. Western astrology
   A. 5,000 years old
   B. Persian Gulf
   C. Characteristics
      1. Twelve-part zodiac
      2. Repeats in 30 days

III. Eastern astrology
   A. 5,000 years old
   B. China
   C. Characteristics
      1. Twelve-part zodiac
      2. Repeats every 12 years

Concluding sentence: Both started long ago; both still believed in.

The thesis sentence (similar to the topic sentence in a paragraph) promises to explain that astrology is very old and world-wide. Paragraph 1 uses definition to contrast astrology with astronomy. Paragraph 2 uses a transition sentence to introduce the first type, Western astrology. It uses a brief chronology, or time sequence, to explain Western astrology and its characteristics. Paragraph 3 does the same with Eastern astrology. Paragraphs 2 and 3 both contain elements of comparison and contrast. The concluding sentence restates the thesis and adds the fact that both systems are still in use today. You will find, when you begin to write longer papers, that you will combine the paragraph patterns and orders that you have been studying and practicing. This short essay uses definition, example, narrative (in the brief history), comparison, and contrast. It even seems to include some cause and effect in the statements about the influence of the stars on people.

Western astrology believes that people born in certain months (they say, "born under the sign of Scorpio," for example) will be certain kinds of people. Here are some of the main characteristics of the different astrological signs.

Aquarius (the water carrier) January 20 to February 19

An independent thinker, very intelligent, friendly, good-humored, and fair-minded; usually a kind person, but sometimes impractical.

Pisces (the fish) February 20 to March 20

An imaginative and original person, generous and honest, very emotional, creative, but sometimes gloomy or jealous.

Aries (the ram) March 21 to April 19

Courageous and enthusiastic; likes adventures; a good organizer who is self-confident but sometimes also selfish.

Taurus (the bull) April 20 to May 20

Determined, even stubborn, yet kind; has a talent for getting money, but sometimes is greedy; a practical person, a lover of beauty.

Gemini (the twins) May 21 to June 21

Witty and happy, with a good sense of humor; a talkative person who is skilled with the hands but is sometimes unkind to others.

Cancer (the crab) June 22 to July 22

Sensitive and idealistic person who is home-loving, romantic, and gentle, but sometimes jealous of others.

Leo (the lion) July 23 to August 22

A born leader, ambitious and yet honest, loyal, generous, and cheerful most of the time, but sometimes bossy.

Virgo (the virgin) August 23 to September 22

Logical and intellectual; a hard worker who likes details; modest and dependable, but sometimes critical of others.

Libra (the scales, or balance) September 23 to October 22

A diplomatic, peace-loving person who hates arguments, has a good imagination, loves beauty, but is sometimes careless.

Scorpio (the scorpion) October 23 to November 21

A hard-working, patient person who is very realistic, loyal, and courageous, with a logical mind; a very loving person, but sometimes selfish.

Sagittarius (the archer) November 22 to December 21

A warm and friendly person who is honest and curious, is fun to have near, likes adventure, but is sometimes forgetful.

Capricorn (the goat) December 22 to January 19

An ambitious and hard-working person who is very orderly and careful; a good organizer, but sometimes very impatient with others.

Eastern astrology believes that people born in certain years have certain characteristics (they say, "born in the year of the rat," for example).

Rat (or mouse) 1924, 1936, 1948, 1960, 1972, 1984
A physically attractive person, hard-working, socially active and highly emotional, but sometimes critical of others.

Buffalo (or ox) 1925, 1937, 1949, 1961, 1973, 1985
Outwardly patient, with regular habits, a perfectionist who is both protective and loyal but never forgives an injury.

Tiger 1926, 1938, 1950, 1962, 1974, 1986
Cautious, good at making money, physically strong and usually large, well liked by others, but often lacking in self-confidence.

Rabbit (or hare) 1927, 1939, 1951, 1963, 1975, 1987
Very good at gambling; holds traditional values, is usually very careful in work, but tries too hard to impress others.

Dragon 1928, 1940, 1952, 1964, 1976, 1988
Appears to be happy in all things in life, but inwardly is not really happy; usually has strong opinions, but tends to be bossy.

Serpent (or snake) 1929, 1941, 1953, 1965, 1977, 1989
A glamorous person who is lively and sensitive to others; an intellectual person, but sometimes selfish.

Horse 1930, 1942, 1954, 1966, 1978, 1990
Usually an attractive person who is popular and clever, likes people, but is a poor family person who may be impatient with others.

Ram (or sheep) 1919, 1931, 1943, 1955, 1967, 1979
A sincere, sensible person who is a lover of nature and of comfort, is usually religious and tender, but has no ambition.

Monkey 1920, 1932, 1944, 1956, 1968, 1980
A talented person with a good memory and a sense of humor; ambitious, with a strong ego, usually trusting, but sometimes too shy.

Rooster (or cock) 1921, 1933, 1945, 1957, 1969, 1981
An intelligent and imaginative person who likes adventure and activity, a good judge of people, but often too honest in what he or she says.

Dog 1922, 1934, 1946, 1958, 1970, 1982
A friendly, sensitive person who can keep secrets; dreamy and gracious, sometimes stubborn, but very quick to anger (and to forget).

Boar (or pig) 1923, 1935, 1947, 1959, 1971, 1983
A studious, kind person who is honest, loyal, and affectionate, likes a quiet life with a few good friends, but sometimes seems unfriendly.

These characteristics are given very briefly. Books on astrology have many more details. Before you begin your writing, be sure to check the meanings of the words used to describe these characteristics. Many of them have special meanings, and you may need some help. Most of them can be found in your dictionary.

Writing Practice (Sentence Combining)

Directions: Combine the short sentences into longer, more mature sentences by eliminating words used many times. Use the suggested conjunctions and transitions or others that you like.

1. a. Astrologers study the positions of the stars. (*both*)
   b. Astronomers study the positions of the stars.
   c. Astrologers study the positions of the planets.
   d. Astronomers study the positions of the planets. (*and*)

2. a. Astrologers make a claim. (*while*)
   b. The claim is to tell the future.
   c. The future is of people on earth.
   d. Astronomers make a claim. (*also*)
   e. The claim is to tell the future.
   f. This future is the positions of the stars. (*but*)

3. a. A great many people have a belief. (*although*)
   b. The belief is in astrology.
   c. Many other people have a belief.
   d. That belief is that astrology is superstition.

4. a. Astronomy is a science. (*though*)
   b. It is a true science.

5. a. Astronomers know something.
   b. They know that the planet Pluto is far away.
   c. It is 3,664,000,000 miles from earth.

6. a. Astronomers laugh.
   b. Astronomers ask a question. (*and*)
   c. Pluto is far away. (*if*)
   d. Could it have an effect?
   e. The effect would be on people.
   f. The people are here on earth.

Writing Practice (Sentence Sequence)

Directions: Arrange the following sentences in the correct time order. Look for dates, repetition of words, and transitions to help you.

7 1. Then the Greeks, and later the Romans, discovered most of the other planets.

5 2. The ancient Greeks, about 400 B.C., believed that the sun and planets all circled around the earth.

10 3. Finally, in 1930 A.D., the last of the planets that circle the sun, Pluto, was discovered.

2 4. Even the most primitive people knew something about the sky thousands of years ago.

1 5. Astronomy is the oldest of the sciences. (*topic sentence*)

4 6. Early people also knew that they could measure time by the position of the moon.

6 7. Later, the Greeks discovered the positions of the nearer planets like Venus and Mars.

8 8. As early as 1750 B.C., the people of the Near East knew how to figure the positions of many planets.

3 9. These early, primitive people knew that the sun gave light and warmth.

9 10. By the year 1781 A.D., people had discovered six planets.

Writing Practice (Guided Writing)

Directions: This type of guided writing is different from the type you have done before. You are to develop a paragraph by picking one of the following topic sentences. Then, use information from the article "Astrology" and your own knowledge to write the paragraph. Use any method of development studied so far, or a combination of methods.

Topic Sentences

1. The two zodiacs, Western and Eastern, are similar in many ways.

2. The two zodiacs, Western and Eastern, differ in many ways.

3. Although astronomy and astrology both study planets and stars, they are not the same.

4. Astrology is an interesting topic. For example, ...

5. If someone really believes in astrology, that belief might "make" him or her act in a certain way.

Writing Practice (Controlled Writing)

Directions: Develop a paragraph about yourself and astrology by completing the following sentence patterns with information from the article.

1. According to the Western zodiac, I have the following characteristics. (*List some of the characteristics. You may need more than one sentence.*)

2. According to the Eastern zodiac, I also have other characteristics. (*List some other characteristics.*)

3. According to astrology, I am. . . . (*List the main characteristics according to your birth date.*)

4. I agree (or disagree) with astrologers' statements about me because. . . .

5. Now write a clear topic sentence for your paragraph.

 ## *Writing Practice (Free Writing)*

Directions: Develop one of the following topics into an expository paragraph. Use the method of development (or the combination of methods) that best seems to fit your ideas.

Compare or contrast (or both).

Show cause and effect (or effect to cause).

Explain by illustrations or examples.

Use analysis.

Use narration, definition, or description to make your paragraph clear and interesting.

1. There is a column giving astrological advice in almost every daily newspaper. Thousands of people earn money by giving astrological advice. Why is astrology so popular?

2. Do you agree or disagree that you are the kind of a person that astrologers say you are?

3. Astrologers claim that there are "good days" and "bad days" according to the stars and planets. Do you have "good days" and "bad days"? Do you think that the stars and planets cause such days? Give some examples to support your topic sentence.

4. Which zodiac is more accurate for you, the Western or the Eastern?

5. Do you believe in astrology? Why?

Chapter Nine

Argumentation: The Art of Convincing

The Proposition

The Proof

Kinds of Arguments

Patterns of Reasoning

Review and Conclusion

People commonly use the word *argument* to mean "a fight with words" or "a dispute." Writers, however, use *argument* in a different way. They use it to mean an attempt to convince someone that a statement is true or right. An argumentative paragraph is similar in pattern, method, and order to an expository paragraph, but it is different in that it tries to prove, not just to explain. *Argumentation* is useful in three ways. First, as a writer in college you will have to convince your instructors of the truth of your statements in term reports, essays, written examinations, and other kinds of required writing. Second, you will find this skill useful once you are out of college. You will be able to use the skills of argumentation in business to convince people. Many professionals, such as lawyers, salespersons, politicians, and writers, use argumentation every day. Third, and perhaps most important, when you have learned how arguments are put together, you will be able to hear and read the arguments of others and know whether or not these arguments are true and valid. You will be able to analyze the statements of others and *know* whether to accept these statements or to reject them.

The skill of argumentation writing has a long history. The famous Greek philosopher Aristotle wrote in the third century B.C., "The good argument has two parts. State your proposition, then prove it." It is not possible to improve on this advice. When you write an argumentative paper, you want your reader to accept your proposition as true, to believe that what you say is right, or to accept your statement and act in a certain way. To do this, you will need to know what a proposition is and exactly how to prove one.

The Proposition

A *proposition* is almost the same as a topic sentence. It carefully limits your topic and presents your controlling idea. How does it differ from the kinds of topic sentences that you have been writing? It must be a statement with which your reader can reasonably agree or disagree. It must be *arguable*. There are three kinds of statements that are not arguable.

1. Statements about matters of taste or personal preference
   a. The statue of Venus de Milo is *beautiful*.
   b. Watching TV is more *fun* than reading.
   c. Hot dogs are *tastier* than hamburgers.
2. Statements of fact
   a. Over 50,000 people were killed in traffic accidents in 1983.
   b. Nguyen is taller than Khalil.
   c. Seoul is the capital of South Korea.
3. Statements that are vague or contain vague words
   a. Cars are the main cause of pollution.
   b. A college education is necessary for success.
   c. The Ford Ranger is the most popular truck in its class.

It is not possible to argue about whether or not a statue or a person is beautiful. Different people have different ideas about beauty. Today in the United States, for example, the Venus de Milo would be considered too fat to be really beautiful. It is useless to try to argue about which is more fun or which tastes better. The most you could do would be to state your preference. It is also foolish to argue about matters of fact. Simply check the facts in a reliable reference book. Or observe; have Nguyen and Khalil stand up and compare their heights. The third kinds of statements are the ones that can cause the most trouble.

   a. Cars are the main cause of pollution.

All cars? Electric cars do not pollute. The "*main cause*"? Consider factories and industry. "*Pollution*"? There are several kinds of pollution: air, water, soil, noise. This statement is far too vague to make a sensible argument. It could be improved by being made more specific. For example, the following statement might be proven:

   Gasoline- and diesel-powered vehicles are a major cause of air pollution in cities.

   b. A college education is necessary for success.

This statement is so vague that it is almost meaningless. At first look, many people might agree with it, but what does it mean? "A college education" might be many things. At least a B.A. degree? A major in humanities or accounting? "Success" might mean making money (how much?), or understanding literature, or finding a spouse, or having a family, or getting a certain job, or just being a happy person. For a statement like this to be considered an arguable proposition, it needs to be more specific.

A bachelor's degree in business is required for most high-level jobs.

Once "high-level jobs" has been carefully defined, this statement could be argued.

c. The Ford Ranger is the most popular truck in its class.

Here is the kind of proposition that advertisements state so often. As it stands, it is too vague. It might be proven if "popular" is defined and if "in its class" is made clear. This kind of statement is usually followed by a list of the outstanding qualities of the Ford Ranger truck.

The Ford Ranger sold more units than any other American-made, one-half–ton truck in 1983.

This clear, specific statement of fact can be checked. An argument is unnecessary.

 ## *Writing Practice (Propositions)*

Directions: Read the following list of possible propositions. If you think the statement would make an acceptable argument, write *C* in front of it. If it is a matter of taste, write *T.* If it is too vague for an argument, write *V.* If it is only a statement of fact, write *F.*

_____ 1. A vegetarian diet can be healthy.

_____ 2. College courses have no relation to real life.

_____ 3. Oxygen is necessary for fire to burn.

_____ 4. Democracy is a failure.

_____ 5. A ten-year-old car is a better buy than a new one.

_____ 6. Classical music is better than rock music.

_____ 7. Professional baseball players are highly paid.

_____ 8. John Travolta is a handsome man.

_____ 9. The California condor is an endangered bird.

_____ 10. Poverty causes crime.

Writing Practice (Propositions)

Directions: Look at the statements you have marked with a *V* in the preceding list. On your own paper, rewrite those statements to make arguable propositions.

Example

Statement 2 might be revised to make the following argument:

2. Required courses such as American history and health education are of no use to me as a computer science major.

Suggestions

1. Make sure that your propositions are really arguable ones, not statements of personal taste or fact. For example, in statement 7 you might state that professional athletes are overpaid for the benefits they give society.

2. Make sure that your statement is clear. Define words your reader may not know. Limit all vague words. For example, in statement 7, "highly paid" could be limited to "the top 10 percent of all wage earners" or to "wage earners who average at least $75,000 per year."

3. Limit the proposition to a single point. In a longer paper you might be able to argue several related topics, but in a paragraph one topic is enough. For example, in statement 7 you could state, "Professional baseball players are overpaid for their value to society." In a longer paper you might include other professional athletes and entertainers and argue that doctors or English teachers are more valuable to society and should be more highly paid.

The Proof

Once your proposition is clearly stated, you must give enough evidence to convince your reader to believe it. Two main kinds of evidence or proof may be presented: *fact* and *opinion*. Of the two, facts are usually the most convincing.

Facts

A fact is something that is known to be really true or to have actually happened. Observations are the basis for what is called fact. Each person makes his own observations, starting with birth. You must be as careful in giving facts as evidence as you are in writing the proposition. One person may observe that strawberries smell and taste "good." Another person may think that they smell and taste "bad." The kinds of observations you use as "facts" are those that most people agree with. A fact is a statement that can be checked or proved.

1. People accept as facts things that they have observed themselves.

2. People accept as facts things that others have observed.

3. People accept as facts the way nature works.

4. People accept as facts things recorded by cameras, television, newspapers, and other devices.

 ### Examples

1. The Eiffel Tower is in Paris. (*observed by self or someone else*)

2. In the year 1979 Shah Mohammed Reza Pahlavi was forced to leave Iran. (*newspaper report*)

3. Julius Caesar fought a war in Britain in the year 55 B.C. (*reported by Julius Caesar*)

4. Night follows day. (*law of nature*)

5. An airplane crashed in Cuba in 1982. (*television report by camera*)

We accept as facts reports from others, including those written long ago and believed as history. There are special kinds of facts called *statistics*. Statistics are numbers collected and arranged to show a trend or to tell what happened.

 ### Examples

There are 212 million people in the United States.

Two out of three marriages in California end in divorce.

The annual rainfall in the Sahara Desert is 0.023 inches.

Thirty-six inches equals one yard. (Fact by definition)

In 1983 there were 48.2 million pupils in primary and secondary schools in the United States.

In 1983 there were 2.46 million school teachers in the United States.

Using facts is a strong way to prove your proposition. You must be careful that the facts are as accurate as possible and that you have enough of them to convince your reader. The number of facts you will need will depend on the kind of proposition you have.

Opinions

The second kind of evidence is *opinion*. An opinion is a belief based on one's own ideas and thinking and not on certain knowledge. If you want to know, for example, which of two teachers is better, you might get the opinion of several of your classmates who have studied with the teachers. (Of course, you would have to define *better*.) When you feel ill, you often go to a doctor to get his or her opinion. Courtrooms use the opinions of experts as evidence. Be careful that the opinions you use as evidence are those of experts. Ask yourself, "Is this person an expert on this subject?" Valid opinions are those of people who have studied a subject or who have experienced an event.

Writing Practice (Fact and Opinion)

Directions: Decide which of the following statements is a fact and which is an opinion. Write *F* in front of the factual statements and *O* in front of the opinions.

_____ 1. Ronald Reagan was elected president of the United States in 1980.

_____ 2. Television actors earn lots of money.

_____ 3. Tokyo is located in Japan.

_____ 4. The man was overweight.

_____ 5. One mile equals 1.609 kilometers.

_____ 6. Small dogs live longer than big dogs.

_____ 7. Christmas is celebrated on December 25.

_____ 8. It is difficult to walk with a broken leg.

_____ 9. Crime is on the increase in large cities.

_____ 10. Heart disease is the greatest cause of death in the United States.

Thinking Practice (Fact and Opinion)

Directions: With the statements that you believe to be facts, what must you do to check their accuracy? With the statements that you believe to be opinions, how could they be made useful as evidence? For example, statement 4 might be used as evidence if you defined *overweight* as "having more than ten pounds of extra fat" (a medical expert's opinion) and gave the man's actual weight.

Kinds of Arguments

You may wonder why it is necessary to argue at all. If you present a clear proposition that is completely understood and enough facts, reports, or expert opinions to support it, why must you argue at all? Clearly, disagreement will always exist in matters of taste, but why argue about other matters? To understand why we disagree, you must know the two basic kinds of arguments: *factual* arguments and *moral* arguments.

Factual Arguments

A factual argument is used to convince someone that a given proposition is true. For example, in the United States and in Russia in the 1960s, scientists argued that it was possible to send a man into space, even to the moon. The purpose of the argument in each case was to convince the government to spend the necessary money. The proposition "If we are given the money to buy or to make certain equipment, we can put a man into space" was proven to be true.

There are four main reasons for disagreement in a factual argument.

1. False reports or incorrect information

 ### Example

It was believed for years that chimpanzees, one of the large apes, ate only plants: fruits, berries, roots, and grass. An observer, Jane Goodall, noticed that they also ate certain insects and small animals. She took pictures of chimpanzees eating meat. It was necessary to revise all of the books about animal behavior that contained the false information.

2. Incomplete information

 ### Example

It was accepted as fact for over 300 years that Christopher Columbus was the first European to come to the Americas. The 1980 edition of *The World Book Encyclopedia* states that he was "the discoverer of America." Further evidence showed that Leif Ericson, a Norse explorer, actually landed in North America in the year 1003. More information, such as reports of where he had been and the remains of Norse buildings (discovered in 1960), proved that the original information was incomplete.

3. Different interpretation or explanation of the same reports

Example

A small gray and white bird called a mockingbird has been observed to sit in a tree in the spring and sing loudly. His behavior has been observed by people and recorded on film and on recording machines. Some people say he is singing because it is spring and he is happy that winter is over. Others say that he is singing to attract a female mockingbird. Still others say that his song is a warning to other birds to stay away from his territory. The report is the same, the interpretations differ; there is cause for argument.

4. Refusal to believe

Example

In 1543 Nicolaus Copernicus, the Polish astronomer, proved that the earth moves around the sun. Even today there are people who do not believe it. They say that it is "obvious" that the earth does not move but that the sun circles in the sky. Many people refuse to believe factual arguments because those arguments conflict with other beliefs.

Model Paragraph (Factual Argument)

I have often thought about buying a new car, but it is much cheaper to drive an old one. I am driving an old 1972 Dodge that I bought for $450.00. The insurance isn't very much, just $185.00 per year. One problem is gas. The old car gets about 12 miles per gallon. With gas costing $1.50 a gallon and my driving amounting to about 9,000 miles per year, I have to spend $964.00 on gas. Also, an older car costs over $100.00 a year to keep running. My friend Manuel just bought a new Nissan Sentra. He had to pay $5,500.00 for it, which means monthly payments of $160.00. He gets better mileage, nearly 25 miles per gallon, at a cost of only $562.50 per year, but his insurance is $465.00. My total expense for a year is $1,245.00; Manuel's is $2,947.50. At the end of three years, when his car is paid for, he will have spent $5,107.50 more than I have spent. His new car will not take him anywhere that my old one can't take me. Accordingly, I plan to keep on driving old cars.

Analysis

This student has made a factual argument for keeping an older car. The proposition is that an older car is less expensive. His main evidence is the expense of the two cars. He uses the *contrast* pattern in his paragraph. The compare-contrast pattern is useful when you want to argue for making a choice. The student has carefully limited his paragraph to the cost of the two cars. He does not include matters of taste (a new car is more attractive) or opinion (a new car will impress people more than an old one).

Outline:

Title: Old Car or New?

Proposition: An old car is less expensive than a new car.

    I. Expenses for an old car
      A. Cost of car
      B. Cost of insurance
      C. Cost of gasoline
   II. Expenses for a new car
      A. Cost of car
      B. Cost of gasoline
      C. Cost of insurance
  III. Total expenses
      A. Old car
      B. New car

Conclusion: In three years a new car costs more and will not go anywhere that an old car cannot.

Writing Practice (Controlled Writing)

Directions: Following the contrast pattern of the model essay, write an argument paragraph in which you present arguments for (*pro*) or against (*con*) one of the suggested topics or one of your own. Be sure to develop a proposition (similar to a topic sentence) that is not a matter of taste, is not a matter of simple fact, and does not contain vague, undefined words. Outline the paragraph before you begin to write it. You may argue either for or against the topic.

    Topics:

    1. Old, comfortable clothes contrasted with new, stylish clothes
    2. Renting a house contrasted with buying a house
    3. Having just one boyfriend or girlfriend contrasted with having several
    4. Going to college contrasted with getting a full-time job
    5. Having children contrasted with not having children

    Notice that, in the paragraph about cars, the term *older* is not specifically defined. The student does tell that his car is a 1972 model; thus it is possible to *infer* or guess that he defines *older* as 12 or more years old (in 1984). It is very important to define such terms as *old, younger, moderate, better, acceptable,* and *unfair,* especially in an argumentative paragraph. The definition must be clear and exact enough that *both you and the reader can agree.* In fact, it is possible that a clear definition will make the argument unnecessary.

 ### Example

A student handed in the following paragraph about the history of writing.

Scribes

People have been writing for thousands of years. *Writers called scribes were used in Egypt to record the names of soldiers.* The Hebrews also used scribes. *Hebrew scribes later became teachers of the law.* Scribes became important in Islamic countries, where *they kept alive the holy Koran as well as writings from the Greeks and Romans.* The Arab writers were very important, and *they were regarded as equal to the greatest warriors.*

The teacher wrote "plagiarism" on the paper and gave the student a failing grade. The unhappy student wanted to know what was wrong. The teacher explained that *plagiarism* meant "to copy someone else's words or ideas and not give them credit." The student protested that she had written the paper herself. The teacher pointed out that the words in italics were copied word for word from a book on writing. The student finally understood the difference between plagiarism and research and rewrote the paper. The argument was over when both people agreed on the definitions of the two terms.

 ### Writing Practice (Definition in Arguments)

Directions: Read the following propositions. Write a definition for each of the underlined words. Make the definition so clear that there will be no argument about the meaning.

1. An *old* car can be expensive to keep going.
2. Sometimes *middle-aged* people are more active than *young* people.
3. This tool is guaranteed to be unbreakable *in normal use.*
4. Today's air pollution is within *acceptable limits.*
5. Abdul is an *average* student.

✔ **Check:**   Discuss your definitions with other students who have done the assignment. Are you in agreement? Did you put specific limits on your definitions?

Model Paragraph (Argument Using Examples as Proof)

Translations

Would you buy an automobile that was named the Doesn't Go? General Motors found that sometimes words translated from one language to another are bad for business. They tried to sell Chevrolet models called Nova and Camaro in Spanish-speaking countries. The cars did not sell well. Finally someone told the people at General Motors that *nova* (the Greek word for "star") means "does not (*no*) go (*va*)" in Spanish. *Camaro* was very close to the Spanish word *camarón,* which means "shrimp." People did not want to buy cars named Doesn't Go or Shrimp. An American machine company tried to sell a pump to Russia. The common name for the pump was *hydraulic ram.* The Russian translation was "wet male sheep." (*Hydraulic* means "run by water," and a *ram* is a male sheep.) The pump did not sell in Russia. In Japan there is an honored job called *kekkon sodansha*; it means "someone who arranges marriages." When a Japanese immigrant to Los Angeles tried to open such a business, he found that the dictionary translation was "someone who makes love in public." When he put up a sign that read, "Public Lover," he did not get the kind of business he expected. Certainly, it takes more than a dictionary to translate clearly and accurately from one language to another.

Analysis

The first sentence is an introduction that catches the interest of the reader. The second sentence states the proposition that sometimes words translated from one language to another are bad for business. The next several sentences give four specific examples of confusion caused by translations from English to Spanish, Russian, and Japanese. The last sentence restates the proposition in different words. Enough examples are given to convince the reader that the proposition is true.

 ## *Writing Practice (Guided Writing)*

Directions: Following the general pattern of the model paragraph (*introduction + proposition + specific examples + conclusion*), write an argumentative paragraph. *After* you have outlined your paragraph, try to develop an introductory sentence that will catch your reader's interest.

Suggested Propositions:

1. Some words do not translate from one language to another.

2. Many expressions do not make any sense when translated from one language to another.

3. Translating from one language to another can cause problems if it is not done carefully.

4. Careless translations from one language to another can sometimes be funny.

5. I often have trouble with English idioms.

Checklist of American Idioms

apple-pie order	at loose ends	beat up	bed of roses
bow out	crop up	dish out	free hand
go for broke	in the pink	off base	look down on
open up	out of shape	point out	puppy love
search me	stand up to	take back	tie up

There are several transitions that are useful in argumentative papers.

To show conclusions	*To show possibility*	*To show certainty*
accordingly	apparently	certainly
as a result	if	evidently
consequently	maybe	no doubt
hence	perhaps	obviously
in conclusion	probably	surely
therefore	usually	unquestionably
thus		

Writing Practice (Free Writing)

Directions: Write a paragraph using statistics as evidence or proof. The general topic is education in the United States. Use the following definitions and the statistics given in Table 9.1 as evidence for your proposition. Study the evidence first. Decide on your proposition. After you have made your working outline, think of an interesting introduction.

American Education

SOURCE OF INFORMATION: The United States Office of Education Survey by the University of Texas, 1975

	Functionally incompetent	Just getting by	Proficient
Getting and keeping satisfactory job	19.1%	31.9%	49.0%
Managing family budget	29.4%	33.0%	37.6%
Awareness of legal, government rights	25.8%	26.2%	48.0%
Ability to keep good health	21.3%	30.3%	48.3%
Reading	21.7%	26.0%	46.1%
Problem solving	28.0%	23.4%	48.5%
Computation	32.9%	26.3%	40.8%
Writing	16.4%	25.5%	58.1%
Overall Competence	19.7%	33.9%	46.3%

Table 9.1
Educational Levels in the United States (U.S. Office of Education, 1975)

PURPOSE: To find out how many Americans can read, write, and figure (do mathematics) well enough to function as adults.

DEFINITIONS:
Literate: able to read and write
Computation: arithmetic (addition, subtraction, multiplication, and division)
Functionally incompetent: unable to do simple daily tasks (for example: cannot fill out driver's license form; cannot make change from $20 bill; cannot write a bank check correctly; has difficulty shopping for food)
Just gets by: can do common tasks, but with difficulty
Proficient: has no problems applying skills to life

FURTHER DATA:
Total population of the United States at the time of the survey was 210 million people.
There were 32.6 million students in primary school.
There were 15.6 million students in high school.
There were 2,340,000 teachers.

Suggestions: Study the data. Did America have a literacy problem? Which areas show the greatest need? What actual number of people had trouble keeping a job? What *inferences* can you make from these statistics about American education? About American people?

Moral Arguments

A *moral* argument differs from a *factual* argument. It tries to convince the reader that something is *right* or *wrong, good* or *bad,* that a certain action *ought* to be followed, or that something *should* be done. It makes use of the same kinds of evidence as the factual argument: observations and reports from reliable sources, laws of nature, statistics, examples, and expert opinions. It tends to use more opinions than factual arguments.

Typical Moral Propositions

1. Selling cigarettes should be made illegal.
2. Nuclear weapons ought to be banned.
3. Abortion is a sin.
4. Give teachers merit pay, and illiteracy should decrease.
5. Cheating is always wrong.
6. Omar Khayyam was a great poet.
7. The cafeteria serves terrible food.
8. The death penalty should be abolished.
9. Violence on television is bad for children.

The proposition of a *moral* argument (sometimes called an *ethical* argument) makes use of modals—*should, ought, must* (see pp. 238–239)—and value words like *right, wrong, good,* and *bad.* The evidence in a moral argument is often expert opinion or authority.

1. The authority of law: certain actions are either right or wrong because of the laws of a city, state, or country. If you disobey the law, you will be punished by the state. People moving from one country to another are often confused because different countries have different laws.

2. The authority of tradition: many arguments use tradition as evidence. "It is traditional for sons to follow the family trade. If you do not, you are wrong." Some traditions are so strong that they are almost as powerful as laws.

3. The authority of religion: many arguments appeal to religious beliefs. You must be careful when you use religious beliefs as evidence for your arguments because they often differ. It is "wrong" for an orthodox Jew to eat

pork, for an orthodox Muslim to drink alcohol, for a Mormon (member of the Church of the Latter-Day Saints) to smoke a cigarette, for a Buddhist monk to eat meat. If you try to convince a Christian not to eat meat because of the teachings of Buddha, you will not succeed. If you use the authority of religion, you must be careful that you have selected the right authority for your reader.

4. The authority of knowledge: many moral arguments use the authority of expert opinion just as factual arguments do. In matters of health a doctor is used. In legal matters a lawyer or a court is used. In matters of correct writing an English teacher is used. You must be careful to use the correct authority. Your English teacher would probably be a poor authority on legal matters, just as lawyers are usually not experts on clear writing.

Writing Practice (Sentence Combining)

Directions: This Writing Practice will let you understand why you have a certain opinion and will show you an effective way to write a moral argument. The first part is sentence combining to show the pattern. The second part lets you write about your own experience. First, combine the following sentences into a paragraph.

1. I believe that it is wrong for people to write on walls and buildings.
2. The kind of writing I am talking about is called *graffiti*.
3. It is done with cans of spray paint.
4. It is done on both public and private buildings.
5. It is wrong because it makes the walls and buildings look dirty.
6. It is wrong because it is done on someone else's property.
7. It is wrong because it costs money to get rid of.
8. It happens more in large cities than in small towns.
9. I have seen graffiti on the wall of the store where I shop.
10. There is graffiti on the garage of the apartment house where I live.
11. The apartment manager had to pay to have the garage repainted.
12. He said that people did not want to rent an apartment that had graffiti on the walls.
13. He said that it made the apartment look like a bad place to live.
14. I think that most graffiti is ugly.
15. I think that people who write graffiti should pay to have it removed.

Suggestion: Group the sentences by meaning and then combine them into mature sentences. The first sentence can be the proposition. The next three explain and define. The next three tell why the writer thinks it is wrong.

Statements 8, 9, and 10 give specific examples of where graffiti is located. The next three sentences give more specific reasons why graffiti is wrong. The last two are the writer's conclusion. Your finished paragraph should have six sentences.

Writing Practice (Controlled Writing)

Directions:

1. Think about one of the following topics. Do not write anything until you have decided what is wrong or right, good or bad, about the topic.
   a. Advertising on television
   b. Violence in motion pictures
   c. The cost of getting an education

2. Now write a single sentence telling *what* you feel about the topic. Do you approve or disapprove of, like or dislike, the topic?

3. Reread your sentence. Does it state exactly what you believe?

4. If any words or ideas in your sentence need to be defined or explained, write another sentence to make the proposition clear.

5. Write another sentence that tells *why* you believe the way you do.

6. Write another sentence that gives a specific example, event, or observation that tells why you believe the way you do. (If you have more than one specific example, write other sentences.)

7. Write a concluding sentence.

8. Read your sentences. Are your reasons and examples honest? Would they convince the reader to agree with you? Check for grammar, spelling, and punctuation.

9. Write your sentences in paragraph form.

10. Give your paragraph a title.

Factual and Moral Arguments Combined

It is possible to combine *factual* and *moral* arguments in the same paragraph, just as it is possible to combine definition and exposition or any other patterns of writing. Two common kinds of argument are heard every day, read in the newspapers, seen on television. The first kind is the argument that starts with a moral issue and uses factual evidence to support it.

Model Paragraph

Mass Education

The main thing that is wrong with education in the United States is the attempt to educate everybody equally. Every state has laws that require young people to go to school. Most states require either graduation from high school or attendance until the age of sixteen. Many states, like New York and California, require students to pass an examination to graduate. The reason for these laws is that an industrial democracy needs educated people to work in the factories and to vote intelligently. What is wrong is that no number of laws can make everybody equally educated. According to the National Education Association, 40 percent of the students in high school will drop out before they graduate. Twenty percent do not have the ability to learn all that they are supposed to learn. These students find school too hard. They believe they are dumb. As a result of always failing tests in school, they stop trying to get any kind of education. It is as wrong to expect everyone to pass the same classes in high school as it is to expect everyone to be six feet tall by the age of sixteen.

Analysis

The proposition states that the attempt to educate everyone equally is wrong (a moral statement). The writer then gives some specific examples of laws and the reasons for them. Then the writer uses statistics from the National Education Association to show why he believes that trying to educate everyone equally is "wrong." He next makes a general statement about the bad effects on students. He concludes with a comparison (analogy). This writer has redefined *wrong* to mean "impossible" and has attempted to convince the reader that there is no point in trying to do the impossible.

It is possible to take what seems to be a moral argument (something is good, bad, better, worse, right, or wrong or should or ought to be done) and change it into a simple statement of like or dislike. Remember, statements of personal preference cannot be argued. But, if you redefined the key term, you can make an argument.

 ## Examples

Jose is a *better* student than Samuel.

Redefine *better* to give it a specific meaning:

1. Has a higher grade point average
2. Takes more units each semester
3. Is not absent as often

The Dodgers are a *better* baseball team than the Giants.

Redefine *better* to give it a specific meaning:

1. Have won more world championships
2. Have hit more home runs

3. Have won more games this year

It is *wrong* to beat children.

Redefine *wrong* to give it a specific meaning:

1. Damaging to children physically

2. Damaging to children emotionally

3. Useless in changing behavior

By redefining *better* to give it a more specific meaning, you can now write a factual argument using the standard kinds of evidence. By redefining *wrong*, you can give examples of child abuse to convince your reader of its wrongness.

Writing Practice (Guided Writing)

Directions: Following the general pattern of the Model Paragraph "Mass Education," write an argument in which you redefine the term in italics to make it possible to use observations (reports), natural laws, statistics, or expert opinions to convince your reader. Choose one of the following topics. You may argue for the statement (*pro*) or against the statement (*con*).

1. Swimming is *better* exercise than jogging.

2. A four-year college is *harder* than a two-year college.

3. There are several things *wrong* with American _____ . (*women, men, education, automobiles, children, television, markets; choose your own subject*)

4. It is *wrong* to cheat in school.

5. Children *ought to* obey their parents.

Patterns of Reasoning

The Rooster and the Fox

Once upon a time there was a very intelligent rooster who lived in a field with many other chickens. One day it began to rain very hard, and all the chickens were getting wet. A clever fox who lived in a nearby cave told the chickens that they could come into his cave and stay dry. Many of the chickens went into the cave. The next day the wind started to blow very hard and made the chickens cold. The clever fox told them that they could come into his cave and stay warm. Many other chickens went into the cave. The next day the sun was very warm and the chickens were hot. The fox said that they could come into his cave and stay cool. The fox noticed that the intelligent rooster did not come near the cave. When he asked why, the rooster replied, "I see many footprints all going into the cave. I do not see any footprints coming out. I will stay outside, thank you, and not become dinner for a fox."

The intelligent rooster used one of the two main patterns of reasoning. He made an observation and came to a conclusion that probably explained what he saw. He made a guess about the future based on what he knew. This kind of guessing is called *inference*. The more information you have, the more accurate will be your inference. Many educators believe that this kind of thinking—from cause to possible effect—is a sign of a mature mind. Many arguments follow this pattern of reasoning.

Examples

Observations

1. The grass of the house next door has not been cut for two weeks.
2. There are old newspapers on the porch.
3. No lights go on at night in the house.
4. The trash has not been put out for two weeks.
5. The windows are all dirty and shut tightly.

Inferences (possible guesses based on the observations)

1. The people are on a vacation.
2. The people have moved away.
3. The people are just careless and sloppy.
4. The people in the house are dead.

Suppose you believe that the people are on a vacation. You could check or *verify* your inference by a closer look at the house. You might look in a window. If you see no furniture, then the people have probably moved out. If there is furniture, then they are probably on vacation. If you see people lying on the floor and not moving, you should call the police.

Reasoning Practice (Inferences)

Directions: Carefully observe Illustration 9.1. Read the list of inferences. Put a *T* in front of the statements you believe to be true and an *F* in front of the statements you believe to be false.

_____ 1. The girl is sick.

_____ 2. The woman is the girl's mother.

Illustration 9.1

_____ 3. The girl is staying home from school.

_____ 4. The girl likes stuffed animals.

_____ 5. The girl is in her mother's bedroom.

_____ 6. The girl has a fever.

_____ 7. The girl is going to be well tomorrow.

_____ 8. The woman is a doctor.

_____ 9. There is a glass of medicine on the table.

_____ 10. The woman is worried about the girl.

 ## Writing Practice (Free Writing)

Directions: Read the list of the most popular television shows in 1982, taken from the show business magazine _Variety._ Make an inference about what kinds of shows Americans like most. Make an inference about the kind of new show you would start if you were able to make that decision. State your inference as a proposition to be proved.

Rank	Series	Type of show
1	"Dallas"	drama (soap opera)
2	"60 Minutes"	news stories (human interest)
3	"Jeffersons"	situation comedy
4	"Joanie Loves Chachi"	situation comedy
5	"Three's Company"	situation comedy
6	"Alice"	situation comedy
7	"Dukes of Hazard"	situation comedy
8	"Too Close for Comfort"	situation comedy
9	"ABC Monday Movie"	motion picture
10	"One Day at a Time"	situation comedy

The more information you have, the more accurate will be your reasoning, and the better will be your inference. It should not be hard to decide what kind of television show might be popular. You must be careful not to pick the kind of show that you like instead of the one indicated by the evidence.

Write a paragraph supporting your proposition.

Induction

This first pattern of reasoning is a common way to learn. Like the intelligent rooster, we gather information or evidence and then reach a conclusion. You probably learned when you were very small that, when you touched something hot, your hand was burned. It did not take long for you to reach a conclusion based on specific observations:

Touch stove: hand burned

Touch cooking pot: hand burned

Touch heater: hand burned

Touch fire: hand burned

General conclusion: "If I touch something hot, my hand will get burned." Writing teachers call this type of thinking *induction,* or *inductive reasoning.* Ordinary people call it learning from experience. It is usual when writing an inductive argument to list the specific examples and then conclude with the general statement.

Model Paragraph (Personal Narrative)

Things Go Better?

Last year I went to a party at my friend's house and drank three bottles of beer. I got a headache. In the summer at the beach I drank four bottles of beer and also got a headache. After school last month I went bowling and had two bottles of beer, but I did not get a headache. Last Friday at a soccer game I drank three bottles of beer and got another headache. I have finally decided that I should limit drinking beer to two bottles unless I want a headache.

Analysis

The writer gives a list of experiences and then tells the general conclusion. He has led the reader step by step through his experiences. Such a pattern, with the proposition stated at the end instead of at the beginning, often makes the argument convincing. Notice that there are enough specific examples to make the conclusion acceptable. Just one experience with beer might not be as convincing. When you write inductive arguments, you will have to decide just how much evidence you will need to convince your reader. The amount of evidence will depend on both the proposition and the reader.

 ### *Writing Practice (Guided Writing)*

Directions: Following the general pattern of the model paragraph (list of examples followed by the general conclusion), write an inductive paragraph of from six to ten sentences. Remember, you are not limited to your own personal experiences; you may use any kind of proof (see pp. 118–120).

Suggested Topics:
1. Kinds of stories on television news
2. Fast-food restaurants in your city
3. Names of American automobiles
4. Required courses for your major
5. Keeping animals as pets

Deduction

The second basic pattern of reasoning may be considered the opposite of induction. It starts with a generally accepted statement that does not need any proof. This general statement is then used to reach a conclusion for a specific case.

Examples

1. a. *Generally accepted statement:* Cigarette smoking can be dangerous to your health.
   b. *Specific case:* Helmut smokes a pack of cigarettes a day.
   c. *Conclusion* (using the generally accepted statement for a specific case): Helmut is endangering his health.

2. a. *Generally accepted statement* (personal experience): Drinking more than two beers gives me a headache.
   b. *Specific case:* Oscar is offering me a third beer.
   c. *Conclusion:* If I drink it, I will get a headache.

This pattern of reasoning is called *deduction.* To use *deductive reasoning,* you make use of what is known or generally accepted as true to find out about what is unknown. In example 1 you might conclude that Helmut *ought* to stop smoking to remain in good health. In example 2 you might decide that you *should* not have another beer (unless you want a headache). When most people reason, they automatically move from induction to deduction or from deduction to induction. The process works both ways. Several experiences cause one to form a general conclusion. Then that general conclusion can be used in a different case (like the example about drinking beer).

 Writing Practice (Induction and Deduction)

Directions: Look at Illustration 9.2, which shows the different kinds of hats worn by people in the United States. Using them as typical examples, write an inductive paragraph about Americans and hats.

Now, using the general statement you have developed, write a deductive statement about the man in Illustration 9.3.

 Writing Practice (Free Writing)

Directions: Write an argumentative paragraph on one of the following topics. Use either the inductive or deductive pattern, or both.

1. The kinds of clothes worn by students at your school
   (*Suggestion:* Pick one item, like shoes.)
2. Clothes or uniforms worn by people in different jobs
   (*Suggestion:* Use your own country for the examples.)
3. The cost of textbooks for all of your classes
   (*Suggestion:* Make an inference about next semester.)
4. Problems caused by different laws in different countries
   (*Suggestion:* Use the personal experiences of your friends or yourself.)

Formal hat
(top hat)

Driving cap

Cowboy hat

Fishing hat

Illustration 9.2

Worker's hat
(hard hat)

Sailor's cap

Illustration 9.3

Review and Conclusion

The argumentative paragraph consists of a proposition that you believe to be true and the evidence you need to convince others. Kinds of propositions that are not arguable are matters of personal taste, matters of fact, and statements containing vague, undefined words. Kinds of evidence include facts (observations by yourself or others, natural laws, and records, such as photographs or writing) and expert opinions. Arguments may be written in any of the patterns of development studied so far (such as narration, definition, comparison or contrast, cause and effect, exposition). Arguments may be either factual (prove something is true) or moral (prove something ought or ought not to be done). Arguments usually use one or both of the two kinds of reasoning: *inductive,* from specifics to a general conclusion; and *deductive,* from a generally accepted statement to a specific case.

When you write an inductive argument, you must be sure that you have enough evidence to convince your reader. How much is necessary will depend on your proposition and your reader. When you write a deductive argument, you must be sure that the general statement is true or mostly true. In the *Writing Practice* for Illustration 9.3, the man in the cowboy hat *may* be a cowboy, but not all people who wear cowboy hats are cowboys. The conclusion would be "This man is wearing a cowboy hat and is *probably* a cowboy."

Learning how argument works will not only make you an effective writer but will also help you to make effective decisions in life. Most differences of opinion are caused by the amount of information people have, the kinds of authorities they accept, and the types of experiences they have had. Using the skills of argumentation will enable you to make the best choices in school, in business, and in your personal life.

PART TWO
THE LONGER PAPER

Chapter Ten

The Longer Composition

By now you should be comfortable writing many kinds of paragraphs. The next step in becoming an effective writer is to learn to put several paragraphs together into a longer composition. You have been working on paragraphs because they are easier to learn than longer compositions. Another reason that you started with paragraphs is that *compositions pattern exactly the same way that paragraphs do!* Narration, description, the main types of exposition, and argumentation are all used in longer compositions. The same methods of order (space, time, climax) are used. The main difference is that you will need more information to write a longer paper and a slightly different kind of controlling idea.

 Model Paragraph

Be Nice!

Would you rather be called a "lazy kid" or an underachieving student (1)? People in the United States are always changing the names of things to make them sound nicer (2). In the 1920s a young person who was a thief was called a "youthful criminal" and was sent to a "reform school" (3). Today he is classified as a "juvenile delinquent" and is sent to a "correctional facility" (4). In fact, there do not seem to be any "jails" any more (5). The places where criminals are sent for "rehabilitation" are now given such names as *men's (or women's) colony* or *honor farm* (6). Even job names change (7). The old-fashioned "garbage collector" is now a "sanitation engineer" (8). Actually, no matter how the names are changed, the realities remain the same (9).

Analysis

Sentence 1: introductory sentence to get the reader's attention

Sentence 2: topic sentence: People in the United States change names (*topic*) to make them sound nicer (*controlling idea*).

Sentence 3: specific example

Sentences 4, 5, 6: more specific examples of name changes

Sentence 7: transitional sentence (from "criminals" to "jobs")

Sentence 8: specific example for job name changes

Sentence 9: concluding sentence (writer's opinion)

The same topic can be expanded into a longer composition by adding more information.

 ## Model Composition

Change in title   Euphemism or Reality?

Introductory paragraph to get reader's interest

Would you rather be called a "lazy kid" or an "underachieving student"? Would you rather work as a "garbage collector" or as a "sanitation engineer"? In each case both terms refer to the same reality, but somehow the second

Definition ⟶ term sounds nicer. This changing of the names of things is called *euphemism,* from a Greek word meaning "beautiful sound." For years people in the United States have been changing harsh or ugly names to pleasant or pretty

Thesis statement names in an attempt to seem more refined, to get more respect, or to hide an unpleasant reality. (1)

First part of thesis statement

After the Americans had finally hacked a country out of the wilderness, they became aware that their language was more suited to the log cabin than

Reference ⟶ to the fine house. According to H. L. Mencken in *The American Language,* as early as 1830 they began to change the names of things. Such common words

Specific examples of word changes for parts of the body like "belly," "bosom," and "leg" were supposed to be vulgar. They practically disappeared from use. Not even tables and chairs had "legs"; they had "limbs." Words used to refer to common animals were changed. No more were there "bulls," "asses," and "bitches." They became (elegantly) "cow-creatures," "donkeys," and "she-dogs." Perhaps they thought that purity of words would lead to purity of thought. (2)

Transitional ⟶
sentence using time order

Later on, at the start of the twentieth century, names were changed for another reason. Certain job titles were changed to allow the workers to have more respect for themselves and their jobs. Who would want to be a "janitor," a "garbage collector," or a "grave digger"? Surely one would get more respect

Job respect: specific examples if one were called a "custodian" (or even a "sanitation engineer"), a "refuse collector" (or another "sanitation engineer"), or an "undertaker" (perhaps even a "mortician") than if one had those other titles. In addition, even the

Other respect:
specific examples

⌈ word *job* became *occupation* or *position*. It is possible that "old people"
would feel better about themselves if they were called "senior citizens," or
⌊ "lazy kids" might do better in school if they were labeled "underachievers."

A question ———►   But does it help society to change prisons to "men's (or women's) colonies"
or to reclassify the poor as the "underprivileged"? The use of euphemisms to
help people feel good about themselves may be socially useful, but it must be
done carefully. (3)

Transitional phrase►
and part of thesis

    Another reason for the use of euphemisms is to avoid the ugly or the
⌈ unpleasant. Certain diseases like leprosy are now called by nicer names, like

Diseases and
death: specific
examples

Hansen's disease. People who once were considered "crazy" or "lunatics" are
now "mentally ill." Even pimples have been changed to "blemishes." It is
understandable to want to say "passed away" or "passed on" instead of
⌊ "dead," but there is a danger in trying to avoid all unpleasantness by changing

Reference ———►   the name. As George Orwell points out in his essay *Politics and the English*
⌈ *Language,* to call the killing of people in an enemy town "pacification" can

Some problems
noted

hide from us the evil of war. To call the test of a nuclear weapon "Operation
Sunshine" is to mislead. To call a deadly missile "The Peacekeeper" is to
⌊ cover up its terrible purpose. (4)

For using
euphemism

    It is a fact of language that changing the name can change the way people
⌈ feel about things. A person who sells houses feels better as a "real estate

Against using
euphemism ———

broker." A student who is "retained" instead of "failed" still has some hope.
The question is "How far should we go in trying to hide ugly reality?" Might it

Closing question►
shows writer's tone

not be better to call some things by their "ugly" names so we do not fool
ourselves? (5)

Analysis

The five-paragraph composition entitled "Euphemism or Reality?" is 590
words long. The writer has an introductory paragraph similar to the introductory sentence in a paragraph. He uses three paragraphs to develop his topic
(similar to the sentences used to develop a paragraph). He ends with a
concluding paragraph (similar to a concluding sentence in a single paragraph).

The Thesis Statement

Note the differences between the paragraph and the composition.
First: The topic sentence of the paragraph has been expanded into a *thesis
statement.* A thesis statement does the same thing for a longer composition
that a *topic sentence* does for a paragraph—and a little bit more. The thesis
statement is more detailed because the writer is going to present more
information.

Topic sentence: People in the United States change the names of things to make them nicer. (*Good enough for a paragraph but not for a more detailed composition*)

Thesis statement: For years people in the United States have been changing harsh or ugly names to pleasant or pretty names in an attempt to seem more refined, to get more respect, or to hide an unpleasant reality. Notice the increase in detail:

1. The process has been going on for years.
2. The process has been "an attempt."
3. There are three reasons for the process.
   a. To seem more refined
   b. To get respect
   c. To hide an ugly reality

Like the topic sentence, the *thesis statement* is a promise to the reader. It is also a guide for the writer in developing the composition.

Second: The words *in an attempt* tell the writer's *attitude* about the process of changing the names of things to make them seem nicer. The *thesis* lets us know that using euphemisms is an attempt and is thus not always successful. We know something about the *tone* (writer's attitude) of the composition. Although some variations are possible, the following list gives the characteristics of an effective *thesis statement:*

1. It is a statement that the writer believes to be true.
   a. A general statement about life
   b. A principle of thought or action
   c. A proposition to be argued
2. It is written as a single, declarative sentence.
3. It limits the topic of the composition.
4. It usually sets the tone (writer's attitude) of the composition.

This writer starts with an introductory *paragraph* and puts the thesis statement at the end of it. He uses a *striking example* to catch the reader's interest and a definition to explain. The second paragraph uses a metaphor to restate the first part of the thesis ("to be more refined"), a reference to H. L. Mencken, and several specific examples. The third paragraph starts with a *transitional sentence* and uses chronological (time) order as promised in the thesis ("For years . . ."). He gives several specific examples of changes of names in an attempt to get respect (job titles and other names). The fourth paragraph starts with a transitional phrase and offers more specific examples and another reference. The concluding sentence of paragraph 4 notes some problems and makes the reader more aware of the writer's attitude toward euphemism. It also serves as a transition to the fifth, or concluding, paragraph. This last paragraph gives the writer's conclusion that using euphemisms may or may not be useful.

The general order of the paragraph is time. The essay is developed by giving many specific examples of name changing in the United States. The writer has completed the promise he made in his thesis statement.

Writing Practice (Thesis Statement)

Directions: Remember that an effective thesis statement is a single declarative sentence that limits the topic and sets the tone. Read the following statements. Assume that they are thesis statements for a longer paper of about 500 words. Each is too general or too vague to be effective. Rewrite them so that they are more specific and make the writer's purpose clear.

Example

Vague: Foreign cars are better than American cars.

Better: Volkswagen automobiles are less expensive, get better gas mileage, and have lower maintenance costs than mid-sized Fords.

1. Old people have many problems to deal with.
2. Good transportation has always aided economic growth.
3. Working in a factory can cause many problems for workers.
4. Television is really stupid!
5. It is very important to have good moral values.
6. War is wrong.
7. I'm going to stay healthy because it costs too much to get sick.
8. Learning a new language causes many problems.
9. It is important to get a good education.
10. Two-year colleges have many advantages.

Sometimes you will find it necessary to present a topic to an audience that is opposed to it. Or the topic may be one about which people have very strong feelings. In that case you may want to use a *controlling question.* If you have a thesis like "Abortion is wrong!" for example, you are likely to make part of your audience angry before you start the moral argument. If you use a question like, "When does life actually start?" the audience will listen or continue to read. You will, of course, have a regular thesis statement, but you will change it to question form.

Writing Practice (Thesis Statements)

Directions: Change each of the following thesis statements to a controlling question. Your purpose is to get your reader to continue reading.

1. For three reasons, abortions should be legalized.
2. The only way to stop criminals from killing is to outlaw handguns.
3. Nuclear disarmament will bring world peace by getting rid of the threat and by getting rid of the means to destroy.
4. Sending students to faraway schools by bus is harmful to the students and does not give them a better education.
5. For three main reasons, divorce is the only way out of an unhappy marriage.

The Introductory Paragraph

The *introductory paragraph* serves the same purpose in the longer composition as the introductory sentence in the paragraph. (See pp. 103–104 for kinds of introductory sentences.) It is supposed to do two things: *introduce* your composition and *interest* the reader so that he or she will want to continue reading. The best advice is to start with a clear thesis statement. Make sure that both you and your reader know what you are going to write about. Outline your composition. Be sure that you have enough evidence to explain or to convince. Write the first draft of the paper. *Then* write the introduction. In other words, *write the introduction last.* An introductory paragraph gives you more space than a single sentence in which to interest your reader.

 ### Model Introductions

The Bible tells us that the devil is the father of lies: he was a liar from the beginning and will be one till the end. He is supposed to have turned lying from a skill into an art. I do not know who was the first person to turn lying from an art form to a political practice, but political lying has become increasingly popular during the past twenty years.

—Adapted from Jonathan Swift, *The Art of Political Lying*

The changes made by death are so sharp and so final, so terrible and sad, that death seems to be a horrible thing. It outdoes all other accidents because it is the last of them. Sometimes it leaps suddenly upon its victims.

Sometimes it comes upon them gradually. All of this makes people speak softly of death. Yet not speaking of death has put mankind in error when thinking about death.

—Adapted from Robert Louis Stevenson, *Aes Triplex*

My friend received another degree this month. She became a B.A., M.A., M.A., or, as we fondly call her, a Bamama. All of these degrees made my friend qualified to be unemployed in yet a better class of jobs.

—Adapted from Ellen Goodman, *Bamama Goes to College*

At the Anglo-Indian day school in Zorinabad to which my sister and I were sent, they changed our names. On the first day the headmistress asked us what our names were. "Premila and Santha," we replied. She told us that she would give us pretty English names. *Premila* would become *Pamela,* and *Santha* would be *Cynthia.* She thought that would be "jolly." Changing my name from *Santha* to *Cynthia* made me have a strange sort of dual personality.

—Adapted from Santha Rama Rau, *By Any Other Name*

Analysis

Each of these brief introductory paragraphs (and an introduction need not be long) make the reader want to read more. What is Swift going to write about political liars? Are there ways of talking about death that will make us not fear it so? Why does having many degrees make one unable to get a job? Does having a different name change one's personality?

Writing Practice (Introductions)

Directions: Select five of the thesis statements that you wrote in the Writing Practice in Chapter Nine where you made the vague statements into effective thesis statements (see page 117). Write an introductory paragraph for each.

Writing Practice (Alternate Assignment)

Directions: Write an introductory paragraph for any of the controlling question thesis statements you developed earlier in this chapter.

Suggestions:

1. Do not use such common or dull introductions as:
   a. I am going to write about. . . .

b. The purpose of this composition is to. . . .

c. I don't know too much about (*topic*), but. . . .

2. Explain or define the topic.

3. Make the limit of the topic clear.

4. Use a brief narration (anecdote).

5. Review kinds of introductory sentences on pp. 103–104 for suggestions. The introductory paragraph can use *exactly* the same ideas.

The Concluding Paragraph

The *concluding paragraph* ends your longer paper. It must make your reader feel satisfied that you have kept the promise you made in your thesis statement. A strong conclusion lets the reader know that you have reached a definite ending, that you have not simply stopped or run out of time or paper. A superior conclusion is clearly related to the main idea of the paper and adds something to it. The conclusion is the last chance you will have to make your explanation clear or to convince your reader. The concluding paragraph of the model composition on euphemism, for example, adds the writer's belief that changing names of things may be useful but must also be done carefully.

Model Conclusions

The following are some adaptations of the concluding paragraphs for the model introductions presented earlier.

Jonathan Swift: After giving several examples of political liars and contrasting them to other kinds of liars, Swift concludes something like this:

Considering that it is natural for some men to lie and for many men to believe, I wonder what to do with the common saying that truth will at last overcome. I believe that, when the common people understand the methods of these liars, they will no longer be fooled, and truth will, indeed, overcome.

Robert Louis Stevenson: After giving some examples of cultures that are not afraid to talk about death and some illustrations from literature, Stevenson concludes:

After all, it is sad and pitiful to worry about death, not to have all of the pleasures of living. It is better to live life and be done with it than to die daily in a sickroom. If the doctor says that you have one month to live, see what can be accomplished in a week. Every heart that has beaten strong and cheerfully has left a hopeful feeling behind it in the world.

Ellen Goodman: Goodman presents many statistics showing the great number of people getting college degrees and the growing difference between educational levels and job levels. She concludes in this way:

> Remember the movie "Goodbye Columbus"? There is a moment when the father, who owns a trucking business, shakes his head watching his son work. Finally he sighs, "Four years of college, and he can't load a truck."
> Just a few years ago that was funny. But at the current rate of educational war, the kid won't even be able to get a tryout without a Ph.D.

Santha Rama Rau: After telling several unhappy experiences that the two little Indian girls had in the Anglo school, Rau concludes:

> Of course I did not forget. I understood it perfectly, and I remember it all very clearly. But I put it happily away, because it had all happened to a girl called Cynthia, and I was never really particularly interested in her.

Analysis

Swift explains how much political lying existed in England. Then he adds the hope that the people will someday stop being fooled by it. Stevenson had tuberculosis and knew that he did not have long to live. He added his personal belief and a tone of hope in his conclusion. Goodman uses two short paragraphs in her conclusion. She uses a closing anecdote and adds the prediction that someday people will need college degrees for the simplest jobs. Rau ties her conclusion to her introduction by stating that the bad experiences she had as Cynthia did not really happen to Santha, her "real" self.

 ## Writing Practice (Conclusions)

Directions: Using the same five thesis statements for which you wrote introductions, write concluding paragraphs. (You may select other thesis statements, if you wish.) Assume that you have written a composition of about three paragraphs.

 ## Writing Practice (Alternate Assignment)

Directions: Write a concluding paragraph for any of the controlling question thesis statements you developed earlier in this chapter.

Suggestions:

1. Do not use weak or common conclusions.
   a. "In conclusion . . ." or "Finally . . ."
   b. "Although I really don't know much about . . ."

2. Do not introduce a new topic or subject in the conclusion.

3. Do not just restate your thesis; add to it.

4. Use a summary as a conclusion only if your paper is very long.

5. Try some of these kinds of conclusions:
   a. Give a forecast of what will or will not happen: "If I am right, then . . ."
   b. Show how the topic is important to the reader.
   c. Use any of the types of introductions on pp. 103–104. They may be used as conclusions, too.

Titles

Have you ever gone to the library or looked through a magazine and been interested in a book or an article just because of its interesting title? Most people have. An interesting title will draw the reader's attention to your composition. A title that will catch the reader's eye is called a "catchy" title. It is often better to write the title last. Many times you will find a useful phrase or idea in your own writing as you compose the paper.

There are four rules or conventions for writing titles:

1. Do not use quotation marks or underline your own title. If you quote someone else, then you may use quotation marks.

2. Capitalize the first and last words and all other words *except* articles and prepositions.

   The Last of the Tigers

   Cats in My Bedroom

3. Use an exclamation point [!] or a question mark [?] at the end of the title if you need it, but do not use a period [.] or a comma [,].

   Losing Can Be Fun, Too!

   Euphemism or Reality?

4. Titles are usually *not* complete sentences, but brief, catchy phrases.

College Writing

Writing a longer composition—an essay, a term paper, a report—is an artificial kind of writing. Most college students are required to use a specific form or combination of forms (description, narration, exposition, argumentation). Usually the topic is assigned by the teacher, and the paper is checked for certain elements.

1. Correctness of grammar and mechanics
2. Organization and order (time, space, climax, general to specific, specific to general)
3. Clear thinking or reasoning
4. Clarity of writing
5. Research or knowledge

The longer composition is expected to have the same *unity* (sticks to the subject of the thesis), *coherence* (is all of one piece, tied together with transitional devices), and *completeness* (fills the promise made in the thesis statement) that a paragraph has. In addition, each paragraph in the longer paper is expected to be carefully *composed*. It is almost always necessary for the student to rewrite and revise his papers. Written English, as expected from a college student, is a dialect of spoken English. It must be clearer and more precise than the spoken word. However, once you have learned this specialized kind of writing (and you should be getting very good at it by now), you will find it useful and helpful in many areas of life.

Writing Practice (Guided Writing—Description)

Directions: First, read the following descriptive essay developed from newspaper accounts and reports from the United States Geological Survey.

Model Composition

Eruption

On the morning of May 18, 1980, Mount St. Helens in the state of Washington rose 9,671 feet into the clear, sunny sky. It was a cone of clean white surrounded by miles of green forest. At nearby Spirit Lake, Harry R. Truman was preparing his cabins for the tourists he expected in a few months. But the beautiful mountain was rumbling. Mount St. Helens is an active volcano.

Since the end of March, the mountain had been shaking and swelling. The north wall of the volcano was swelling at the rate of five feet a day. The United States Geological Survey planted instruments on the mountain and stationed men in observation posts nearby. David Johnson was six miles away watching closely. Robert Landisburg, a photographer, was even closer making a detailed record of the changes in the mountain. That morning he was trying for just a few more pictures. Suddenly at 8:32 there was a strong jolt, a severe earthquake caused by the earth movement in the volcano.

There was a terrific roar, heard up to 200 miles away. With a sudden blast, the entire north wall of the mountain exploded outward. Hot gasses, ash, and huge rocks burst out of the volcano at a speed of 200 miles an hour. David Johnson called Vancouver on his radio, "This is it. . . ." Those were his last words. The flaming explosion tossed the trailer of his observation post like a matchbox off the ridge and into a canyon. His body has never been found. The photographer snapped a few last pictures, rewound his film, put everything into his backpack and turned to flee. His body was found seventeen days later along with the interesting pictures that cost his life. Harry R. Truman, his cabins, and part of Spirit Lake were buried under tons of hot ash.

The north side of the mountain collapsed like a sled of earth and giant rocks destroying vacation homes in its path. The blast knocked down the forest of evergreen trees for 200 square miles. The trees within three miles of the explosion simply vanished, snatched from the mountain side as if by some giant hand. Then the force turned upward. A cloud of ash rose 30,000 feet, then 50,000, finally to a height of 60,000 feet. The ice and snow on the peak mixed with the hot gas and ash and created an estimated 46 billion gallons of hot mud. The mud rushed down the streams and rivers uprooting forest giants, tossing the trucks and buildings of a lumber camp about like children's toys; it surged on, crumpling an entire train and filling houses to the roof with sticky hot mud.

The huge cloud of volcanic ash was charged with electricity. Lightning bolts shattered down adding to the destruction. The cloud spread swiftly. By 9:30 A.M. the town of Yakima, 85 miles away, was as dark as if it were midnight. Then the ash began to fall. It left 600,000 *tons* in the city of Yakima. It ruined almost all of the crops in the beautiful valley. It reached the Pacific within three days and caused floods in the rivers. So much ash fell in the Columbia river that it had to be closed to ships until the Navy could remove the material. By the 21st the ash reached the Atlantic Ocean. In seventeen days it had circled the world, dusting the northern part with ash from a few inches to several feet deep. There was no life left within seventeen miles of the eruption. The deer, beavers, small animals, even the fish in the 26 lakes and 150 miles of streams were killed by the ashfall.

Yet, because the United States Geological Survey had been watching and warning, very few people were killed. People had been told to leave their homes and camps, for the volcano was going to erupt. The destruction to property and crops seemed great, but, according to geologists, this was a minor explosion when compared to others. The eruption of Krakatoa in 1883 sent over 18 cubic kilometers of ash into the air and darkened the whole world. Its blast killed 36,000 people. Mount Pelee on the island of Martinique blew up in 1902, destroyed the entire town of St. Pierre, and killed 30,000 people. By contrast, Mount St. Helens sent only one cubic kilometer of ash into the skies, and only 61 people lost their lives.

Today, the once proud and beautiful Mount St. Helens is a short, grey, barren, ugly spot, without trees, without wildlife, covered with ash and mud. But there are some signs of renewal. A few plants are pushing their green leaves through the ash. There are a few rabbits and small animals seen running through the broken forests. Fish are appearing in the changed streams and lakes. The cities once filled with ash or mud are clean again. But Mount St. Helens is not finished. Every now and then there are rumbles and fumes and the earth trembles. It may erupt again.

Analysis

The purpose of of this composition is to show that, even though the destruction was great, the eruption of Mount St. Helens was not a major geological event. Within the pattern of chronology or time, the writer has described the events as they happened. The writer uses contrast by describing the mountain as it was in the first paragraph and how it is now in the last one.

Now, write a descriptive composition of from three to five paragraphs. You may wish to improve and enlarge on one of the topics you wrote for Chapter Three. The description does not have to be about a natural disaster.

Alternate Topics:

1. A place that you know well
2. A person that you know well
3. The school you are attending (Add some interest by describing it on a windy, rainy, or very hot day.)
4. Yourself

 ## Remember

Descriptive writing should serve some purpose. Give your description a point.

 ## Writing Practice (Guided Writing—Narration)

Directions: Like description, narrative writing serves a purpose. It is often written to entertain, as in stories and novels. However, except in creative writing classes, you will do very little of that kind of writing in college. One of the most common forms of narration is the historical narrative. Historical narratives may be about many things other than the history of a country. The example that follows is about the history of computers. It is adapted from a pamphlet by the United States Department of Health, Education and Welfare.

 **Model Narrative**

Artificial Intelligence

The first mechanical device to help calculation was the abacus, an arrangement of beads on wires or strings. Used as early as the first century B.C., it is still common in oriental countries. When arithmetical signs were developed in the fifteenth century, it was possible to use two numbered scales to compute. This device, called the slide rule, became a great help to engineers and mathematicians. In 1812 two British mathematicians, Charles Babbage and John Herschel, were using slide rules and checking some logarithmic tables for errors. The job was long and difficult. Babbage said, "I wish that these calculations had been done by a steam engine." And so was started the idea that was to be his main interest in life, the elimination of error through mechanical calculation.

Babbage's first project was called the Difference Engine. Unfortunately, it could not be built. It was designed to have the parts fit together exactly. The methods and machines at that time could not construct such precise parts. Even clocks at that time were slowly fitted together by hand. To overcome this difficulty, Babbage designed new machine tools. He hired and trained a technical assistant. But these preparations cost money, and the sum that the British government provided soon was gone. After ten years of work and some £35,000 of government money, the government stopped the project.

Babbage, however, had money of his own, so he designed the Analytical Engine, which was to use the punch cards invented in 1800 by Joseph Jacquard for use in his automatic weaving machines. The design was excellent. The machine would have been the first general-purpose computing machine. It was to have a memory unit of 1,000 numbers each 50 digits long. Again, it was too complicated for the technology of the time and was never finished. Although Babbage never finished his machine, his enthusiasm spread to others.

Herman Hollerith, inspired by Babbage, designed *and built* the first machine that could do data processing. Data in the form of "yes" or "no" answers were transferred to punch cards that were fed into a machine that could tell the positions of the holes. In 1896 Hollerith formed the Tabulating Machine Company, which was one of several businesses that later became IBM. His inventions started a whole new kind of computing machines.

From then on, advances came rapidly. People like William S. Burroughs, Leonardo Torres, and Vannevar Bush improved these mechanical computers. In 1943 John Mauchly and J. Presper Eckert, Jr. of the University of Pennsylvania proposed the next step, an electronic difference analyzer. Built in secrecy at the university, the new device was called the Electronic Numerical Integrator and Calculator (ENIAC). Completed in 1946, the huge device was made of 18,000 vacuum tubes and 1,500 relays. Around 1950 the computer became a general tool. The speed and ability of these computers using cathode ray tubes and magnetic drums surprised most people, yet experts in the field guessed that only 50 companies would find use for them.

But computer languages were developed in the late fifties, integrated circuits in the mid-sixties. These integrated circuits put the power of 1,400 transistors, resistors, and diodes onto silicon chips an eighth of an inch square. Everybody began to use computers. Private businesses began to use computers to process orders, inventories, and payrolls. Computers set the type for newspapers and processed checks for banks. Airlines used computers to make and record seat reservations. Computers were used in medicine to help doctors find out just what kind of illness people had.

Today's experts believe that computers will find many non-business uses as people learn how to use them. Home computers may someday turn on and off heating and cooling systems, call the fire or police department in case of emergencies, and do tax statements. By the end of this century computers will be used more and more. They will be even smaller and more powerful. A single silicon chip, only a few millimeters square, will be able to follow 20 million instructions per second, using 10 million cells of internal memory storage. Scientists also predict that programming techniques and software development will also advance along with this new technology. They claim that we are just now really entering the age of computers.

Suggestions: Like other narratives, the historical narrative uses time order. The essay above moves chronologically from the past to the present. The final paragraph is a prediction of the future uses and development of computers. You must take care to have accurate facts in your historical narrative.

Possible topics:

1. The development of the personal computer
2. The growth of computer software in the last ten years
3. Teaching of computer science in elementary schools
4. Your own experience with computers (personal narrative)
5. The growth of jobs in the computer field.

Noncomputer topics: You may wish to write a historical narrative on the development of some other device than the computer.

1. Automobiles
2. Solar heating
3. Building technology
4. Antibiotics
5. Space exploration

 ### Writing Practice (Guided Writing—Exposition)

Directions: Read the following model expository composition. Then write an expository composition of from three to five paragraphs. You may expand any of the expository paragraphs you wrote for Chapters 5, 6, 7, or 8, or you may develop a new topic.

Suggestions: The following topics are typical of writing assignments given in college. One of them may interest you.

1. Tell how something works (a rotary engine, a mechanical pencil, the human heart).
2. Explain the cause of something (why you got a certain grade in a class, why you are attending college, inflation).
3. Compare or contrast—or both (two forms of government, moral behavior in two countries, science and art).
4. Explain by giving one example or several illustrations (effective use of slang, self-improvement by reading, scholarships for worthy students).
5. Explain a scientific process (like the following model paragraph).

 ### Model Composition

The Individual[2]

In a recent science fiction movie the hero stepped into a "clone machine" and was duplicated. There were two identical human beings. Such a process actually exists. Called *cloning,* it is the attempt to make exact copies of groups of living cells. As strange as it seems, some scientists are making progress in developing this process.

Cloning is not really new. Any gardener who has taken part of a plant, called a cutting, and made it grow into a new plant has cloned the old plant. The cells of the new one are identical to the cells of the old one. The horticultural laboratory of Toshio Murashige of the University of California at Riverside has been growing special plants from single cells for a long time. The lab duplicates plants that grow strong or that have special features.

It is easier to clone plants than animals because plant cells seem to have the ability to grow into complete adult plants. Yet in 1952 researchers were able to clone frogs from the cells of tadpoles, the water-breathing young form of frogs. They were able to take a frog egg and separate the cells into other individual but identical eggs. When these eggs matured, the individual frogs had *exactly* the same cell structure.

The latest development occurred at the University of Geneva in Switzerland. Two scientists there claim to have cloned mice. They removed an egg from a mouse, separated the cells, and encouraged each cell to grow into another egg. Then the eggs were put into a female mouse. There were 542 separate steps required, all using a microscope. The researchers claimed that the mice, when they were born, were identical.

The Geneva scientists and others have found that it is impossible to make clones from adult creatures. The cells must be taken from eggs or the unborn young. Older cells do not seem to have the ability to reproduce that young cells have. There is no chance to make duplicates of geniuses and have a world full of outstanding people. In any event, even if it were possible, the duplicate would be a baby, not a full-grown person with all of the training and education of the original.

It may be best that we cannot clone people. Imagine what would happen to your life if an exact copy of you appeared. Indeed, what if two or three appeared?

Suggestions: This composition explains the misunderstood process of cloning. The title is strange until you understand the meaning of ^{2}, or "squared." The introduction uses a striking example to catch interest. The conclusion is a closing question. In your composition, try to follow the general pattern of the model. Notice the use of definition and specific references to actual persons and places. This is a nontechnical paper that emphasizes the development of the process, not a detailed, step-by-step explanation of how it is done.

Writing Practice (Guided Writing—Argument)

Directions: Read the following argumentative composition and the comments that follow. Develop an argumentative paper following the general plan of the model essay. You may expand any of the argumentative paragraphs you wrote for Chapter Nine by adding further examples and details, or you may pick another topic. Select a topic that you know something about and have a strong belief about. The best argumentative paper is one that is honest.

Model Composition

Why Teach Failure?

Last week my nine-year-old daughter came home from school with tears in her eyes. She was sad because her report card showed that she had an *F* in music and a *D* in "cooperation." Although her other grades were passing, she was sure that she was a failure. I explained that no one in our family had much musical talent. The only instrument I can play is the radio, and, after all, music is not a terribly important subject. Still, she was sobbing, convinced that she was a "failure." It seems to me that our present grading system *teaches* children to think of themselves as failures and needs to be changed.

The present system of grading in the United States is artificial and damaging to students. First, it requires *all* students to be placed in one of five classifications in *all* subjects:

A = outstanding or superior

B = better than average

C = average

D = barely passing

F = failure

Such a division of everybody into only one out of five classes is artificial. There is so much variation in the ability of people to do different things that it is almost impossible to make such a separation. This system is artificial because it is based on teaching children to memorize facts (which often have no real meaning for them). They are taught that there is a "correct" answer for each question. Where would we be if we still believed that the "correct" way to get food was to hunt animals and gather fruit? It is artificial because it places great importance on grades rather than on thinking. A study at Columbia University showed that *over* 55% of college students cheated to get good grades. An ad in a recent newspaper offered a method to "Help your children get higher grades." Not "to learn more" or "to be able to think better." It is damaging to children because, like my daughter, they are told that they have "failed." A child cannot tell the difference between not being able to sing and *being* a failure.

In spite of some opposition, there is a need for a change. If we can let children know that some may be good in one subject and others good in something else, they will not think of failure as a total statement about themselves. It is a good thing for us that such "failing" and "barely passing" students as Albert Einstein and Thomas Edison did not accept the judgments of their teachers. Those who oppose a change in our traditional grading system have such old arguments as, "It is traditional" or "We have to have some way to tell the better student from the poorer student." In answer to the first argument: the only way we have progressed is by challenging tradition. In answer to the second: there are other ways to tell the "better" from the "poorer" student than by using the A-to-F system.

Many educators and psychologists like John Holt and William Glasser have developed systems for grading that allow for differences between people, do not make students feel like failures, and still let them learn to think, do well what they are able to do well, and progress at their own speed. The University of California at Santa Cruz has not used letter grades for years. These systems often differ, but generally they allow for a mark showing "understood the subject" or "understood and has done extra, original work in the subject." There is no failure. If a student does not "pass" the class, there is no mark recorded. He or she may try it again or change to another subject. With such a system, students are able to find their own strengths. They learn what they can and cannot do well. They begin to believe in themselves for what they *can* do, rather than believing that they are failures for what they can *not* do.

A change from the A-to-F way of grading to a new, realistic system would help people feel better about themselves. It would enable them to find their own strengths. It would stop them from feeling like failures. It would encourage new ideas and creativity. It might even go a long way toward stopping many of the social problems brought about by people who *think* of themselves as failures.

Analysis

This paper is organized the way many argumentative papers are. The first paragraph is a personal narrative or anecdote. It catches the reader's interest and concludes with the thesis statement. The second paragraph tells about how things are now and why they should be changed. The third paragraph tries to overcome the arguments against change. The fourth paragraph offers a solution to the problem, and the fifth paragraph concludes by telling how a change would be better and closes with a statement of even more benefits if a new system is used.

Suggestions: Organize your argumentative paper carefully. Outline it before you write it. Try to present the thesis clearly. State the way things are now, and tell why they should be changed. Think of reasons why others would not want things to change; then offer evidence why these reasons are not good ones. Finally, present your plan to make things better or to do something differently. The introduction must catch the reader's interest, and the conclusion might add something more to the thesis statement. Notice that this writer uses references to famous people (Einstein and Edison), a comparison (we might still be hunting and gathering), and references to authorities (Holt and Glasser) to support his argument. The writer has a personal interest in this topic because his daughter has a problem. The most effective argumentative papers are those in which the writer really cares about the topic.

PART THREE

SUMMARIES AND EVALUATIONS

Chapter Eleven

The Summary

Suppose you are about to have an examination in one of your classes. What is the best way to study for it? Suppose you have to write a book review for a class. What is the best way to present the main ideas of the book you are reviewing? Suppose you have to write a technical paper that requires you to present several ideas you must learn by doing research. What is the best way to present these ideas? The standard form for most technical papers requires an *abstract* at the beginning of the paper. What is an abstract?

Perhaps the most effective way to study, to prepare a book review, or to present a technical paper is to use a *summary*. A summary is a brief statement that gives all of the important points of a longer work. The summary presents the main ideas in the same order as the original. Brief statements of longer works are sometimes called *abstracts, digests, precis,* or *condensations.* The differences in meaning are very small. Most technical summaries are called abstracts, whereas literary summaries are called digests or condensations and usually use the exact words of the original author. A precis is a concise summary, an abstract, and is usually shorter than a general summary. A precis or abstract may not use the original author's exact words but does use the original ideas in their original order. A summary, then, is a brief restatement of the original in your own words. Usually it is about one-fourth the length of the original but may be even shorter.

To make a summary, follow these steps:

1. Read the original carefully.
2. Either underline the important sentences, phrases, and words (in your own book) or copy them on a sheet of paper (someone else's book).

3. Copy the important material on a sheet of paper, leaving space for changes.

4. Write these important parts in sentence form.

5. Using the skills you have learned in sentence combining and using the necessary transitions, rewrite the sentences into a continuous paragraph.

6. Check your summary to make sure that it only contains ideas that appear in the original.

 ## *Model Compositon*

Citizen of the World

I am one of those people who spends much time in coffeehouses and taverns talking to and observing others. One time I met half a dozen gentlemen who were talking about the different kinds of people in Europe. One of these men stated that he had all of the wonderful qualities of the English in his person. He went on to say that the Dutch were all greedy and hungry for money. The French were not to be trusted. The Germans were a bunch of drunks. The Spanish were too proud. In bravery, kindliness, generosity, and every other virtue the English were better than the rest of the world.

The rest of the company, all Englishmen, accepted his statements as truth. I sat there and said nothing, so my companion asked me if what he had just said was not true. I replied that I could not judge until I had spent some time in those other countries. Perhaps I might find that the Dutch were thrifty and saved their money, that the French were very polite, that the Germans were hard-working, that the Spanish were very calm and quiet—even that the English, although brave and generous, might be too bold and too happy when things went well and too sad when they did not. When I said this, I soon lost the goodwill of my companions, and they all left me alone.

I paid my bill and went home. There I began to think about the silliness of national prejudice. I thought of that ancient wise man who, when asked what "countryman" he was, replied that he was "a citizen of the world." We have now become so English, French, Dutch, Spanish, or German that we are no longer citizens of the world. We are so much members of one small society that we no longer think of ourselves as members of that grand society that includes all of humankind. (*330 words*)

Summary Sentences:

1. I spend much time talking to people in coffeehouses.

2. One time I met six gentlemen.

3. One of them spoke about the bad qualities of other nations.

4. He spoke of the Dutch, French, German, and Spanish.

5. He said that the English were the best.

6. The others accepted his statements.

7. I was asked my opinion.

8. I said I would have to visit those countries to know.

9. Perhaps those other people had good qualities.

10. Perhaps the English had some bad qualities.

11. The others did not like what I said and left.

12. I paid my bill and went home.

13. I though of the wise "citizen of the world."

14. There is too much national prejudice.

15. We no longer think of ourselves as part of humankind.

Summary:

National Prejudices

I spend much time talking in coffeehouses. Once I met six gentlemen, one of whom spoke of all the bad qualities of the Dutch, French, Germans, and Spanish and concluded that the English were the best. While the others agreed, I said I would have to visit the other countries to be sure. Perhaps the English had some bad qualities, too. The others did not approve and left. I paid my bill, went home, and thought of the wise man who said he was a "citizen of the world." National prejudice does not let us think of ourselves as part of all humankind.

The original has over 330 words. This summary leaves out the specific details about the bad qualities of the different nationalities, as well as much of the personal narrative. This summary is slightly over 100 words. If you wanted to keep to one-fourth the size of the original, you would condense the first summary.

National Prejudices

One of several men I met in a coffeehouse listed the bad qualities of the Dutch, French, Germans, and Spanish, concluding that the English were best. I disagreed until I could observe these other nations, pointing out that the English had some flaws. Disapproving, they left, and I went home remembering the man who was "a citizen of the world." National prejudice prevents us from being part of all humankind.

This second summary has cut the size down to 70 words, less than one-fourth of the original. It keeps the essence of the original by leaving out most details and personal narration. It keeps the same order of this purposeful narration, including putting the topic sentence at the end (inductive reasoning; see page 135).

Summarizing Description

 ## Writing Practice (Guided Summary)

Directions: Read the following expository composition, which describes and explains mythology. Write a coherent summary of no more than one-fourth the length of the original.

 ## Model Composition

There is no culture or tribe, however primitive, that does not have its mythology. From the cold North to the sunny South, across the seas to the far West and the distant East, all people have traditional stories about gods, strange beings, ancestors, and heroes. These myths, so widespread and often so similar, seem to serve two main purposes.

The first purpose that myths serve is to answer difficult questions. For some of these questions there is still no answer accepted by everybody: What is the origin of humankind? Is there life after death? If so, what is it like? Where did the skills of reading, writing, and growing food come from? Most mythologies have man created by a god. In China it was Yu-ti, the "Ancient One of Jade," who made the first person out of clay. In the Near East Marduk made man from earth and the blood of Kingu, another god. The people of Central America believed that Nohochacyum, the "Grandfather," created human beings from the earth. The ancient Hebrews (and many Christians today) think that Yahweh made human beings out of dust from the four corners of the earth. Each of these cultures has a complex and complete story about what happens to people after they die. In many cultures there are many gods: a god of storms, a god of knowledge or wisdom, a god who told human beings how to grow food, gods of the sky and the stars.

Another function of mythology is to explain social customs and ways of behaving. Without going into too much detail, it can be noted that in all cultures humankind was created by a god. The god might be humanlike or even, as in Africa, a giant beetle. It is, therefore, the duty of human beings to worship the gods and to serve them. The ways of serving the gods form the rules of social behavior. Almost all cultures have a myth about a great flood that destroyed the wicked people of the time. If someone is wicked, then he or she might be destroyed by the gods. In almost every culture there is an evil god or demon who is opposed to the good gods. This evil being tempts people to do wrong. So it is the duty of people to fight the desire to do wrong. All cultures tell stories of great persons of the past, heroes and heroines, who have done what the gods wanted and serve as models for the proper way to act.

Sometimes modern people smile at these myths, but even today we do not agree about the "truth" of many of the questions that are answered by mythology. Perhaps we are making our own mythology about why we do the things we do, about what we accept as right or wrong. Doesn't each country have its own heroes, great leaders, artists, even sports figures, who serve as models? Perhaps the day of mythology is not over. (*500 words*)

Suggestions:

1. Find the thesis statement in the introductory paragraph.
2. Find the topic sentences for paragraphs 2 and 3.
3. After each topic sentence, list the *main* examples, definitions, or illustrations that the writer uses to support the topic sentence.
4. Find the main idea in the concluding paragraph.
5. Combine all of the material in suggestions 1–4 into a paragraph of not more than 125 words. (Use your own words; if you use the author's exact words, use quotation marks.)

Summarizing Narration

Writing Practice (Guided Summary)

Directions: Read the following narrative composition, adapted and modernized from "A Dissertation on Roast Pig" by Charles Lamb. Following the suggestions, write a coherent summary of about one-fourth the length of the original.

Model Narrative

Roast Pig

Humankind, says a Chinese manuscript, for the first 70,000 ages, ate their meat raw, clawing or biting it from the animal. The manuscript goes on to say that the art of roasting was accidentally discovered in the following manner. The swineherd, or keeper of pigs, Ho-ti went out in the woods one morning to collect acorns for his hogs, leaving his house in the care of his eldest son, Bo-bo. This great clumsy boy, who was fond of playing with fire, let some sparks escape into the straw and burned down the house as well as the pigpen. The house was not important because it was made of dry branches and easy to rebuild. The pigpen, also reduced to ashes, contained nine newborn pigs considered to be the best in China, and Bo-bo was wondering what he would say to his father when he smelled the new and different odor that seemed to be coming from the pigpen. He stooped down to feel one of the pigs, to see if there were any signs of life. He burned his fingers and put them in his mouth to cool. Some of the bits of pig skin stuck to his fingers, and for the first time in his life (indeed, in the world's life, for no person had done it before) he tasted roast pig. He finally understood the truth—that it was the roast pig that smelled and tasted so delicious. He was cramming whole handfuls down his throat when his father came home and began to beat him for being so careless. In spite of the blows, Bo-bo would not stop eating until the pig was gone.

"You useless son, what are you eating? Is it not enough that you have burned down the house, but you must eat fire as well!"

"Oh father, the pig, the burnt pig, do come and taste how nice the burnt pig eats."

Ho-ti cursed his son, and he cursed himself for having a son that would eat burnt pig. But Bo-bo pulled another pig from the ashes and began to eat, still shouting, "Eat, eat, eat the burnt pig, oh father." Ho-ti trembled and took the pig from his son. He also burned his fingers and put them in his mouth. Then both father and son sat down to the mess and did not leave until they had eaten all of the newborn pigs.

Bo-bo was made to promise not to tell the neighbors, who would have thought them very strange indeed to eat burnt pig. But the neighbors noticed that Ho-ti's house burned down more often than before. In fact, every time there was a new litter of pigs, there was a fire. At length they watched and discovered the terrible secret, and the father and son, along with some burnt pigs, were sent before the judge at Pekin. The judge and jury did the same thing that Ho-ti and Bo-bo had done. They tasted the pigs and immediately reached a verdict of not guilty.

The judge, a clever man, went out and secretly bought all of the young pigs he could find. In a few days His Lordship's house was seen to be on fire. Soon there was nothing but fires all over the district. Pigs and material for houses became more and more expensive. This process of burning houses continued, says my manuscript, until a wise man discovered that it was not necessary to burn a whole house down to make cooked (*burnt,* they called it) pig. By such slow ways, concludes the manuscript, do the most useful arts make their way among humankind.

Suggestions: To write a summary of a narrative, it is necessary to leave out many of the interesting details. You must put in only the important parts that make the story understandable. The first 100 words can be summarized in this way:

A Chinese manuscript says that meat was first roasted instead of being eaten raw when Bo-bo, the son of Ho-ti, a swineherd, accidentally burned down the house. (*26 words*)

Continue with the summary. If necessary, rewrite your first summary to keep the final version under one-fourth (about 150 words).

Summarizing Compare/Contrast

 ## Writing Practice (Summary)

Directions: Read the following compare-contrast composition adapted from an essay by Juan Montalvo of Ecuador showing some similarities and differences between George Washington and Simon Bolivar. Underline the main ideas. Combine the main ideas into a summary no more than one-fourth the length of the original. Use your own words; if you use Montalvo's *exact* words or phrases, use quotation marks to give him credit.

 ## Model Composition

Washington and Bolivar

Washington and Bolivar had in common the same goal, the desire to bring liberty to a country and bring about a democracy. It is the breadth and success of the one in reaching his goal and the difficulties without measure of the other that makes the difference.

The fame of Washington does not rest so much on his greatness as a military leader as it does on the success of the work he carried on and achieved with such happiness and good judgment. The fame of Bolivar was marked by the noise of arms and the splendor of a glorious figure, the feeling of trumpets and horses and the noise of a warrior fighting the evils of tyranny. Washington had around him such notable men as Jefferson, Madison, and Franklin, that spirit of both sky and earth. These and the rest gave him good advice and help. Bolivar, on the other hand, had to tame his lieutenants, each of whom wanted to save his own land from tyranny by himself. There were men like Jose Paez, who helped free Venezuela and then turned against Bolivar. Washington founded a republic that has lasted to become one of the major countries of the world, partly because the men who followed Washington were great citizens, philosophers, and politicians. Bolivar founded a nation that is still free but never became as great because the men who came after him did not work together to build a single nation.

Washington was less ambitious (he refused a third term) and more modest; he appears more respectable and majestic to the world. Bolivar was more ambitious (he accepted a third term) and more elevated. Although both are to be honored for the glory of the New World, Bolivar will remain, because of the greater difficulties he had to overcome, a more splendid, glowing, beloved figure than Washington. (*350 words*)

Suggestion: Review Chapter Six to see which pattern Montalvo uses to compare and contrast these two leaders. Your summary should use the same pattern. When you write your summary, be sure that you have found the writer's thesis statement—it will help you decide which parts are important and which you can easily omit.

Summarizing Cause and Effect

Writing Practice (Summary)

Directions: Read the following cause-and-effect composition. Find the thesis statement and the topic sentences of each paragraph. Write a summary of not more than one-fourth the length of the original. If you use the *exact* words of the writer, give him credit by using quotation marks.

Model Composition

What Next?

In Washington, D.C., there is a small office on the fourth floor of an old building stuck between railroad tracks and busy freeways. From this office of the Department of Agriculture comes information about the changes and shifts in population. It is the office of the department that handles *demography,* the study of the size, growth, density, and changing patterns of human populations. This work shows us not only what has happened and what is happening, but also what we can expect in the future.

Calvin L. Beale, who works in this office, discovered that the population of the United States was moving *from* the cities *to* the small towns and rural areas. He made his discovery in the 1970s, but not many people believed him until the 1980 census proved him right. Many city planners wish now that they had listened to him, for the centers of many American cities are bare and empty. If the planners had listened to Beale, they could have planned for a gradual change in population.

Leon F. Bouvier of the Population Reference Bureau has been studying population trends worldwide, with some interesting conclusions. First, world population is still growing at a 3 percent rate. (That means a possible doubling in twenty-five years.) Second, people are moving more and more from country to country. Most of the movement is from countries of little economic opportunity to industrial countries. In Kuwait 75 percent of the population are temporary immigrants. In the Ivory Coast 25 percent of the people are foreigners. France has 3.8 million immigrant workers, and West Germany over 6 million. The United States has taken in 100,000 refugees per year since 1974 and over 600,000 per year since 1980. In addition, there are about 400,000 illegal immigrants. The society of the United States is changing.

Demographers simply state the facts, but everybody should think about what those facts mean. In the United States, will these millions of immigrants stay in limited ethnic groups? Will they mix with the general Anglo-American culture? Will there be a multiracial culture with two, maybe three, main languages? Will there be racial conflicts? Should there be a limit on further immigration? Should the schools teach in English only or in more than one language? These and other questions have to be answered. It is better to use the work of the demographer and try to find some solutions before the problems get too big to handle. The study of population trends reaches far beyond that cluttered little office in Washington, D.C., to cover the whole world. (*470 words*)

Analysis

This composition differs a little from other cause-and-effect papers you have been reading. It has a slightly different kind of introduction called *location,* or *setting,* which is similar to the *scene* for a narrative or anecdote. This kind of introduction is common in journalism (newspaper and magazine writing). The writer then gives his information (cause). He does not tell the effects of the cause, though. He asks the reader a series of questions. Given these causes, what might happen? This cause–possible effect pattern is often used in argument. The writer would next offer some answers to the questions and try to convince the reader what ought to be done (moral argument). The concluding sentence refers back to the opening location.

 ## Writing Practice (Summary)

Directions: Read the following expository composition. Find the writer's thesis statement (in this case, it is phrased as a controlling question) and the topic sentence for each paragraph. Using them as a basis for your organizing, write a summary of the composition. Make it no more than one-fourth as long as the original.

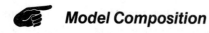

Model Composition

Wonderful Poison

On the wall of an Egyptian temple is a 3,000-year-old painting of a man drinking; by his side is a pot of beer. One of the earliest bits of writing ever found in ancient Iran is a recipe for making wine. People have been making and using alcohol at least as long as they have known writing. To judge from the fact that many people too primitive to have developed writing also make beer and wine, we were probably drinking long before we started writing. Where does this stuff come from and what effect does it have on us so that we continue to use it?

The active ingredient in beer and wine is alcohol ($C_2 H_5 OH$), which is produced naturally. Many plants, such as the pineapple, have natural alcohol in their juice. If grape juice has yeast added to it, either natural yeast from the grape skins or yeast from another source, the sugar in the juice will *ferment* and produce alcohol. This alcoholic juice is called *wine* and will not spoil or turn sour the way unfermented juice will. Different alcoholic drinks (beer, whiskey, brandy, gin, vodka) are made from different plants and are processed differently, but they all have in common the one ingredient alcohol.

Alcohol has a definite and predictable effect on people. It is absorbed directly into the bloodstream, where it affects the central nervous system quickly. Although beer or wine may contain some protein or carbohydrates, pure alcohol has no food value other than calories (seven calories per gram). The body burns up these calories in the liver, nowhere else. The result of this process is that alcohol stays in the bloodstream until it is used up, at the rate of one-third to one-half ounce per hour. The rate varies with the size of the person, but generally it takes three hours to completely use up one and one-half ounces of alcohol. So what does alcohol do? It is a depressant; it slows down the functioning of the brain. It works directly on the control center, attacking first the higher functions like speech and reasoning, then the grosser functions like walking, and finally the basic functions like breathing.

Because of the slow rate of use by the liver, it is possible to build up concentrations of alcohol in the blood. The amount of alcohol in the blood, called the blood alcohol level, or BAL, is measured as the percent of alcohol in the total bloodstream. As the percentage increases, so does the effect on the body.

0.00%–0.05%	No noticeable effect
0.06%–0.10%	Relaxation of judgment and social restraint
	Reduced anxiety (cares and worries forgotten)

0.11%–0.15%	Reaction time greatly slowed
	Lack of coordination
0.16%–0.20%	Difficulty in walking straight
	Speech slurred, vision blurred
0.21%–0.30%	Great mental confusion
	Nearly unconscious
0.31%–0.35%	Completely unconscious
0.36%–0.45%	Shutdown of basic functions
	Death

For some people there is one additional effect: alcohol seems to be *addictive*. *Addictive* means that, after repeated use of a substance, certain people "need" that substance in the body to function in a normal or near-normal manner. If alcohol can be addictive, it is medically a poison; if as little as four-tenths of one percent can cause death, why do people drink it?

People seem to drink alcoholic beverages for two main reasons. The first occurs in primitive societies, where the blurred vision, the seeing of images that do not really exist (hallucination), and the loss of contact with the higher brain functions is considered a religious experience. The second is far more common. It is the drinking of small amounts to reach the stage of relaxation (up to 0.1 percent). There is a feeling of calmness. Cares and worries seem to go away. Anxieties are reduced. Although some people may show anger or sadness, most are relaxed and happy. This social function of alcohol has made one doctor call it "that wonderful poison." (*710 words*)

Analysis

This composition is a technical process paper showing how alcohol affects the human nervous system. Notice that it does not make any moral statements about whether the use of alcohol is good or bad, right or wrong. There is no clear concluding paragraph; the last sentence refers to the title and serves as a conclusion.

Summarizing Argumentation

Writing Practice (Summary)

Directions: Read the following argumentative composition. Find the writer's proposition and notice the pattern of his argument. Write a summary that is not more than one-fourth the length of the original.

 **Model Composition**

Earthquake

In 1983 a major earthquake completely destroyed the business section of the California town of Coalinga, as well as hundreds of private houses. No building in the town escaped some damage. California is earthquake country! The people of California do not ask *if* there will be another major earthquake, they ask *when* and *where* it will happen. If Coalinga, with its 5,500 people, could be destroyed, what would be the effect on the over 2 million people living in urban Los Angeles? It is time for the people of Los Angeles to make plans for "the big one."

The City Council of Los Angeles made a start by forming an Earthquake Safety Study Committee. The committee found that over 8,000 buildings in the city were unsafe: factories, stores, and dwellings, including apartments and hotels. In the event of an earthquake of 6.0 strength (on the Richter scale of 1.0 to 10.0) there would be an estimated 8,500 deaths and 34,000 injuries. The cost of the damage would be more than $1,200,000,000. Most of these buildings would suffer damage because they were built before 1934, when building laws were made stronger. They have weak foundations; the mortar holding the bricks together is not as strong as it was; some have suffered from earlier quakes. The committee concluded that conditions are not very good.

However, there is a cure. Most of these buildings can be reinforced, made safer by adding steel rods and by making the foundations stronger. Many owners of dangerous buildings have already made these improvements. It is hard to be accurate, but the cost has been between $6 and $10 per square foot. At an average cost of, say, $8 per square foot, it would take a total of $700 million to make downtown Los Angeles safer.

Property owners, insurance people, and other citizens have asked, "Where is the money going to come from?" The federal government will give disaster loans, but only *after* the destruction. Are the owners supposed to bear the cost? Will they raise the rents to make up the expense? Will banks loan the money at low interest rates? At what point will an owner say that it is too costly to fix his building and just walk away? Is it really the business of the city council to pass a law requiring all buildings to be made safer?

Many of these questions and objections are honest, but the people who ask them miss the main point: What will be the cost if nothing is done? Is the loss of property and human lives worth less than the cost of reinforcement? Clearly, it is the duty of the city council to the citizens to protect them by passing earthquake laws and making Los Angeles a safer place to live. (*500 words*)

Analysis

The writer follows a standard argument pattern. He opens with some startling statistics, presents conditions as they are now, offers a solution to the problem, states some objections, and concludes with reasons why these objections are not good. Notice the use of factual argument, inferences made from those facts, and the change to a moral argument (the *duty* of the council) at the end.

Summary writing, as mentioned in the first part of this chapter, is a most useful skill. It allows you to understand the main parts of any kind of writing. It also allows you to decide the value of any kind of writing by using your summary as a basis for analysis.

Chapter Twelve

The Evaluation

Understanding the Work

Analyzing the Work

Evaluating the Work

Evaluation means just what it sounds like: to put *value* on, to tell what something is worth, to tell whether or not it is useful. Many times you will be asked to evaluate a paragraph, an essay, a book, an experiment, or a report. Once you learn how to evaluate, you will be able to tell whether or not something was worth reading, and you will be able to support your judgment. The process of evaluation has two main parts: understanding and analysis.

Understanding means that you must know exactly what the author has written. You must understand the ideas, the sentences, the words. If you do not understand one word in a sentence, the meaning of that sentence is not quite clear. If you do not understand one sentence in a paragraph or composition, the whole meaning is not quite clear. To really understand what you read, you will have to use your dictionary often.

Analysis, as you know, means to take something apart, look at the parts, and see how they work together to make the whole. An analysis has been presented for many of the model paragraphs you have studied so far. You are going to practice writing that kind of analysis, but in a little more detail.

Understanding the Work

1. Make sure that you know the meaning of what you have read. Usually it will take two or more readings to understand completely.

2. Make sure that you know the writer's *purpose* for writing. Although purposes sometimes are mixed, there are three common reasons for writing:

a. To entertain or to amuse the reader (usually narration)

b. To inform or to explain (usually description or exposition)

c. To convince or to persuade (usually argumentation)

Remember that it is possible for a narration to have the purpose of doing more than just entertaining. It may try to teach or explain, like fables and myths. Argumentation may use exposition to teach or inform in order to make you believe the argument.

3. The key to understanding is to find the writer's topic sentence (or thesis statement), the proposition (in an argument), or the point or purpose (in a narrative).

Analyzing the Work

1. Once you have found the purpose—what the writer is trying to do—see how he or she does it. An excellent way to find out how the writer works is to make either an outline or a summary. A summary will leave out all of the details and will let you see the pattern used.

2. Ask yourself what *pattern* is used.

a. Primarily description-definition?

b. Primarily example-illustration?

c. Primarily comparison-contrast?

d. Primarily cause-and-effect?

e. Primarily analysis?

f. Primarily argument?

g. A combination of some of these patterns?

Evaluating the Work

1. Look carefully at the writer's purpose and method; then ask yourself how effectively he or she accomplished that purpose:

a. Are the examples clear and understandable?

b. Is the information complete, or did the writer omit something?

c. Is the writer honest, or did he or she lie?

d. Is the writer's pattern of reasoning correct? (Do his or her inferences make sense?)

2. Thinking carefully about what the writer tried to do and how well he or she did it, decide whether you agree with the thesis or proposition, disagree with it, or agree with only part of it.

3. Finally, ask yourself if what the writer did was worth doing. Did it have any value to you? To someone else, perhaps?

The process of evaluation answers four questions about any piece of writing.

1. What is the writer trying to do?
2. How does he or she do it?
3. How well does he or she do it?
4. Was it worth doing?

 ## Model Evaluation

Sea Secrets

The oceans cover just over 70 percent of the surface of the earth, and until recently we have only been able to see the top. Only in the last few decades have people been able to go below the surface to find out what strange creatures might live in the seas. There are secrets in the seas that we are just beginning to understand.

Last year a strange creature was found washed up on the sands near the city of Acapulco. The residents thought it was a sea serpent. Dead from some unknown cause, it was over 14 meters long. This monster had a red crest 2 meters high running the length of its slender body. The head was topped with rays or feelers even longer. Experts from the University of Mexico examined it and said that it was a giant oarfish, a rare but not unknown kind of deep-water fish that lives in the Pacific Ocean. However, oarfish are usually no more than 2 or 3 meters long. What made this one grow to nearly five times its normal size?

Even stranger things have happened. There is an early fish called the *coelocanth* (see-low-kanth). Fossils of this fish had been found, and scientists believed that it had lived 18 million years ago. However, in 1938 a fisherman off Capetown, South Africa, let down his nets to a depth of 45 fathoms and brought up a strange fish. It was colored a bright blue, had a large bony head, and had legs! Astounded scientists said it was, indeed, a coelocanth, thought to have been extinct for millions of years. It was a "living fossil." Even more recently another "living fossil" was found in the Mariana Trench off the Philippine Islands. This one was a primitive shellfish living at a depth of 11,730 meters. It was believed to have become extinct 400 million years ago! The same expedition that discovered the shellfish took photographs of other creatures living at that depth. These creatures had glowing lights and moved swiftly away from the cameras. They have not yet been identified.

These and other discoveries make one wonder just how much we really do know about this planet that is our home. Are there other giant animals living in the sea? What makes them grow so large? Are there other animals still living that were thought to have been extinct for millions of years? How do they manage to survive? Finally, how many of the "facts" we "know" about our world are really true? (*435 words*)

—Peter Ossen

There are several words in this composition that probably are not in your vocabulary or have meanings that are different from the ones you know. To understand the essay, you must find out what they mean. Here are a few; if there are others, look them up in your dictionary.

1. Paragraph 1
   decade   a period of ten years
   creature any living thing
              (notice that the writer used the word in paragraph 2 to mean a *dead* animal)

2. Paragraph 2
   residents   people who live in a place
   sea serpent a sea snake (a serpent is a snake)
   monster   any large or ugly thing
   crest   in this use, a kind of growth along the body
   rays   long, slender growths
   giant   much bigger than normal

3. Paragraph 3
   fossils   remains of long-dead creatures that have turned to stone
   fathom   a sailor's measure of about two meters
   extinct   no longer living; used to refer to a whole group of animals
   astounded very surprised

4. Paragraph 4
   shellfish   any animal that has a shell, usually in the water

The writer uses quotation marks around several words in this composition: *living fossil, facts,* and *know.* This device tells the reader that the writer knows that he may not be using the words exactly. A "living fossil" could not really exist because a fossil is an animal that has been in the earth so long that it has turned to stone; it could not be alive. When he uses quotation marks around *facts* and *know,* he is letting the reader know that they are not really facts and that we really do not know. His purpose seems to be to inform or explain, perhaps to teach us that what we think we "know" may not be completely accurate.

Summary

Until the last few decades, we have explored only the surface of the sea. There are secrets in the depths that we are just beginning to understand. (*thesis statement*) Last year an oarfish was discovered in Mexico that was five times larger than normal. In 1938 a coelocanth, thought to have been extinct for 18 million years, was caught off Africa. A shellfish thought to have been extinct for 400 million years was discovered off the Philippines. Other creatures, as yet unidentified, were discovered there, too. These discoveries should make us ask how much we really know about the world we live on. (*100 words*)

Analysis

The writer uses an expository pattern, primarily giving examples and using description to make the examples clear. The last paragraph seems to be a kind of argument. (Proposition: Some of our information about the world may not be accurate.)

 ## Model Evaluation

Sea Secrets

The essay "Sea Secrets" by Peter Ossen presents some of the recent discoveries about strange forms of life in the sea. He states, "There are secrets in the sea that we are just beginning to understand." He uses examples of a giant oarfish found in Mexico, a coelocanth discovered off the coast of Africa, and a shellfish and strange glowing creatures found near the Philippine Islands. The oceans cover over 70 percent of the planet's surface, and it is only within the last few decades that we have been able to explore the depths. Ossen asks why some fish grow to giant size and wonders if there are more strange "secrets" in the seas. His specific examples are accurate and may be checked in any up-to-date reference book. In his conclusion he asks, "Finally, how many of the 'facts' we 'know' about our world are really true?" Yet there is a difference between *new* knowledge, what we have recently learned, and *old* knowledge, what we believed to be true. Most scientists would say that the statement "The coelocanth is extinct" is a theory, not a fact. In spite of this minor confusion about scientific thinking, Ossen's essay presents interesting information to the general reader.

Analysis

This evaluation briefly tells the content of the essay, shows how the writer supports his thesis, and judges how valid the examples are. The evaluation also points out that the writer should make the difference clear between *fact* and *theory.* Two quotations from the essay are used: the thesis and the conclusion. Both are clearly shown by the use of quotation marks. The evaluation says that the essay is worth reading by a general reader.

Notice what the evaluation does *not* do.

1. It does not simply retell the composition. The summary is less than half of the total evaluation.

2. It does not argue with the essay; as the following paragraph does:

   I think this writer is wrong. Sure, we may not know too much about what is happening on the ocean's bottom, but we sure know a lot of other things. Look at the advances we have made in medicine and transportation. So we don't know a lot about funny fish. I don't think it is very important anyway!

3. It is not limited to a statement of taste like the following paragraph:

   This is a really interesting essay. I learned a lot about fish and things that live in the ocean. This is one of the best essays we have read this semester. I thought it was really good!

You may, of course, say that you like or dislike any composition that you are evaluating, but your opinion should have some support. ("I did not know that people were exploring the depths of the ocean. I now plan to find out more about these discoveries.") And, your opinion should be a very small part of the evaluation (roughly 10 percent).

Writing Practice (Evaluation)

Directions: Read the following narrative adapted from *Gulliver's Travels* by Jonathan Swift. After making sure that you understand it, write a summary. Then, using the summary as a guide, write an evaluation.

Model Narrative

The Immortals

Next I traveled to the land of Luggnagg. The people there are quiet and generous, and they are kind to strangers. I had many friends among them. One day one of my friends asked me if I had seen any of their Struldbrugs, or immortals. I said that I had not, and asked if he would tell me how it was possible for a person to be immortal, that is, to live forever. He told me that sometimes, but very rarely, a child was born with a red mark above the left eyebrow. This mark was a sign that the child would never die. The mark grew larger and changed color; at twelve years of age it turned green, at twenty-five it turned deep blue, at forty-five it grew coal black and was as large as a half-dollar. After that it never changed. These births were very rare. There were only 1100 in the whole kingdom. They could happen in any family, and the children of the immortals were normal.

I cried out in amazement: Happy nation, where each child has a chance to be immortal! Happy people, who could enjoy examples of wisdom and virtue! Happiest of all those the Struldbrugs, who would never have to worry about death.

The friend smiled at me with the sort of smile that people give to the ignorant. Another young man who was with me asked what kind of life I would lead to make the most out of being immortal. I answered that first I would study the way to become rich. In 200 years I would be the richest man in the kingdom. Then, not having to go to work every day, I would study arts and sciences until I became an expert. Finally, I would write down all of the changes in fashion, language, and politics until I could offer good and sound advice to the rulers. I would be wise. I would gather together other Struldbrugs, and we would make great discoveries in medicine, astronomy, and inventions.

At last my friend said that he wanted to point out some mistakes that I had made. The system of life that I had described was not possible. My system was based on the idea that all men wished to live as long as possible, and it supposed that the Struldbrugs lived in youth and health. But this was not so. They commonly act like mortals until about 30 years old; after that they grow more and more sad and unhappy until they reach 80. At 80 they are looked upon as dead by the law. They are not allowed to hold any public office and are given money to live on. At 90 they lose their teeth and hair but continue to have all of the diseases they had before. Soon their memory fails them. As the language of the country is always changing, after 200 years they are not able to talk to anyone and live like foreigners in their own country.

Later I saw five or six of different ages, the youngest being a little over 200 years old. Not one of them wanted to ask me any questions, although they were told that I was a great traveler. They were the most horrible sight I had ever seen, and the women were more terrible than the men. After I had seen them, my desire to live forever was very much less. (*560 words*)

Suggestions: This is a fictional narrative, and the author's purpose is to entertain and to teach something. Whether or not a composition is entertaining is a personal matter and will vary from reader to reader. An evaluation will give a summary of the story, tell how the writer tried to achieve his or her purpose (in a narrative, writers try to make the story seem to be true), tell if he or she did succeed, and tell the worth of the story (was it interesting to read, and did you learn anything?).

Writing Practice (Evaluation)

Directions: Read the following expository essay; it follows a comparison pattern. Write a summary and, using the summary as a guide, evaluate the composition. Use the guidelines (the four basic questions) on page 181.

Model Composition

Heat Rays

More often than not, the ideas that writers invent are later developed by men of science. A striking example is the heat ray. In 1897 H. G. Wells wrote a science fiction novel called *The War of the Worlds* in which creatures from Mars attacked the earth. They destroyed towns, cities, and armies by using a heat ray. Here is Wells's explanation:

> It is still a matter of wonder how the Martians are able to kill men so swiftly and silently. Many think that in some way they are able to create an intense heat in a special tube that does not get hot itself. This great heat they project in parallel rays by means of a special mirror, much as a lighthouse projects a beam of light. Whatever can burn flashes into flame at its touch. Metal runs like water; it softens iron, cracks and melts glass, and water immediately explodes into steam.

In 1958, over sixty years later, two American scientists developed what they called "light amplification by stimulated emission of radiation," better known by its initials, *laser*. Here is how a laser works.

> The molecules or atoms of certain materials (gas, liquid, crystal) are placed between two mirrors and stimulated, or "excited," by outside energy in the form of high-energy flash lamps. When the excited molecules or atoms drop back to a normal state, they give off energy in the form of heat or light. The light energy bounces back and forth between two mirrors in a tube until there is enough energy for them to come out of a special mirror at one end of the tube in parallel rays. Although the tube itself does not get hot, the light can reach a temperature of over 10,000 degrees Fahrenheit. That is enough to melt steel and cause water to burst into steam.

Other examples spring readily to mind: Jules Verne's description of an atomic submarine in *20,000 Leagues Under the Sea,* written in 1870; and the remarkable *New Atlantis,* written by Sir Francis Bacon in 1627, which predicted airplanes, submarines, radio, and genetic science. Reading literature, especially science fiction, and comparing the ideas to inventions we now use daily will show a great many more examples of literary creations made real. (*410 words*)

Writing Practice (Evaluation)

Directions: Read the following argument against war. Find the writer's proposition and the support used for it. Using the four questions on page 181, write an evalution of the argument.

Model Composition

War

In the past 5,000 years men have fought 14,523 wars in spite of the fact that wars are both stupid and cruel. Wars are fought largely by the young men of a country. Wars, by their very nature, require that some will die and others will be hurt. What could be more stupid than for a country to send its young men off to be either killed or hurt? More than soldiers are hurt, too. There is another kind of pain, the pain of the mothers, the sisters, and the wives of these young men who are dead or crippled. In addition to the personal pain is the fact that no one ever really wins a war. A country may change leaders for a short time. One country may control another for a short time. A few people may make a lot of money by selling guns and arms. A few professional soldiers may become famous for a short time. But sooner or later the new leaders grow old and die; the countries change control; the blood money is spent; the old soldiers die; and the world is the same as it was before. What happens then? The country spends millions to rebuild from the destruction of the war, and the whole stupid, cruel process starts all over again. Today, one out of four people have been involved in some kind of war or other. It is a fact that war is stupid; it also seems to be a fact that people are stupid. Otherwise they would put a stop to wars. (*250 words*)

Suggestion: The difficult part of writing an evaluation is to read carefully and to understand the pattern and the evidence used by the writer. Your evaluation must be based on the evidence the writer offers. Your agreement or disagreement with the proposition should not be based on what you already believe but on the evidence presented by the writer. It is possible for you to agree with the proposition yet disagree with the evidence. In that case, the argument is not effective.

Writing Practice (Evaluation)

Directions: Read the following argument. It is written in the form of a personal essay, but the proposition is clearly stated. Find the proposition, analyze the pattern, and decide whether you agree or disagree and why. Write an evaluation.

Model Composition

The Best Years

Last week I was idly watching the evening news on television. The news was about a prize for some scientific discovery; I forget what it was. The announcer, his name was Ralph Story, made a comment that caught my attention. "All great discoveries," he said, "are made by people between the ages of twenty-five and thirty." Being somewhat over the age of thirty myself, I wanted to disagree with that statement. Nobody wants to think that he is past the age of making any discovery. (I'm not sure what I could discover, but I did not want to be left out just because of my age.) The next day I happened to be in the public library and went over to the reference section. I ended up spending several hours looking up the ages of famous people and their discoveries and actions. Ralph Story was right.

First I looked at some of the scientific discoveries. One of the earliest discoveries, the famous experiment that proved that bodies of different weights fall at the same speed, was made by Galileo when he was twenty-six. Madame Marie Curie started the investigation of radium that led to a Nobel Prize when she was twenty-eight. Albert Einstein was twenty-six when he published his world-changing theory of relativity. Hideki Yukawa predicted the existence of a new particle in the atom at the age of twenty-six. Well, enough of that. I wasn't going to make any scientific discoveries at my age. Yet I wondered if those "best years" were true in other fields.

So I went to the section on politics. Surely it took the wisdom of age to make a good politician or leader. Perhaps it does, but look when these people *started* their careers, discovered what to do with their lives. Napoleon took command of the mobs of the French Revolution at age twenty-six. Winston Churchill was elected to the House of Commons at the age of twenty-six. Abraham Lincoln gave up the life of a country lawyer and was elected to the state legislature at the age of twenty-six. Simon Bolivar joined the revolutionaries who fought in the city of Caracas and started the movement to liberate Latin America at what age? Twenty-six!

Even religious leaders made choices before the age of thirty. Siddhartha Gautama, the Buddha, left his life of riches and splendor as the son of a raja and started his life's work of teaching before he reached the age of thirty.

St. Francis of Assisi left his happy life and became a wandering saint at age twenty-six. Mohammed beheld the vision of God that started the Muslim religion before he was thirty. I was convinced.

I was convinced, but not too happy. It seems that between the ages of twenty-five and thirty people have learned enough to let them make these discoveries and choices, but they are not old enough to be set in their ways. They will still take risks, make great changes, try new methods. After thirty, I guess, most people do not want to try new ways. Then I thought of people like Bassho, Shakespeare, and Cervantes, who were still writing wonderful works at the ripe old ages of forty-five and fifty. I thought of Picasso, who was trying new ways of painting and creating sculpture when he was *ninety!* Perhaps there is still hope for me. (*610 words*)

Suggestion: Earlier you were told not to use statements of personal taste in an evaluation unless you gave some support (page 184). Many students write sentences like these:

I thought that this was a well-written composition.

I really liked this essay.

This story bored me.

I recommend this book to everyone.

Such statements belong in an evaluation *only* if you can give some support for them.

 ## Example

(Weak Statement in an Evaluation of the Essay "War")

This essay really points out the evils of war. Wars are cruel and stupid. Imagine, nearly 15,000 wars. I agree that "no one ever really wins a war." I know that, when my friend was supposed to go to Viet Nam, he went to Canada instead. If they had asked me to go, I would have gone to Canada, too.

Comment: This writer has not really evaluated the essay. He has expressed his personal experience and views that have nothing to do with the essay.

 ## Example

(Thoughtful Evaluation of the Same Essay)

I wonder how this writer got the exact number of wars fought in the past 5,000 years. Such a figure is doubtful to me. It is possible for a country to "win" a war. Two examples are the American and French wars for independence. The people made sacrifices but gained freedom. Although I agree that wars cause pain and suffering, they are not fought for "stupid" reasons.

Comment: This second writer evaluates the essay; he does not just give his own emotional statements.

If you want to comment that a composition is "well-written," make sure that you know what good writing is. You would have to mention vocabulary, use of figures of speech, sentence structure, organization, style, and many other things. If an essay was boring to you, tell why. Was it too childish? Were the ideas or the vocabulary too difficult? Were the ideas or the information something that you already knew? Was the narration one that you had read before?

If your instructor asks for your opinion in an evaluation or book review, be sure that you tell *why* you feel the way you do about the subject. You might like an essay because it gave you some new information; perhaps the ideas will be of value to you in your daily life. Perhaps it made you think, or laugh, or cry, or get angry.

Writing Practice (Opinion)

Directions: If you wish, add your personal opinion about one (or several) of the evaluations you have written for this chapter.

HANDBOOK
FOR PROCESS AND PATTERN

An Outline of English Grammar

Section One

Grammar is a study of language. It is the study of the way words are arranged into sentences to give meaning to speech or writing. Grammar attempts to develop the rules by which thoughts, ideas, or emotions may be spoken or written by one person and understood clearly by another. Although there is some similarity, different languages have different grammars. The words are arranged in different patterns. The grammar you will need to study is the English grammar used in the United States by educated speakers and writers. It is a dialect of English used in North America.

Most people learn the grammar of their native language without any effort or study. They learn it from their parents and friends as they grow up. Most people know all of the basic sentence patterns by the time they are three years old. However, when they have to learn another language, they must study the grammar of the language and build a vocabulary. They must study the rules for building sentences; the way verbs change to show past, present, and future; the placement of modifiers in sentences; and many other patterns and structures.

There are two ways to learn the grammar of another language. The first is to learn it the way you learned the grammar of your own language—from friends, relatives, and people you happen to meet. The other way is by studying it formally. One good way to study is to divide that study into five parts:

1. The ways words work in English
2. The four main word classes of English
   Nouns (including pronouns)

Verbs

Modifiers (adjectives and adverbs)

Structure words (articles, prepositions, conjunctions, modals, and others)

3. Sentence parts and their basic patterns

4. Variations (questions, commands, exclamations)

5. Combinations of the basic patterns

There are three problems that can cause confusion when you try to learn English. The first is that several words may refer to the same thing. For example, several other words may refer to the single animal known as a *dog*:

canine: the general term for all dogs (from the Latin or scientific words *canis familiaris*)

pup or puppy: a young animal

mutt: usually a bad term, an ugly dog

cur: usually a stray dog with no owner

mongrel: a dog of mixed types, not purebred

In addition, there are many different kinds, or breeds, of dogs. Each has a specific name.

Hound	Spaniel	Great Dane
Poodle	Pit bull	Terrier
Pekinese	Boxer	Saint Bernard

There are over a dozen more.

The second problem with many English words is that a single word such as *dog* may have more than one meaning.

1. Any domesticated member of the canine family (*noun*)

2. Specifically, the male animal of any canine class (including the wolf and the fox), as opposed to the female, called a *bitch* (*noun*)

3. A device used to hold logs in a fireplace (*noun*)

4. A hooked or U-shaped device used to hold heavy objects (*noun*)

5. A verb meaning "to follow closely" (*He dogged my footsteps.*) (*verb*)

6. A verb meaning to use the device in number 4 (*verb*)

7. An adjective used to describe another noun (*dog house, dog cart, dog collar*) (*adjective*)

8. An adverb used to describe an action in a sense similar to usage 5 (*She studied the lesson doggedly.*) (*adverb*)

9. A number of different meanings in many informal or slang expressions:

To put on the dog (display wealth)

A dog's life (an unhappy life)

You lucky dog (you happy person)

So the single word *dog* has at least eight similar but different meanings. It can pattern as a noun, as a verb, as an adjective, or as an adverb. Most words in English can change from one class to another, being used as nouns, verbs, and modifiers. They can also be changed by adding extra letters and syllables to the end (called *suffixes*) or to the front (called *prefixes*). Later on you will see how these changes are regularly made in English.

The third possible problem with the way words work in English is that many words are spelled the same but have different meanings when they are said or pronounced differently.

 ## Examples

Ob*ject*: something that can be seen or touched
Ob*ject*: to show that one does not like something

Tear (*tare*): to rip something apart
Tear (*teer*): water that comes from the eyes

*Con*duct: a way of acting or behaving
Con*duct*: to lead or show the way

Polish (*poh-lish*): of or related to Poland
Polish (*pah-lish*): to make shine

Words like these may cause you some trouble. Just remember, if the word does not seem to make sense, check your dictionary for another meaning.

It is possible to learn such a language. First, there are only four main classes of words. There are only four parts to English sentences. There are only five basic sentence patterns. Once you understand these basic parts, you will be able to put them together in a great many ways to write clear, understandable English. The place to start is with the four main classes of English words.

 ## Meaning Practice

Directions: To see the many possible meanings of common English words, use your dictionary to find at least two different meanings for the following words.

Well	Close	Frog	Clip	Felt
Read	Cold	Bat	Fast	Graze

Meaning Practice

Nouns

Directions: Using your dictionary or a larger one, see how many meanings you can find for the common word *hand.*   *5*

The first large class of words is called *nouns.* The word *noun* comes from a Latin word, *nomen,* which means "name." To name is the function of this class of words.

1. They name persons:
   Charles M. Cobb
   Nguyen Dinh Hoa
   Jun Maeda
   Lena Levindowski
   Khalil Sajat

2. They name things:
   crocodile
   flower
   automobile
   diode
   computer

3. They name abstract qualities and ideas:
   love
   hate
   beauty
   democracy
   kindness

4. They name actions:
   swimming
   sleeping
   dancing
   studying
   jogging

Note

The present participle form of most verbs may be used as a noun.

When nouns name a *specific person, place,* or *thing,* they always begin with a *capital* letter and are called *proper nouns.*

Examples

John Doe, New York, France, Nippon, Fido, Hamlet, Christmas

Nouns that begin with a small, or lowercase, letter are called *common nouns*. This second subclass includes all of the nouns that are not proper nouns, including words like *grass, sand, water,* and *beauty*.

Nouns have two special characteristics. First, nouns change form to become *plural*. *Plural* means more than one person, place, or thing. When there is only one person, place, or thing, the word used is *singular*.

Singular Form	Plural Form
duck	ducks
window	windows
magazine	magazines
house	houses

Question: What is one way nouns can be made plural?

Answer: ___use s in the end of the word.___

Singular Form	Plural Form
fox	foxes
church	churches
goddess	goddesses
bush	bushes

Question: What is another way nouns can be made plural?

Answer: ___Use es in the end of the word___

Singular Form	Plural Form
fly	flies
baby	babies
beauty	beauties
city	cities

Question: What is another way nouns can be made plural?

Answer: _Take off the y & use ies in the_
end of the word.

Singular Form	Plural Form
foot	feet
mouse	mice
child	children
knife	knives

Question: Why do some nouns have these unusual ways to form plurals?

Answer: These forms have been in English for hundreds of years. They are old-fashioned plurals that have never changed.

Exceptions: There are several words that do not change form. The same word is used for both singular and plural.

Singular Form	Plural Form
Chinese	Chinese
deer	deer
sheep	sheep
fish	fish

Question: How can you learn these exceptions and the few others?

Answer: You will have to memorize them. There is no rule.

Second, nouns change form to show ownership. This form is called the *possessive.* The usual way to show possession with nouns is to add an apostrophe and an *s.* (See page 300 for other uses of the apostrophe.)

 Examples

the car of (belonging to) Kim	Kim's car
the dress of Alicia	Alicia's dress
the work of one hour	one hour's work
the pay of one week	one week's pay
the friend of everybody	everybody's friend
the hat of (one) girl	the girl's hat
the hats of (many) girls	the girls' hats
the toy of the baby	the baby's toy
the toys of the babies	the babies' toys

Note

When you change the plural form that ends in *s* to the possessive form, it is necessary to add only the apostrophe.

Classes of Nouns

Nouns may be put into several classes: proper nouns, common nouns, singular nouns, plural nouns, and possessive nouns. In addition, nouns may be classified as *count nouns* and *noncount nouns*.

Count Nouns: Count nouns are simply names for things that can be counted (one, two, several, many). They pattern with *a, an,* or *the* in the singular, and they form the plural by adding *s* or *es*.

a boy	the boy	the boys
an apple	the apple	the apples
a horse	the horse	the horses
an engine	the engine	the engines
a girl	the girl	the girls

See page 250 for more information about when to use *the* with singular count nouns.

Noncount Nouns: Noncount nouns are simply those things that cannot be counted. They do *not* pattern with *a* or *an* when used alone but may take *a* or *an* when other words or phrases are used in front of them. They do *not* form a plural (with a few exceptions).

water	some water (*never* a water)
money	much money (*never* many)
the grass	a lot of grass
sand	a little sand (*never* few)
information	a great deal of information
love	a little love

Compound Nouns: Sometimes a noun will have more than one word. These nouns are called *compound nouns. Compound* means anything having two or more parts. Right now there is no agreement about how to write compound nouns. Some dictionaries will advise using a hyphen [-]; others will not.

Examples

mother-in-law	swimming pool
Salvation Army	breakout
root beer	human being

Even though a compound noun is really a noun with a modifier (*swimming* tells what kind of a pool it is), when words have been used together for a long time, they are often called compound nouns and are treated as a single idea. You can check your dictionary to decide whether to write *trash collector* or *trash-collector*. If you hear these words spoken, the stress is usually on the word that normally acts as a modifier.

Making Nouns

You already noticed that the *-ing* form of a verb (present participle) may be used as a noun. There are many other endings that can change other words into nouns. Here are some of the more common ones.

-ation	-ism	-er
-ment	-ness	-ian (*or* -ion)

 Examples

Verb	*Noun Form*
develop	development
relax	relaxation
criticize	criticism
swim	swimmer

Adjective	*Noun Form*
happy	happiness
sad	sadness
logical	logician

 Noun Practice (Singular to Plural)

Directions: In the following sentences, change the nouns in *italics* from singular to plural. Write the complete sentence on your paper. Do not forget to change the form of the verb and, in most cases, to omit the articles *a, an,* and *the.*

Example

0. The *child* put some sand into a *box*. (*singular*)
0. The children put some sand into boxes. (*plural*)

1. The *goat* is an important *animal* in the Middle East.
2. A *goat* can eat a *weed* or a *shrub* and still be healthy.
3. A *farmer* is happy to have a *goat*.
4. He can get a fine *product* from the *animal*.
5. The meat is cooked on a *spit* with *tomato* and with *onion*.
6. The *hide* makes soft leather easily cut with a *knife*.
7. Milk from a *goat* is more healthful than milk from a *cow*.
8. The *female* is called a *nanny*.
9. The *male* is called a *billy*.
10. The *baby* is called a *kid*.

Noun Practice (Singular to Plural)

Directions: Change the following nouns from singular to plural:

1. city	6. church	11. bus
2. cliff	7. wife	12. copy
3. reply	8. valley	13. radio
4. bush	9. fox	14. bath
5. woman	10. business	15. industry

Note

Some of these nouns are irregular. When in doubt, check your dictionary

Noun Practice (Possessive)

Directions: In the following sentences, change the noun and prepositional phrase in *italics* to make them possessive. Remember the pattern:

hair of the goat	the goat's hair
leg of the man	the man's leg
warmth of the sun	the sun's warmth

Write the complete sentence on your own paper.

Example

0. The hair *of the goat* protects it from the cold *of the night.*

0. The goat's hair protects it from the night's cold.

1. The hair *of the animal* makes rugs and tents.
2. The milk *of the goat* is more healthful than the milk *of the cow.*
3. The feet *of all goats* are sharp and pointed.
4. The climate *of the area* is very dry.
5. The friends *of the farmer* are usually small.
6. Yearly rains fill the small ponds *of the desert.*
7. The water *of the ponds* soon sinks into the sands *of the desert.*
8. So the diet *of these animals* is limited.
9. They eat the tops *of the weeds* and the dry leaves *of the shrubs.*
10. The desert goat is the friend *of the farmer.*

Noun Practice (Possessive)

Directions: Change the following phrases to the possessive form by adding the apostrophe or the apostrophe + *s.*

1. a school for boys
2. pay for a year
3. a car that Sam bought
4. a dress that Maria owns
5. the bad habits that Pete has
6. the smell of a goat
7. a house that Lee has
8. the directions that the teacher gave

9. a box for a fox
10. the noise of a class
11. the voice of my mother
12. the shoes of a child
13. the paragraph of Bess
14. the noise of two classes
15. the bark of a dog

Noun Practice (Count and Noncount Nouns)

Directions: The words *a few* and *few* are used with plural count nouns. The words *a little* and *little* are used with noncount nouns. Use *few, a few, little,* or *a little* with each of the following words. Change the word to plural if necessary.

Example

  0. coffee   *a little coffee*

  0. dollar   *a few dollars*

  1. furniture

  2. idea

  3. animal

  4. snow

  5. music

  6. friend

  7. wind

  8. city

  9. book

10. money

Noun Practice (Count and Noncount Nouns)

Directions: The word *many* is used with count nouns, and *much* is used with noncount nouns. Use the words in the preceding list with either *many* or *much*.

Note

The words *a lot of* or *lots of* are used with either count or noncount nouns, but these words are considered by many to be informal usage, not precise.

Personal Pronouns

The word *pronoun* means "in place of a noun." The function of pronouns in English is to take the place of nouns. There are thousands and thousands of nouns. Pronouns, however, make up a very small class of words; there are only eight kinds, and they have stayed almost the same for hundreds of years.

Personal pronouns are the only kinds of words that change form completely. These changes are called *case changes*. Most nouns, for example, become plural by just adding *s* or *es*. Pronouns change completely.

Pronouns also change form to show whether they are the subject or the object of the sentence or to show possession. Nouns show possession, as you have seen, by adding an apostrophe and an *s*. Pronouns *never* use the apostrophe.

<u>Personal Pronoun Patterns</u>

Person	Subject	Object	Possessive
Person speaking (*first person*)	I	me	my, mine
Person spoken to (*second person*)	you	you	your, yours
Person spoken about (*third person*)	he	him	his
	she	her	her, hers
	it	it	its (*no apostrophe*)
Plural Forms			
First person	we	us	our, ours
Second person	you	you	your, yours
Third person	they	them	their, theirs

 Examples

1. Charlie is wearing Charlie's hat. (*proper nouns*)
2. *I* (*subject*) am wearing *my* (*possessive*) hat. (*personal pronouns*)
3. *He* (*subject*) is wearing *his* (*possessive*) hat.
4. Lena gave it (*pronoun replacing* hat) to Charlie. (*proper nouns*)
5. *She* (*pronoun*) gave it to *him* (*pronoun*).
6. Do *you* have *yours*?
7. *They* took *mine*.
8. Every dog will have *its* day. (*no apostrophe*)

The following old-fashioned "familiar" forms are not much used in English today, although they are still used in some languages: *thou, thee, thy,* and *thine* (second person).

Question words (*interrogative pronouns*) also change:

Subject	Object	Possessive
who	whom	whose

Examples

Who is going with me?

With *whom* are you going?

Whose car are we going in?

Some *demonstrative* pronouns change form from singular to plural:

Singular Form	Plural Form
that	those
this	these

 ### Examples

That chair (over there)   *Those* chairs (over there)

This table (right here)   *These* tables (right here)

These changes are called *case changes*. Your instructor may tell you to put a pronoun "in the objective case." With this chart you will be able to do so. After a while, you will know how to make the proper changes.

 ### Remember

Personal pronouns *never* use the apostrophe to show possession.

Other Classes of Pronouns

Do not worry too much about the following classes of pronouns. Just be aware that they exist. The only problem that most people have with pronouns is deciding when to use *who* or *whom* and *I, me, him, her, he,* and *she* correctly. Check to see if the word is the subject of a sentence (use *subjective* case) or the object of a sentence or phrase (use *objective* case).

Indefinite Pronouns: These pronouns do not refer to a definite person or a definite amount; for that reason they are called indefinite.

anyone	everything	one
anything	few	other
both	many	several
each	much	some
either	neither	someone
every	nobody	something
everybody	none	

Example

Anyone can make a few mistakes.

   Relative Pronouns: These pronouns are used to refer to a noun already mentioned:

   who   which
   whom   what
   whose   that

 Example

The man *who* helped me is the one *that* I thanked.

   Interrogative Pronouns: These pronouns are the same as the relative pronouns (except *that*); when they are used to ask a question, they are called *interrogative* pronouns.

 Example

   Who is it?
   What was that?
   Which is it?

   Demonstrative Pronouns: These pronouns are used to point out something. They have a singular and a plural form:

   this   these
   that   those

   Reflexive Pronouns: The addition of the word *self* (*selves* in the plural) to a personal pronoun turns the action of the statement back to the subject.

   I shave *myself.*   We shave *ourselves.*
   Did you hurt *yourself?*   They hurt *themselves.*

   Reciprocal Pronouns: These pronouns show that the actions are exchanged by two or more subjects.

   Let us help *each other.*
   We like *one another.*

   Intensive Pronouns: This use of pronouns is for emphasis.

I *myself* climbed the mountain. (I really did it.)

We need a rest *ourselves.* (We are tired, too!)

You will have noticed that grammarians (people who study grammar) like to put words into many classes. Some pronouns are classed by the kinds of things they refer to or replace (personal pronouns), some by the way they are used in a sentence (relative and interrogative pronouns are almost the same), and some by the way they change the meaning of another pronoun (reflexive and intensive pronouns). What you or your instructor choose to call a pronoun will depend on both the meaning and its use in a sentence. Again, do not worry too much about the names of these eight kinds of pronouns. Just learn to use them correctly.

Pronoun Practice (Case Changes)

Directions: Choose the correct form of the pronouns between the parentheses. Draw a line through the *incorrect* forms. Refer to page 206 for the correct forms of the subjective, objective, and possessive cases.

Example

0. Will you please give (~~I,~~ me, ~~myself~~) the book?
1. My sister and (*I, me, myself*) bought a book.
2. She liked it as well as (*I, me, myself*) did.
3. (*Us, We*) children had never read *The Odyssey.*
4. The story interested (*us, we, ourselves*), both (*she and I, her and me*).
5. The Greeks, to (*who, whom, whose*) the story was well-known, liked it.
6. We learned about the old times as a result of (*us, we, our*) reading the book.
7. The story is about Odysseus, (*who, whom*) traveled for ten years.
8. There were problems about (*he, him, his*) getting home.
9. He fought monsters larger than (*he, him*) was.
10. (*Whoever, Whomever*) reads this story will find it interesting.

Pronoun Practice (Demonstrative and Possessive Pronouns)

Directions: Choose the correct demonstrative pronoun by drawing a line through the one that is not correct. Remember, *this* and *these* refer to something that is close; *that* and *those* refer to something that is far away.

1. (*This, That*) book is in (*my, mine*) hand.
2. (*These, Those*) over there are (*my, mine*) also.
3. (*This, That*) one in the library is (*her, hers*).
4. (*These, Those, They*) belong to (*her, hers*).
5. (*These, Those*) I am holding are (*they, their, theirs*).

Verbs

The next large class of words in English is called *verbs*. Generally, these are the kinds of words that show some kind of action. They are usually divided into three subclasses: *transitive* verbs, *intransitive* verbs, and *linking* verbs.

Transitive Verbs

Transitive means to transfer from one thing to another. *Transitive* verbs transfer the action from the "actor," the subject of the sentence, to the person or thing "acted upon."

 Examples

1. Jeffrey *throws* rocks.
2. Pierre *dropped* the dishes.
3. Nadya *broke* her toe.
4. Carlos *builds* houses.
5. Troung *needs* a pencil.

It would not make sense to write the following as complete sentences.

1. Jeffrey throws. (What?)
2. Pierre dropped. (What?)
3. Nadya broke. (What?)
4. Carlos builds. (What?)
5. Troung needs. (What?)

The action of the verb is incomplete. The reader wants to know *what* is being thrown, dropped, broken, built, or needed. These kinds of verbs must have an *object* to make the sentence complete. Transitive verbs are words for actions that need an object, or something acted upon.

Intransitive Verbs

Intransitive verbs are those words that show an action that does not need an object, or something acted upon.

 ### Examples

1. Alfredo *runs* swiftly.
2. Lida rarely *works.*
3. Jennifer *reads* all of the time.
4. Rahim *studies* very hard.
5. Antonia *sleeps* in class.

These verbs do not need an object to make sense. The reader does not feel that something is left out if you write the simplest kind of sentence that you can, simply a subject and an intransitive verb.

1. Alfredo runs.
2. Lida works.
3. Jennifer reads.
4. Rahim studies.
5. Antonia sleeps.

Some verbs may be either transitive or intransitive. That is, they sometimes use an object and sometimes do not.

 ### Examples

0. Mr. Habib breathes. (*intransitive*)
0. Mr. Habib breathes dust and smog. (*transitive*)

0. Rahim studies. (*intransitive*)
0. Rahim studies books. (*transitive*)

Linking Verbs

Linking verbs are used to show what is often called "a state of being." The other verbs show some kind of action—running, studying, throwing, working. Linking verbs simply link or join the subject of a sentence to a modifier (a noun or an adjective).

Examples

1. Ronald Reagan *became* President.
2. Generalissimo Franco *appeared* dead.
3. You *look* happy.
4. Kwang *seemed* tired.
5. I *remained* calm.

The main linking verbs in English are

>   to be
>   to seem
>   to appear
>   to look (in the sense of "to appear")
>   to become
>   to remain

Verb Practice (Kinds of Verbs)

Directions: In each of the following sentences, find the verb. Decide if it is transitive (needs an object), intransitive (does not need an object), or linking (shows a state of being). On the line in front of the sentence write the letter for the kind of verb it is.

>   Transitive verbs   = *T*
>   Intransitive verbs = *I*
>   Linking verbs   = *L*

___I___ 1. Odysseus sailed across the wine-dark sea.

___I___ 2. Once he fought a one-eyed giant.

___L___ 3. The giant, the son of the sea god, was Polyphemus.

___L___ 4. Polyphemus seemed such a monster because he ate people. (*two verbs*)

___LT___ 5. Odysseus used his brains and blinded the monster. (*two verbs*)

___L___ 6. Polyphemus, of course, was not very happy about that.

___L___ 7. His father, the sea god, was not very happy about it either.

___T___ 8. The sea god gave Odysseus bad luck.

___L___ 9. For ten years Odysseus went from country to country and from city to city.

___T___ 10. Finally, after ten long years of traveling, he arrived at his home.

Suggestion

Study the diagram in Illustration I.1 to help make the differences clearer between these three classes of verbs. Go back and check your work.

Characteristics of Verbs

All verbs, whatever class they belong to, have three characteristics that identify them as verbs.

1. Verbs change form to show whether the action (or state of being) takes place in the present, took place in the past, or will take place in the future.

Transitive Pattern:

Subject	Verb	Object
Salvador	threw	a ball.

A transitive verb needs an object to answer the question "What?" about the verb.

Intransitive Pattern:

Subject	Verb
Salvador	danced.

Intransitive verbs need no object. We do not ask, "What did Salvador dance?"

Linking Pattern:

Subject	Verb	Complement
Salvador	seemed	happy.
The dog	appeared	dead.
Simon	became	a general.

The way to tell if a verb is a linking verb is to put the complement in front of the subject. If it makes sense, the verb is a linking verb.

Examples

happy Salvador

dead dog

general Simon

Illustration I.1
Three Verb Patterns

Present	Past	Past Participle
I jump.	I jumped.	jumped
We walk.	We walked.	walked

The -*ed* form is both the simple past and the past participle in regular verbs. See page 225 for irregular forms.

2. Verbs pattern regularly with the -*ing* ending to form what is called the *present participle.*

Base Form	Present Participle
To run	Running
To jump	Jumping
To bark	Barking

3. Verbs regularly add an *s* to the base form to be used with *he, she,* or *it* (third person singular, present tense).

Base Form	Third Person Singular
Run	He runs. She runs.
Jump	He jumps. She jumps. It jumps.
Bark	It barks.

In English this is the only change made in the present tense of regular verbs. (See "Agreement," page 233, for more details.)

✓ **Check:**   If you have difficulty finding the verb in a sentence, try this test. Put the word in one of the following blank spaces. If the sentence makes sense, the word is a verb.

1. Let us __*go*__ .
2. Let us __*do*__ it.
3. They (*he, she*) __*are*__ happy.

Verb Tenses

Tense refers to the form of the verb showing *when* the action of that verb takes place. Many languages have separate verb forms for each tense. English has only one change possible in the base form of regular verbs.

Base: I walk. (*present tense*)

Past: I walked. (*past tense*)

To show other tenses, such as the future, it is necessary to add other words to the base form. These *auxiliary* words are also verbs.

> *Future:* I will walk.
>
> I shall walk.

We also use the present participle (the *-ing* form) in some tenses.

> *Progressive forms:* I am walking.
>
> I will be walking.

To place an event in time, three main verb tenses are used in English.

Simple present: The event is taking place right now.

Simple past: The event took place in the past and is now over.

Simple future: The event will take place at a later time.

Each of these simple tenses has two other forms to place the time of the event with greater accuracy:

Progressive: The event is in *progress* or continues over a period of time.

Perfect: One event happens before another event begins.

The diagrams and examples in Illustrations I.2–I.13 will show how the nine tenses work in English.

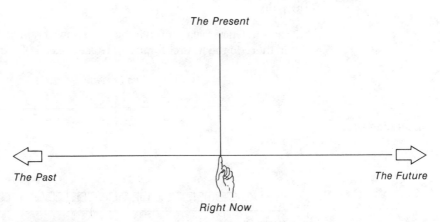

Illustration I.2
Basic Tense Diagram

Simple Present

Using a verb in the simple present tells that the event is taking place at the present time, right now (see Illustration I.3).

 Example

I see a bunch of bananas.

Antonio is at the zoo.

Illustration I.3
Simple Present Tense

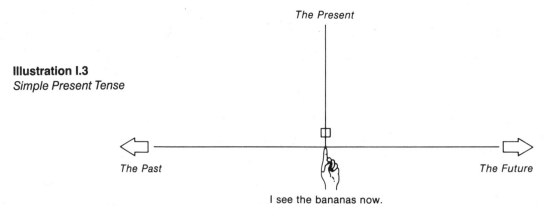

The Present

The Past   *The Future*

I see the bananas now.

The simple present tense is also used to tell that an event or action takes place all of the time. It happened in the past; it is happening right now; it will probably continue to happen in the future (see Illustration I.4).

 Example

It rains in Guatemala. (It is raining there now; it rained there in the past; it will rain there in the future. It rains in Guatemala all of the time.)

Illustration I.4
Simple Present Tense (Ongoing Action)

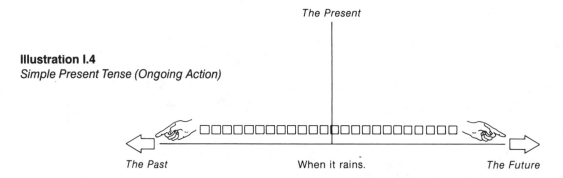

The Present

The Past   When it rains.   *The Future*

Simple Past

Using a verb in the simple past tells that the event took place at one time in the past and is now over or completed (see Illustration I.5). The time could have been just a few minutes in the past or thousands of years ago.

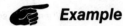 **Example**

I saw a bunch of bananas yesterday (last week, last year).

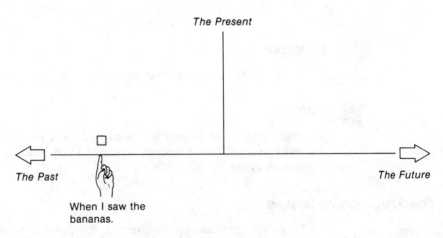

Illustration I.5
Simple Past Tense

Simple Future

Using a verb in the simple future tells that the event or action will take place at some later time. It has not happened yet. (See Illustration I.6.)

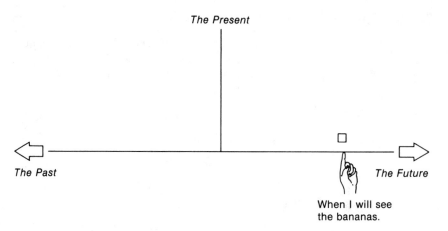

Illustration I.6
Simple Future Tense

 Example

I will see the bananas in one hour (tomorrow, next year).

 Note

In formal usage, *shall* is used with the first person and *will* with the second and third persons. This difference is not used very much in informal writing and speech today.

The Progressive Tenses

There are three progressive tenses: the present progressive, the past progressive, and the future progressive. They are called *progressive* because they tell that the event or action continues for a period of time, or is in *progress.*

Present Progressive: The present progressive tense uses the auxiliary verb *to be* and the present participle (*-ing* form) of the verb. It tells that an event began in the past and is still happening right now. It will probably continue to happen in the future. (See Illustration 1.7.)

 Example

Antonio is watching the gorillas. (*auxiliary verb* is + *present participle* watching)

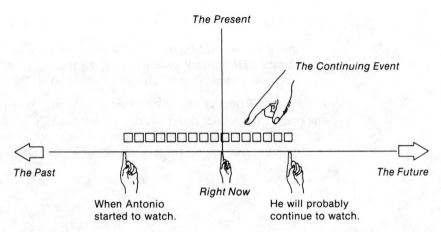

Illustration I.7
Present Progressive Tense

Past Progressive: The past progressive tense uses the auxiliary *be* in the simple past tense with the present participle (*-ing* form). Using a verb in this tense tells that the action started at a certain time in the past, was in progress at a definite time in the past, and is over now. (See Illustration I.8.)

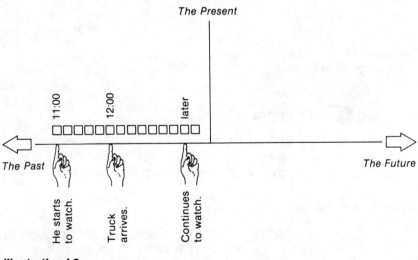

Illustration I.8
Past Progressive Tense

Example

> Antonio was watching the gorillas when the banana truck arrived. (*For example:* He started watching at 11:00; the truck arrived at 12:00; he probably continued to watch them after the truck arrived.)

> **Future Progressive:**   The future progressive tense uses *will* + *be* + the present participle. Using a verb in this tense tells that an event or action will start at a definite time in the future, will be in progress for a certain time in the future, and will probably continue for some time into the future. (See Illustration I.9.)

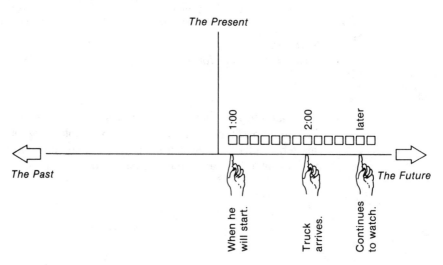

Illustration I.9
Future Progressive Tense

 Example

> Antonio will be watching the gorillas when the banana truck arrives. (*For example:* He will start to watch at 1:00; the truck will arrive at 2:00; he will probably continue to watch them until later.)

The Perfect Tenses

> The perfect tenses use *have* with the past participle (*-ed* form) of the verb. These tenses are used to tell about an event or action that has been completed by the present, in the past, or in the future.

Present Perfect: Using a verb in the present perfect tells that an event or action began in the past and is over at the present time. (See Illustration I.10.)

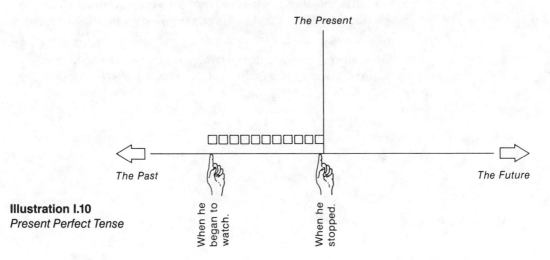

Illustration I.10
Present Perfect Tense

Example

Antonio has watched the gorillas by now. (He watched them earlier—the time is not important—and he is no longer watching them.)

Past Perfect: Using a verb in the past perfect tense tells that the event or action began in the past and was completed when another event or action began, also in the past. (See Illustration I.11.)

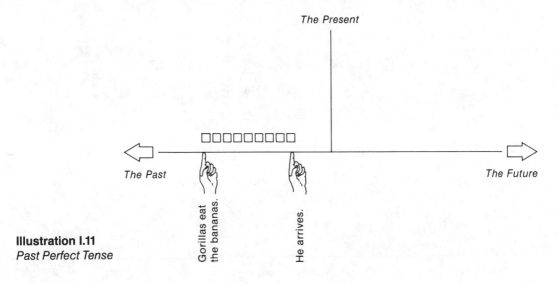

Illustration I.11
Past Perfect Tense

Example

The gorillas had already eaten the bananas when Antonio arrived. (The action began in the past and was over when he arrived, also in the past.)

Future Perfect: The future perfect tense uses *will* + *have* + the past participle (*-ed* form). It tells that two or more events or actions will take place in the future. This tense tells which of the events will be over first. (See Illustration I.12.)

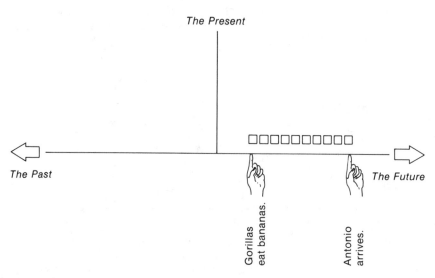

Illustration I.12
Future Perfect Tense

Example

The gorillas will have eaten the bananas by the time Antonio arrives to watch them. (They will eat at some future time. Later, in the future, he will arrive to watch them.)

 ### Note

To eat is an irregular verb; the past participle uses *-en* instead of the regular *-ed*.

The Perfect Progressive Tenses

The perfect progressive tenses are the perfect and the progressive forms joined together. They are formed by using *have + been +* the present participle (*-ing* form) of the verb. These tenses are used to tell that one action or event is in progress immediately before another event takes place. The diagram in Illustration I.13 shows how all three work.

 ### Example (Present Perfect Progressive)

The gorillas have been eating for one hour. (They started eating one hour ago and are eating right now.)

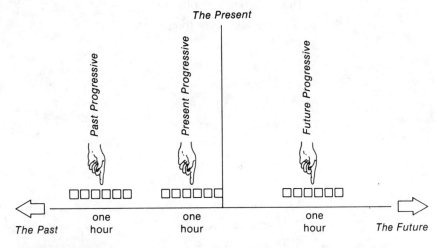

Illustration I.13
Perfect Progressive Tenses

Example (Past Perfect Progressive)

Antonio had been watching for one hour when the truck arrived. (At some time in the past he started to watch. After he had watched the gorillas for one hour, the truck arrived.)

Example (Future Perfect Progressive)

Antonio will have been watching the gorillas for one hour when the truck arrives. (At some future time, Antonio will start to watch the gorillas. After he has watched them for one hour, the truck will arrive.)

Verb Practice (Tense Changes)

Directions: Answer the following questions on your own paper. If the question is in the past tense, answer with the past tense of a verb. If the question is in the future tense, answer with the present perfect tense of a verb.

Examples

Did she marry Abner? *Yes, she married Abner.*

Will they move to a new house? *Yes, they have moved to a new house.*

1. Did you go to school today? *Yes, I went to school today.*
2. Will you have a test tomorrow? *Yes, I have taken test.*
3. Will you pass the test? *Yes, I have passed the test.*
4. Did you go to the party? *Yes, I went to the party.*
5. Will you go to the next one? *Yes I have gone to the next one.*
6. Will your friends go? *Yes my friend has gone.*
7. Did you break anything? *No I did not break anything.*
8. Will you eat something? *No, I have eaten.*
9. Did she really ask that? *No, she did not really ask that.*
10. Did they surprise you? *Yes, they surprised me.*
11. Will there be any extra food? *Yes, they have taken some extra food.*
12. Did they freeze it? *Yes, They freezed it.*
13. Will he get any of it? *Yes, he has gotten some of it.*
14. Did you want more to eat? *Yes, I wanted more to eat.*
15. Will you get fat? *Yes, he has gotten fat*

Verb Practice (Tense Changes)

Directions: Change the present tense verbs in the following sentences to one of the past tenses.

1. A traveler <u>lands</u> on a strange island in the sea. *landed*
2. There <u>is</u> a witch on the island. *was*
3. She <u>is</u> a very evil person. *was*
4. She <u>has</u> a magic wine. *had*
5. This magic wine <u>changes</u> men into pigs. *changed*
6. She <u>gives</u> the traveler some wine. *gave*
7. He <u>is</u> a clever man and <u>does</u> not drink it. *was, did*
8. The witch <u>says</u> she <u>loves</u> clever men. *said, loved*
9. The traveler <u>stays</u> with her for nine years. *stayed*
10. Finally, he <u>builds</u> a boat and <u>sails</u> away. *builted, sailed*

Irregularity

Most English verbs follow a regular pattern in changing from the infinitive or base form to the past or the past participle.

Base Form	Past Tense	Past Participle
walk	walked	walked
jump	jumped	jumped
play	played	played

A few verbs still use the older, irregular form for the past as well as a modern, more regular form.

Base Form	Past Tense	Past Participle
dream	dreamt	dreamt
	dreamed	dreamed
learn	learnt	learnt
	learned	learned

Other verbs still use the old, irregular forms only.

Base Form	Past Tense	Past Participle
bend	bent	bent
bleed	bled	bled
say	said	said

Other verbs are even more irregular.

Base Form	Past Tense	Past Participle
begin	began	begun
bite	bit	bitten
write	wrote	written

These verbs do not follow the regular pattern when they change. It is necessary for you to learn the different forms so that you can use them correctly in a sentence. Many native speakers of English have trouble with these irregular verbs. So here is a list of the most common irregular verbs in English. Read the list to become familiar with them. When you use one in your writing, check the list to see if you have the correct form.

Base Form	Past Tense	Past Participle
awake	awoke (*or* awakened)	awoke (*or* awakened)
become	became	become
begin	began	begun
bind	bound	bound
bite	bit	bit (or bitten)
bleed	bled	bled
blow	blew	blown
break	broke	broken
bring	brought	brought
burst	burst	burst
buy	bought	bought
catch	caught	caught
choose	chose	chosen
cling	clung	clung
come	came	come
creep	crept	crept
deal	dealt	dealt
dig	dug	dug
dive	dove (*or* dived)	dived
do	did	done
draw	drew	drawn
drink	drank	drunk (*or* drank)
drive	drove	driven

eat	ate	eaten
fall	fell	fallen
feed	fed	fed
feel	felt	felt
fight	fought	fought
find	found	found
flee	fled	fled
fling	flung	flung
fly	flew	flown
forget	forgot	forgot (*or* forgotten)
freeze	froze	frozen
get	got	got (*or* gotten)
give	gave	given
go	went	gone
grew	grew	grown
have	had	had
hear	heard	heard
hide	hid	hidden
keep	kept	kept
know	knew	known
lay	laid	laid
lead	led	led
leave	left	left
lend	lent	lent
lie	lay	lain
lose	lost	lost
make	made	made
pay	paid	paid
ride	rode	ridden
ring	rang	rung
rise	rose	risen
run	ran	run
say	said	said
see	saw	seen
seek	sought	sought

sell	sold	sold
send	sent	sent
set	set	set
sew	sewed	sewn (*or* sewed)
shake	shook	shaken
shave	shaved	shaved (*or* shaven)
shine (*transitive*)	shined	shined
shone (*intransitive*)	shone	shone
sing	sang	sung
sink	sank (*or* sunk)	sunk
sit	sat	sat
slay	slew	slain
sleep	slept	slept
slide	slid	slid
sling	slung	slung
slink	slunk	slunk
sow	sowed	sown (*or* sowed)
speak	spoke	spoken
spend	spent	spent
spin	spun	spun
stand	stood	stood
steal	stole	stolen
sting	stung	stung
strike	struck	struck (*or* stricken)
strive	strove	striven
swear	swore	sworn
sweep	swept	swept
swim	swam	swum
swing	swung	swung
take	took	taken
teach	taught	taught
tear	tore	torn
tell	told	told
think	thought	thought
throw	threw	thrown

wear	wore	worn
weave (*transitive*)	wove	woven
weave (*intransitive*)	weaved	weaved
weep	wept	wept
win	won	won
wind	wound	wound
wring	wrung	wrung
write	wrote	written

Even though these verbs are irregular, some of them follow a pattern. Here are some of the verbs from the main list that fall into groups.

Base Form	*Past Tense*	*Past Participle*
I. begin	began	begun
run	ran	run
sing	sang	sung
ring	rang	rung
sink	sank	sunk
swim	swam	swum
drink	drank	drunk
II. bring	brought	brought
buy	bought	bought
catch	caught	caught
fight	fought	fought
teach	taught	taught
think	thought	thought
III. bleed	bled	bled
feed	fed	fed
lead	led	led
speed	sped	sped
read	read	read (*pronounced* red)
IV. deal	dealt	dealt
feel	felt	felt
keep	kept	kept
kneel	knelt	knelt
leave	left	left

mean	meant	meant
meet	met	met
sleep	slept	slept
V. break	broke	broken
choose	chose	chosen
freeze	froze	frozen
speak	spoke	spoken
wake	woke	woken
VI. blow	blew	blown
draw	drew	drawn
fly	flew	flown
grow	grew	grown
know	knew	known
throw	threw	thrown
VII. lay	laid	laid
pay	paid	paid
say	said	said
VIII. drive	drove	driven
ride	rode	ridden
rise	rose	risen
write	wrote	written
IX. sell	sold	sold
tell	told	told
X. find	found	found
wind	wound	wound

The following group of verbs does not follow exactly the same pattern, but they are all similar.

dig	dug	dug
hang	hung	hung
stick	stuck	stuck
sting	stung	stung
strike	struck	struck
swing	swung	swung

One of the most important irregular verbs in English is the verb *to be*. Many languages, like Spanish or French, have more than one verb to do what this one verb must do in English. One Eskimo group in Canada has five "to be" verbs.

The verb *to be* is irregular in six separate ways.

Singular Form	*Present Tense*	*Past Tense*	*Future Tense*
First person	I am (1)	was (2)	will be
Second person	you are (3)	were (4)	will be
Third person	he is (5)	was	will be
	she is	was	will be
	it is	was	will be

Plural Form			
First person	we are	were	will be
Second person	you are	were	will be
Third person	they are	were	will be

Infinitive	*Present Participle*	*Past Participle*
to be	being	been (6)

To be is a linking verb; it links or connects different parts of a sentence. It is not like most verbs, which have one main meaning. *To be* has seven different uses in English.

1. The cactus *is* green.
   Links noun to adjective showing quality *or* property *of the noun.*

2. Mexico *is* larger than Panama.
   Links noun to adjective making an assertion *or statement.*

3. He *is* Charles the Second.
   Links noun to noun showing identity.

4. Hiawatha *was* an American Indian.
   Links noun to noun showing membership in a class.

5. I *am.*
   No linking, but used to show existence.

6. Mice *are* everywhere.
   Links noun to adverb showing location.

7. How *are* you?
   Links adverb to noun seeking condition.

Verbals

Often in English the parts of verbs called the *infinitive,* the *present participle,* and the *past participle* function as other parts of speech. When they function in these ways, they are called *verbals.*

The Infinitive

The *infinitive* form of the verb may be used as a noun.

 Examples

To swim is my favorite exercise.

To dive, however, frightens me.

He wanted *to drive* the car.

The infinitives *to swim* and *to dive* pattern just as if they were nouns. The infinitive *to drive* is the object of the verb *wanted.* It patterns the same way as a noun would. (*He wanted some money.*) Notice that it takes an object, *the car.* This pattern is called an *infinitive phrase.*

The infinitive may be used as an adjective.

 Example

The money *to be earned* is wonderful.

The infinitive phrase is used like an adjective to modify *money.*

The infinitive may be used as an adverb.

 Example

To be healthy you need to exercise.

The infinitive phrase modifies the rest of the sentence just as an adverb would.

The Participle

The *participle* form of a verb may be used as an adjective.

Examples

> The *crying* babies.
>
> A *completed* work of art.
>
> The horse *running the fastest* will win the race.

The participial phrase "running the fastest" modifies the noun *horse.*

The *present participle* may also be used as a noun. When you use the *-ing* form of a verb as a noun, it is called a *gerund.* The gerund is the same form as the present participle.

 ### Examples

> *Swimming* is a healthy exercise.
>
> *Making money* is the goal of many people.

The gerund *making* and its object *money* function as a noun, the subject of the sentence.

It is possible to use infinitives, participles, and gerunds together in a single sentence.

 ### Example

> To tell the truth, heading into the sunset on a sailing ship has always been my dream.

Agreement

Agr stands for "agreement." In English sentences there must be what is called *agreement* between the subject of a sentence and its verb. Here is the standard pattern for a regular English verb in the present tense.

Singular Form

First person	I talk
Second person	You talk
Third person	She *talks*
	He *talks*
	It *talks*

Plural Form

First person	We talk
Second person	You talk
Third person	They talk

Unlike many other languages, the only change in the form of the regular English verb is in the third person singular. Instead of changing the verb form, English puts a noun or pronoun in front of the verb to show who or what does the action.

 Examples

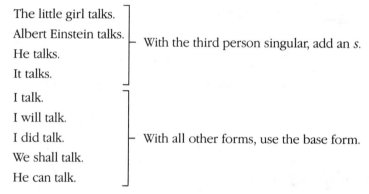

The little girl talks.
Albert Einstein talks.
He talks.
It talks.

With the third person singular, add an *s*.

I talk.
I will talk.
I did talk.
We shall talk.
He can talk.

With all other forms, use the base form.

The question is, Why do English teachers write *agr* all over students' papers if it is so easy to do it correctly? In simple sentences like those above, there is usually no problem. When sentences get complicated you will have problems with agreement.

Problems with Agreement

1. Placing a phrase between the noun and the verb can cause a problem.

    A box of apples __*is*__ on the table.
                    (*is/are?*)

    "Of apples" is a phrase modifying *box*. It is not "apples are," but "box is."

    A box of apples *is* on the table.

    A group of people __*is*__ dancing on the floor.
                    (*is/are?*)

    There is just one group (*singular*) so the correct form would be *is*.

    A group of people *is* dancing on the floor.

2. A sentence with more than one noun used as a subject (*compound subject*) can cause a problem.

Thunder and lightning _____*frighten*_____ me.
(*frighten/frightens?*)

The double (compound) subject requires the plural form of the verb.

Thunder and lightning *frighten* me.

Suggestion

If you temporarily put the word *both* or *all* before the verb when you are writing a sentence with a compound subject, it will help.

Thunder and lightning (*both*) frighten me.
Her beauty, grace, and charm (*all*) _____*make*_____ her attractive.
(*make/makes?*)

The words *both* and *all* are plural, so you would use the form of the verb for plural subjects.

Her beauty, grace, and charm make her attractive.

3. Sometimes you will write a sentence that will have one singular and one plural subject.

Neither Oswald nor his sisters _____*drink*_____ beer.
(*drink/drinks?*)

Neither his sisters nor Oswald _____*drinks*_____ beer.
(*drink/drinks?*)

The rule in English is to have the verb agree with the *last* noun in this kind of sentence with a compound subject.

Neither Oswald nor his sisters drink beer.
Neither his sisters nor Oswald drinks beer.

Verb Practice (Subject-Verb Agreement)

Directions: Read the following sentences. In each one there are two forms of the verb. Select the form that agrees with the subject by drawing a line through the *incorrect* form.

Example

0. The boys in the car (~~is~~/are) driving too fast.

1. The favorite sport of many Americans (~~is/are~~) watching television.

2. Each person (~~watch~~/watches) more than four hours daily.

3. Many kinds of programs (~~is~~/are) shown each day.

4. Sports shows and an occasional comedy (~~is/are~~) presented.

5. Neither sports shows nor comedies (offer/~~offers~~) much information.

6. There (~~is~~/are) dramas and news shows also.

7. A group of children (see/sees) cartoons in the morning.

8. The adults (follow/~~follows~~) daily "soap operas."

9. Neither "soap operas" nor comedies (interest/~~interests~~) many people.

10. There (~~is~~/are) news and adventure shows for them.

11. A hundred dollars (~~buy~~/buys) a cheap television set.

12. Anyone who likes television (spend/spends) hours watching it.

13. A child, as well as his parents, (find/~~finds~~) television interesting.

14. Seeing too many television shows (make/~~makes~~) people lazy.

15. Almost everybody in the United States (~~enjoy~~/enjoys) some of the shows.

 Verb Practice (Subject-Verb Agreement)

Directions: In the blanks in the following sentences write the correct form of the verb that appears after the sentence. Use the present tense.

1. On the street *there are* ten motorcycle riders. (*to be*)

2. At the end *there is* one rider dressed in red. (*to be*)

3. There *is* a two-foot space between each rider. (*to be*)

4. Neither the one in red nor the others *ride* for fun. (*to ride*)

5. Not only "Red" but also the others *race* for money. (*to race*)

6. One judge and one timekeeper *organized* the race. (*to organize*)

7. Judging and keeping time *to decide* who wins. (*to decide*)

8. One of the riders *started* before the others. (*to start*)

9. Each of the others *waited* for the signal. (*to wait*)

10. The early starter as well as the rest *of them* finally ready. (*to be*)

Suggestions

Look for the five common trouble spots.

1. Prepositional phrases between subject and verb.

   A child with two parents *is* happy.

2. Inverted word order (subject at end).

   Over there *are* my parents.
   There *is* only one left.

3. Indefinite pronouns *one, each, either,* and *neither* are always singular.

   Neither child *has* a bicycle.

4. Compound subjects are usually plural.

   Watching television and racing motorcycles *take* most of my time.

5. Correlative conjunctions *either/or, neither/nor,* and *not only/but also* are very tricky. The verb agrees with the subject that is nearest.

   Either the judges or the timekeeper *was* wrong.
   Either the timekeeper or the judges *were* wrong.

Auxiliaries

An *auxiliary* is something that is used "to give support, to help, to aid." This last class of structure words does just that; they are used to help other verbs. Sometimes they are called "helping verbs." There are two subclasses of auxiliaries, *verb auxiliaries* and *modal auxiliaries.* Some books put these words in a separate class, but most classify them with verbs. Using these auxiliaries gives a great flexibility to English.

They are used to make complicated tenses.

They are used to show emphasis.

They are used to show the feelings of the writer (*suggestive force*).

Verb Auxiliaries

Helping verbs (auxiliary verbs) pattern with the present and past participles of other verbs (the *-ing* and *-ed* forms). There are only three auxiliary verbs:

To be (is, am, are, was, were)

To have (have, has, had)

To do (do, does, did)

To be patterns with both the present and past participles:

I am dancing.	I was dancing.
You are dancing.	You were dancing.
He (she, it) is dancing.	They were dancing.
I am finished.	I was finished.
You are finished.	You were finished.
He is finished.	They were finished.

To have patterns with the past participle:

I have danced.	I had danced.
You have danced.	You had danced.
He (she, it) has danced.	They had danced.

To do patterns with the base form of the verb:

I do dance.	I did dance.
You do dance.	You did dance.
He (she, it) does dance.	They did dance.

Auxiliaries also pattern in combinations to form the progressive tenses (see page 218):

I have been dancing.	We had been dancing.
You have been dancing.	You had been dancing.
He has been dancing.	They had been dancing.

Modal Auxiliaries

Modals (modal auxiliaries) are used with verbs to show the future tenses, for English has no way to change the base form of the verb itself as many other languages do. Modals are also used to change the meaning of the verb slightly. They give verbs a "suggestive force."

There are only ten modals:

Modals	Meaning
can, could	ability to do something
may, might	possibility of doing something permission ("May I go?")

must, ought   obligation to do something

shall, should   strong resolve to do something
               (*shall* is also simple future)

will, would   simple future (*will*)
               intention to do something dependent on other factors

 ## Examples

1. I *can* do it myself. (I am able to do it.)
2. I *could* do it if you let me. (I have the ability.)
3. I *may* do it if it does not rain. (It is possible but not sure.)
4. I *might* go if there is time. (It is possible but not sure.)
5. You *must* pass the test. (You have no choice.)
6. You *ought* to study harder. (You have an obligation.)
7. Your skill *shall* be rewarded. (It will definitely happen [*formal style*].)
8. My skill *should* be rewarded. (You have an obligation to reward me.)
9. We *will* go tomorrow. (We will definitely go.)
10. We *would* go but have no car. (We planned to go, but something happened.)

Notice that all of these words, when used as modals, indicate actions that take place in the future.

It is easy to remember the twenty-one auxiliary verbs and modals; they are the words used to start *all* yes or no questions in English.

1. *Is* it raining in the mountains?
2. *Am* I going with you?
3. *Was* your uncle in jail again?
4. *Were* there flowers in the vase?
5. *Have* we any more cookies in the cupboard?
6. *Has* the baseball game started yet?
7. *Had* Abdul arrived by nine o'clock?
8. *Do* you go to school early?
9. *Does* the bus stop here?
10. *Did* you wash the car?
11. *Can* you pick me up tonight?
12. *Could* we study together?
13. *May* I please borrow ten dollars?

14. Might the airplane crash?

15. *Must* you talk so long on the telephone?

16. *Ought* we to wear shoes to school?

17. *Shall* we arrive in time for the party?

18. *Should* children go to bed early?

19. *Will* you please bring me breakfast in bed?

20. *Would* you please come here?

21. *Are* there any more words that start yes or no questions?

Modifiers

The third large class of words in English is called *modifiers*. The word *modify* means "to change." Modifiers change the meaning of the words to which they are attached. A modifier may be a single word, a phrase, or a clause.

There are two kinds of modifiers: *adjectives* and *adverbs*.

Adjectives

Adjectives are words used to change or restrict the meaning of nouns and pronouns.

 Examples

I own an automobile (*noun*). (*We do not know what kind of an automobile.*)

I own a large, green, noisy automobile. (*Adding adjectives makes the qualities of the automobile more specific.*)

We saw the birds.

We saw a thousand beautiful birds.

We saw the large man-eating birds.

Adjectives change form to compare more than one thing. There are two ways to use adjectives to compare. The first uses the endings (suffixes) -*er* and -*est*. There are, then, three forms for some adjectives: *positive, comparative,* and *superlative.* A few examples will make the process clear.

Positive Form	Comparative Form	Superlative Form
good	better	best (*irregular*)
hot	hotter	hottest

cold	colder	coldest
tall	taller	tallest
old	older	oldest

Positive form:	used to modify one noun or pronoun
Comparative form:	used to compare two nouns or pronouns
Superlative form:	used to show which of two or more nouns or pronouns is placed above the rest

Yesterday was warm; tomorrow will be warmer; the next day will be the warmest.

Many writers prefer to use comparative degree for two things or persons and the superlative for three or more.

The suffixes *-er* and *-est* are used to form the comparative and superlative of one-syllable adjectives. For words of three or more syllables, *more, most, less,* and *least* are used.

Positive Form	Comparative Form	Superlative Form
destructive	more destructive	most destructive
intelligent	more intelligent	most intelligent
beautiful	more beautiful	most beautiful

The form to show *negative* comparisons is the same with either one-syllable or many-syllable words.

hot	less hot	least hot
tall	less tall	least tall
old	less old	least old
destructive	less destructive	least destructive
intelligent	less intelligent	least intelligent
beautiful	less beautiful	least beautiful

Two-syllable adjectives may use either *-er* and *-est*, or *more* and *most*. Generally, adjectives ending in *y* use the suffixes: *ugly, uglier, ugliest.* Other two-syllable adjectives use the other method: *subtle, more subtle, most subtle.* It is not grammatically correct to combine both methods.

I am the most intelligentest.

He was more older than I.

Remember that nouns and participles may also be used as adjectives.

I have a *gold* ring.

She wore a *silk* dress.

We saw the *sleeping* animals.

He lives in a *hidden* valley.

When nouns and participles are used as adjectives, they do not change to become comparative or superlative. There are no such words as *golder* or *sleepinger.*

Adverbs

The other group of modifiers is called *adverbs.* The word *adverb* means "added word," but if you think of it as meaning "added to a verb," it will help you to remember the difference between adjectives and adverbs. Adverbs are used to modify verbs, other adverbs, and adjectives.

 Examples

Miguel writes *cleverly.* (*The adverb modifies the verb that tells how Miguel writes.*)

We have an *amazingly* intelligent cat. (*The adverb modifies the adjective* intelligent.)

The cat, however, runs *exceptionally* slowly. (*The adverb modifies the other adverb* slowly.)

A great many, but not all, adverbs end in *-ly.* This ending is often used to change the adjective form to an adverb form.

Adjective Form	*Adverb Form*
a sudden change	to change suddenly
a quick answer	to answer quickly
a happy greeting	to greet happily

Adverbs are usually used to show *time* (when), *place* (where), *degree* (how much), and *manner* (how).

The following are some commonly used adverbs of *time:*

after	ever	then
again	never	till
always	now	tomorrow
before	still	yesterday

The following are some commonly used adverbs of *place:*

east	here	south
far	near	there
forward	north	west

The following are some commonly used adverbs of *degree:*

almost	even	much	
enough	little	only	well

The following are some commonly used adverbs of *manner:*

easily	gently	quietly	nicely

Several of the adverbs of manner used to modify adjectives or other adverbs add very little meaning to the word being modified. Because they are used only to *intensify* the adjective or adverb that does add meaning, they are often called *intensive* adverbs.

The animals in the zoo are   alarmingly wild.

                                     awfully*

                                     incredibly

                                     frighteningly

                                     quite

                                     rather

                                     really*

                                     terribly

                                     very*

(*Good writers rarely use such meaningless intensive adverbs as *awfully, really,* or *very,* as they add so little meaning to the sentence.)

Problems with Modifiers

The structure of the English language can cause some problems in using modifiers. *Adjectives* are used to modify nouns and pronouns. *Adverbs* are used to modify verbs, adjectives, and other adverbs. The form you use tells the reader your meaning.

Kwang wrote a *lovely* letter. (*a very nice letter*)

Kwang wrote a *love* letter. (*a letter about love*)

Problem: Many words use the same form for both adjective and adverb.

far	fast	little
only	early	deadly

Solution: Put the modifier next to the word in the sentence that you want it to modify.

Joshua eats very little. (Little, *the adverb, tells how much he eats;* very, *an adverb, modifies* little.)

Little Joshua is a boy. (*adjective*)

Joshua is a *little* boy. (*adjective*)

Problem: Some adverbs have two forms:

quick/quickly   loud/loudly   slow/slowly

Solution: In general, use the *-ly* form of the word as an adverb and the other form as an adjective.

Joshua blew a *loud* blast on his horn. (*adjective*)

Joshua blew his horn *loudly.* (*adverb*)

Problem: Nouns are commonly used to modify other nouns. They pattern the same as other adjectives. When you hear them spoken, the noun used as a modifier is usually stressed.

Modifying Noun	Noun Being Modified
garage	door
forest	fire
telephone	book
flower	garden

Solution: For better writing, you should use the noun form only if there is no standard adjective form.

Tami needs a *birth* certificate. (*There is no other form; use* birth.)

There were two people in the *senator* election. (*There is an adjective form,* senatorial; *use it.*)

There were two people in the *senatorial* election.

Problem: Sometimes you will need to use an adjective and a noun to modify another noun.

Solution: Put the regular adjective first, then the noun used as a modifier, and then the word to be modified.

new state bridge (*not* state new bridge)

beautiful gold ring (*not* gold beautiful ring)

Problem: Sometimes you will want to use phrases or clauses to modify words.

Solution: Use them exactly as if they were single-word modifiers.

Special Problems

1. Adjectives with linking verbs. When you use a linking verb (see page 211), using an adjective or an adverb can change the meaning of the sentence.

   Nikolas looked *happy.* (Happy, *an adjective, describes Nikolas. He is a happy person.* Looked *is used as a linking verb.*)

   Nikolas looked *happily.* (Happily, *an adverb, tells how Nikolas was looking. He was looking in a happy manner.* Looked *is used as an action verb.*)

2. *Bad* and *badly.*

   Many errors happen when people use the linking verb *feel* with *bad* or *badly.* Always use the adjective *bad* with this verb.

   I felt bad when I failed the test.

   Karim feels bad because his cat just died.

   To write, "I felt badly," means that your sense of feeling, or touch, is not working well. Use *badly* to modify other verbs.

   Elise cooks badly.

   I drive badly when I am in traffic.

3. *Good* and *well.* Many people misuse these words. *Good* is the adjective form and is never used as an adverb. *Good* must never be used to modify a verb.

   I did well on the examination. (*But:* It was a good examination.)

   Elise cooks well. (*But:* Elise is a good cook.)

   Everything is going well in school. (*But:* School is good for me.)

4. Similar problems: *sure* and *surely, near* and *nearly, real* and *really.* In common speech (called *informal usage* or *colloquial speech*) many people use the adjective forms *sure, near,* and *real,* instead of the correct adverb forms *surely, nearly,* and *really.* However, in college writing the proper form should be used.

   We surely tried to win the game.

   The other team did not do nearly as well as last time.

   We played really well.

Modifier Practice (Adjectives to Adverbs, Adverbs to Adjectives)

Directions: Change the following adjective forms to adverbs, the adverbs to adjectives, and the nouns to verbs.

Examples

0. a happy greeting   to greet happily
0. to grip strongly   a strong grip
1. a sudden change   *To change suddenly*
2. a possible cause   *To cause possibly*
3. a probable result   *To result probably*
4. a safe journey   *To journey safely*
5. a cheerful welcome   *To welcome cheerfuly*
6. to depart quickly (*use* departure)   *A quick departure*
7. to fight angrily   *A angre fight*
8. to run effortlessly   *A effortless run*
9. to fit perfectly   *A perfect fit*
10. to look intently   *A intent look*

 Modifier Practice (Adjective and Adverb Placement)

   Directions: Use a caret (^) to show where the adjectives or adverbs following the sentence should be placed. Adjectives usually go just before the noun they modify. Adverbs may be placed elsewhere.

 Examples

0. Manireh and Hrand went to the ^ seashore. (*sunny*)
0. They rushed ^ to the sand. (*quickly*)
      (*or*)
0. They ^ rushed to the sand. (*quickly*)

1. They saw the bright^sea. (*shining*)
2. They spread their^towels on the sand. (*large, hot*)
3. Manireh wore a^bathing suit. (*new*)
4. Hrand kept on his^trousers. (*old, ragged*)
5. The sun was^warm. (*yellow*)
6. Manireh soon had^arms and legs. (*red, sunburned*)
7. Today was the first time she^had been to the beach. (*ever*)
8. She was^sunburned. (*badly*)
9. She wanted to leave^. (*quickly*)

10. Hrand saw that she was in pain. (*suddenly*)
11. They picked up their towels. (*quickly*)
12. They both ran to the car. (*hurriedly*)
13. Hrand looked for the keys to the car. (*in his pockets*)
14. He looked once. (*only*)
15. He knew that he had lost them. (*in the sand*)
16. Manireh's bathing suit was small. (*new, too*)
17. Hrand's trousers were ragged. (*old, too*)
18. He found the keys. (*suddenly, missing*)
19. He opened the door of their car. (*swiftly, old*)
20. They drove all the way home. (*happily*)

Modifier Practice (Misused Forms)

Directions: In the following sentences cross out the misused modifiers. On your own paper write the sentences correctly.

1. This was sure a wet winter. *This was sure a winter before.*
2. It was more rainier than ever before. *It was more rain than ever before*
3. I had a happily experience. *I had a happy experience.*
4. One day the distant clouds looked darkly. *one day the distant clouds looked dark.*
5. I could see the rain in the distance real good. *I could see real good in the rain.*
6. It came more closer and more closer. *It came more closer & closer.*
7. Finally, I got soakingly wet. *Finally, I got soaky wet.*
8. The water rushed rapid down the street. *The water rushed rapidly down the street.*
9. I jumped really good over the running water. *I jumped real good over the running water.*
10. I rushed home quick to get dry. *I quickly rushed home to get dry.*

Modifier Practice (Sentence Combining)

Directions: Combine the following groups of sentences into one sentence (for each group). Try to reduce one sentence to an adjective or an adverb.

Example

0. I jumped over the water. My jump was quick. I dried myself. I was thorough.

0. I quickly jumped over the water and dried myself thoroughly.

1. I took off my clothes. They were wet. I dried myself. I was thorough.

2. I put on other jeans. They were dry. I put on another shirt. It was dry. The pants and shirt were warm.

3. I went to the front-room window. I hurried.

4. I watched the rain. The rain poured down. It was fierce.

5. The house across the street shook. It was an old house. The shaking was sudden.

6. The foundation was old. It was washing away. The rain was heavy. The rain was washing it away.

7. The corner of the house sank. It was the left front corner. The sinking was gradual.

8. The corner dipped. The dipping was toward the street. The dipping was low. Then it was lower.

9. The house was very old. The house moved toward the street. The street was full of rain.

10. The house floated to the river. It floated gently. It floated down the street.

Structure Words

The fourth large class of words in English is called *structure words* and includes four subclasses.

Determiners (also called *noun indicators*) determine that a noun will be the next word.

Conjunctions are words used to join other words and parts of sentences.

Prepositions link nouns to other words in phrases.

Auxiliaries (verb and modal) are sometimes classed as structure words. See pages 232 and 238 in the section on verbs for their use.

The spelling and even the meaning of nouns, verbs, adjectives, and adverbs has changed over the years. We add thousands of new nouns each year and drop hundreds more. Verbs take on new meanings as our culture changes. Structure words, in contrast, stay largely the same.

This class of words is called structure words because they give structure or organization to the language. The British writer Lewis Carroll made playful use of this feature when he wrote a nonsense poem called "Jabberwocky." The poem starts like this:

'Twas brillig and the slithy toves
    Did gyre and gimble in the wabe;
All mimsy were the borogroves,
    And the mome raths outgrabe.

It is absolute nonsense! Yet it seems to mean something because the structure words give it the organization of English. For example *the* tells the reader that a noun will follow. We know that *slithy toves* and *mome raths* are names for things. We know that *gyre* and *gimble* show some kind of action; they are verbs.

Structure words help to tell the difference between two actions.

 ## Examples

I threw the ball *to* him.

I threw the ball *at* him.

Structure words make meaning clear. Here are two newspaper headlines.

1. Hunter returns empty hands

2. Ship sails today

What does the first headline mean? Is there some person named Hunter? Does he or she return empty hands? Whose hands? Does the second headline mean a ship is sailing? Does it mean to ship or send sails for a sailing ship? Add structure words and the meaning becomes perfectly clear.

1. The hunter often returns with empty hands.

2. The ship sails today. (*Or* Ship the sails today.)

Determiners

Three kinds of words *determine* that a noun will follow: articles, certain adjectives, and some possessive pronouns. Articles can be the most confusing of the three.

Articles

Articles are sometimes classed as adjectives. There are only three: two *indefinite* (*a, an*) and one *definite* (*the*). The indefinite article *an* is an old form of the word *one*. It still carries much of the same meaning. The form *a* has the same meaning as *an*. The difference is that *an* is used before words starting with a vowel or a vowel sound, whereas *a* is used before the words starting with a consonant or a consonant sound. The definite article *the* is used to point out or refer to a specific person, place, or thing. It is usually pronounced "thee" before a vowel and "thuh" before a consonant. When someone says to you, "He is the bald-headed man," both you and the speaker know that a particular man is being referred to.

Using Articles

a, an, some, The

Use *a* or *an* before singular nouns that you can count (*count nouns*). (Remember, it means "one".)

a boy   an apple   a book   an egg

Do not use indefinite articles before nouns that you cannot count. Instead of articles, use the adjective (sometimes pronoun) *some*. There are many other words that you can use before count nouns (*few, many*), but *some* is very common.

some water   some sand   some grass

If the count noun is *plural,* then use *some* (or one of the other similar words) in front of the noun.

some boys   some apples   some books

See page 201 for more information on count and noncount nouns. Using the indefinite article can change the meaning of some nouns that are either count or noncount nouns. Noncount nouns usually do not require an article.

He has a paper. (He has one paper.)

He has paper. (He has a quantity of paper.)

The definite article *the* is used in many different ways, but generally *the* is used when the writer and the reader have a definite or specific person, place, or thing in mind.

The moon is bright tonight. (*Both reader and writer think about the same moon.*)

The man is running. (*a specific man*)

Some man is running. (*We do not know which man. It could be any man.*)

The is used when a noun is mentioned for the second time if it has been mentioned before.

I saw *a* tiger at the zoo. *The* tiger was swimming in *a* pond. *The* pond was large enough for three tigers.

Sometimes the use of a definite article can change the meaning of a noun. When it is used before a singular noun, it can make that noun refer to a whole general class.

> *The* human hand is a remarkable tool. (*refers to all human hands, or human hands as a class*)

> *The* horse has been replaced by *the* automobile. (*Horses in general have been replaced by automobiles in general.*)

When an abstract noun (*liberty, love, justice*) is used in the sense of "in general," no article is necessary.

> *Liberty* is desired by all men.

> I have *love* for my country.

> There is no *justice*.

Structure Word Practice (Articles)

Directions: Decide which of the blanks in the following paragraph needs an article. In some cases it may be correct either to put one in or to leave it out.

The man who makes his own ✓ brick wall or barbecue often finds it necessary to clean *the* cement or ✓ dirt from *the* wall that he has just built. *The* hydrochloric acid will do the job. It works by dissolving *a* thin layer of ✓ mortar or ✓ dirt. To use it, mix ✓ one part of *the* acid with ten parts of ✓ water in *a* glass container. Always add ✓ acid to *the* water. Adding ✓ water to *the* acid will cause it to boil. Always wear ✓ rubber gloves, and do not get any of *the* acid on *the* skin or ✓ clothes. It will make *the* hole in them. When finished, wash *some* bricks with *the* water.

Adjectives and Possessive Pronouns

Adjectives that pattern like these—*this, that, any, each, some, few*—may also be used as determiners, as may the numbers *one, two, three,* and so on. In addition, any of the possessive pronouns may be used as a determiner: *my, our, your, their, its* (no apostrophe), *his,* and *her.*

Structure Word Practice (Determiners)

Directions: Following the rules for using determiners, fill in the blanks in the following poem with articles, adjectives, or possessive pronouns. Remember, using a definite instead of an indefinite article may change the meaning. In some cases you may decide to use another word or no determiner.

The Monkey

One hungry monkey sat near *the* stream
With such *a* hunger it made him dream.
He dreamed of *some* food he would like to eat,
Of *some* apple, *some* peach, *some* bananas so sweet.
He had *few* apples, but not *any* peach.
Some fruit was growing out of *his* reach.
He took *her* stick, hung by *his* tail;
He used *one* stick as *his* whip or *his* flail
To knock *some* fruit right out of *their* tree.
So it fell with *that* most delightful sound,
Where he could reach it on *the* ground.

Conjunctions

The word *conjunction* comes from *conjoin,* which means "to join together"—and that is exactly what conjunctions do. They join together other elements of a sentence. There are two main classes of conjunctions: *coordinating* and *subordinating.*

Coordinating Conjunctions

Coordinating conjunctions are used to join equal parts of sentences, such as two nouns, two verbs, or two modifiers. They are also used to join larger elements, such as two phrases, two clauses, or two sentences. Five words are usually classed as coordinators, and each has a slightly different meaning.

1. *And* means "also," "in addition to," "with." It has the same meaning as the plus sign in arithmetic.

   Boys *and* girls go to school. (*joins two nouns*)

2. *But* means "on the contrary," "differently." It means that the two elements joined are somewhat different.

   Some children can run *but* cannot swim. (*joins two verbs showing a difference*)

3. *For* means "because of," "since." It shows that one element may be the cause of or reason for another.

The children will run, *for* they cannot swim. (*shows the reason they will run*)

They will stay home, *for* it is raining. (*shows why they are staying home*)

4. *Nor* means "and not." It has a negative force.

They will not swim, *nor* will they run. (*often patterns with* not)

5. *Or* means "one or the another." It offers a choice of two or more.

The children will be allowed to swim *or* run. (*They have a choice.*)

Coordinating conjunctions may, of course, join more than two elements.

boys *and* girls *and* adults (*three nouns*)

tall *and* fat *and* ugly (*three adjectives*)

swim *and* ride *and* run (*three verbs*)

It is possible to mix coordinating conjunctions:

tall *and* fat *but* beautiful

short *but* happy *and* cheerful

There is a subclass of coordinators called *correlatives,* or "paired conjunctions." There are four pairs:

1. Both/and

Both little boys *and* little girls can play.

2. Either/or

Either a boy *or* a girl can be the captain of the team.

3. Neither/nor

Neither boys *nor* girls can enter this house.

4. Not only/but also

Not only can she run *but also* she can swim.

Subordinating Conjunctions

Subordinating conjunctions are a much larger class of words. *To subordinate* means to make of less importance or lower rank. Subordinators are most often used to join sentences rather than to join just single words. When a subordinator is attached to a sentence, it makes that sentence incomplete.

More detailed information about their use is given on page 274. Here are some commonly used subordinators:

after	because	so that	whenever
although	if	unless	where
as	lest	until	whether
as if	since	when	while

Some adverbs (conjunctive adverbs) may also be used as coordinators. More will be said about them in the section on sentence structure.

Prepositions

Prepositions are used to join nouns or pronouns to some other word in a sentence. School children are sometimes taught that a preposition is "anything a rabbit can do to a hill." If you allow for burrows and tunnels, a rabbit can go

in
on
into
to
from
over
behind
by
across
under

a hill

These words are typical prepositions. Prepositions almost always pattern with an article and a noun to form a *prepositional phrase*.

Preposition	Article (*Determiner*)	Noun (*Object of Preposition*)
under	the	hill
over	the	rainbow
behind	a	tree

Prepositional phrases are used as modifiers. They can be used in the same way that a single-word adverb is used.

We climbed *over the wall*. (tells where *we climbed*)

She sleeps *in the afternoon.* (tells when *she sleeps*)

He reads *with difficulty.* (tells how *he reads*)

Prepositions can also be used as adjectives. They can describe a noun, telling about its contents or composition.

a box *of* apples (*contents of the box*)

a bolt *of* lightning (*composition of the bolt*)

a handful *of* flowers (*what the hand is full of*)

a flock *of* birds (*what the flock consists of*)

In either of these patterns it is possible to make your writing more descriptive by placing a modifier (or several) between the article and the noun. You may also use a conjunction to compound either the prepositions or the objects of the preposition:

over the *crumbling* wall

in the *early* afternoon

with *great* difficulty

a box of *old* and *rotten* apples

a handful of *beautiful* flowers

a flock of *singing* birds

across the hills and valleys

through the *stinking* mud and *dirty* water

above and beyond the call of duty

Here is a list of the most commonly used words that function as prepositions in English. There are, of course, many more.

about	at	down	off	toward
above	before	during	on	under
across	behind	for	onto	until
after	below	from	over	unto
against	beneath	in	round	up
along	beside	inside	since	upon
alongside	between	into	through	via
amid	beyond	like	throughout	with
among	by	near	till	within
around	despite	of	to	without

There are also a few combinations of words that are used as if they were one-word prepositions.

according to	because of	in view of
apart from	contrary to	on account of
ahead of	in front of	out of
back of	in place of	up to
(in back of)	in spite of	

A word that is usually used as a preposition may also be used as another class of word. When these words pattern with a verb, they are called *adverbial particles* or *verb particles* to distinguish them from their use as prepositions. When they are used with a verb, they change the meaning of the verb.

 ### Example

Catch as a verb means "to seize after a chase" or "to stop with the hands." *Catch up* means "to reach the same level or position."

These verb-particle combinations are especially common in informal English. There are hundreds; here is a partial list.

Two-Word Verb	*Meaning*
ask out	ask someone to go on a date
bring up	raise children; mention a topic
call in	ask to come to an official place
call off	cancel
call on	visit someone
check into	investigate
cheer up	make someone feel happier
clean up	make clean and neat; finish
do over	repeat, do again
drop off	leave someone (something) at a place
figure out	find an answer by reasoning
get along with	exist pleasantly with someone
get over	recover (from an illness)
give up	stop trying
hand in	submit an assignment
look after	take care of something or somebody
look into	investigate
pass away	die
pass out	distribute; lose consciousness

pick out	select
point out	indicate, call attention to
put off	delay, postpone
put up with	tolerate, get along with
run across	meet by chance, find
run into	meet by chance
run out (of)	finish the supply
show up	appear, come
show off	attract attention to oneself
shut off	stop a machine or light
take after	resemble, be like
take off	remove (clothing); leave
take over	take control or be in charge
tear down	destroy, demolish
think over	consider very carefully
throw up	regurgitate, vomit
try on	put on clothing to see if it fits
turn down	reject, refuse
turn in	hand in assignment; go to bed

It is possible to string together many prepositional phrases to make a longer descriptive sentence.

Example

In the late summer of that year, we lived *in a house in a village* that looked *across the river and the plain to the mountains.*

—Ernest Hemingway, *A Farewell to Arms*

Structure Word Practice (Coordinating Conjunctions)

Directions: In the blank spaces write the correct coordinating conjunction (*and, but, or, nor, for*).

The Young Chemist

A student had just started to study chemistry. He had learned a little *but* not very much. He liked the laboratory *and* studied hard, *but* he did not like the math *for* the lectures. All the time it was either study math *or* listen to lectures. It was not too bad, _but_ he would rather work in the lab. One day he got some bottles, flasks, _and_ test tubes, _and_ he was going to experiment. Another student watched him _and_ asked, "What are you doing?" "I am going to mix water with phosphate _or_ maybe acid, _and_ maybe this green stuff," he replied. His friend asked, "Do that _for_ what will you make?" The student said, "It will be a universal solvent." "What is a universal solvent?" asked the friend. "Well," answered the student, "it is a liquid that will dissolve everything." The friend thought _for_ a minute _and_ then asked, "_for_ what will you keep it in?"

Structure Word Practice (Prepositions and Adverbial Particles)

Directions: Write the correct preposition or adverbial particle in the blanks in the following story. If there is a phrase in parentheses, use one of the two-word verbs from the list on pages 256–257.

Smart Food

Nadya was having trouble _in_ college. She was going to (*stop trying*). Thinking _over_ her problems, she decided to ask the smartest man she knew what made him smart. The man, with the name _of_ Mr. Schultz, sold fish _in_ the market _of_ the corner. He said, "I can (*find an answer by reasoning*) your problem. You don't eat enough fish heads." Nadya did not (*investigate*) his statement but asked, "Will you sell me some _of_ them?" "Sure," said Schultz, "at a cost _of_ only fifty cents each." So Nadya ate one _of_ them on Monday, two _of_ them on Wednesday, and three _of_ them on Friday. She did not feel any smarter and was about to (*cancel*) the attempt.

"You need to eat more heads _than_ these fish," said Schultz. Nadya reached _in_ her purse, took money _out_ of it, and bought twenty fish heads. "That should last me _for_ next week," she thought. The next week she (*indicated*) to Schultz that he was selling fish heads _to_ her _for_ fifty cents each, but he sold the whole fish _to_ thirty cents. "See," he replied, "when you (*consider very carefully*) the matter, you are finally starting to get smart."

Some Words about Words

To study grammar, it is necessary to put words into classes. The various people who study grammar disagree about these classes. A single word, as you have seen, may be called an adjective, a determiner, a noun indicator, or an article. Happily, most people who study grammar and most teachers use the traditional terms, the *eight parts of speech*.

	Word Class	Definition	How Classified
1	Noun	a word that names a person, place, or thing	by the meaning
2	Pronoun	a word that takes the place of a noun	by the meaning
3	Verb	a word that shows action or state of being	by the meaning
4	Adverb	a word that tells how, when, or where about a verb, an adjective, or another adverb	by the meaning or function
5	Adjective	a word that modifies a noun or another adjective	by the meaning or function
6	Conjunction	a word that joins words, phrases, or clauses	by the function
7	Preposition	a word that shows the relationship of a noun to some other word in a sentence	by the function
8	Interjection	a word that shows strong emotion	by the meaning or intent

This system was developed many years ago and has some faults. Some words, such as *conjunctive adverbs,* seem to fit into more than one class. This book uses the four main classes; they are easier to understand and to learn.

One very important thing to learn about English grammar is that almost any word can be used as almost any part of speech. The part of speech a word is called can depend on its position in a sentence.

She is my *mother.* (*functions as a noun*)

You *mother* that boy too much. (*functions as a verb*)

Look at the *mother* hen. (*functions as an adjective*)

There are endings (suffixes) and beginnings (prefixes) that are used to shift a word from class to class while keeping the original idea of the word.

 ## Examples

Noun	Verb	Adverb	Adjective	Negative
love	to love	lovingly	lovelier	loveless
lover	loved	loverly	loveliest	unloved
loveliness			lovely	
loving	loving		loving	

It is possible to make over a dozen words from the one word *love*. One of the reasons that English has the largest vocabulary of any language is that words can regularly shift from class to class.

Shifting Words

You can increase your vocabulary by learning some of the prefixes and suffixes used to shift words from class to class. Verbs, nouns, adverbs, and adjectives can be formed by using such prefixes and suffixes.

In addition, there are several prefixes that make words negative.

im + potent (*strong*) = impotent (*not strong*)

in + advisable = inadvisable

un + clear = unclear

il + logical = illogical

ir + religious = irreligious

Unfortunately, there is no firm rule about which prefix goes with which word.

Verb Makers

Words can be turned into verbs by adding prefixes or suffixes (note the spelling changes):

be + calm = becalm

beauty + fy = beautify

scrutiny + ize = scrutinize

haste + en = hasten

Increase your vocabulary of verbs by remembering that *re-* means "to do something again."

re + cover = recover

re + gain = regain

re + do = redo

Noun Makers

Here are some ways to make nouns from other words.

1. The suffix *-er* or *-or* makes nouns from verbs.

   act + or = actor

   edit + or = editor

   do + er = doer

2. The suffix *-ness* added to some adjectives makes a noun (note the spelling changes).

   quiet + ness = quietness

   great + ness = greatness

   lazy + ness = laziness

3. The suffix *-ful* added to certain words makes a noun that indicates amount.

   cup + ful = cupful

   room + ful = roomful

   arm + ful = armful

4. The suffix *-ment* may change a verb to a noun.

   advance + ment = advancement

   employ + ment = employment

   enforce + ment = enforcement

5. The present participle of most verbs is regularly used as a noun.

   I *swim* every day. (*verb*)

   Swimming is great fun. (*noun*)

   He *is working* today. (*verb*)

   Working is a pleasure to some people. (*noun*)

Adverb Makers

The most common way to make adverbs is to add *-ly* to the adjective form (note the spelling changes).

quick + ly = quickly

common + ly = commonly

hasty + ly = hastily

Adjective Makers

Four suffixes are used to make adjectives:

1. Add *-able* (sometimes *-ible*) to a verb.

   drink + able = drinkable

   catch + able = catchable

   teach + able = teachable

2. To show quality, add *-ful* to a noun.

   pain + ful = painful

   doubt + ful = doubtful

   help + ful = helpful

3. Some nouns show quality by adding *-y.*

   wind + y = windy

   dirt + y = dirty

   sand + y = sandy

4. To show what something is made of, some nouns add *-en.*

   wood + en = wooden

   gold + en = golden

   silk + en = silken

Sometimes the suffix *-en* is not added.

wooden bowl *or* wood bowl

golden ring *or* gold ring

silken dress *or* silk dress

Vocabulary Practice (Class Shifting)

Directions: Using the words already written as a start, fill in the blanks with different forms of the words. Some words will not change to all classes.

(There is no verb *to logic* and no negative form for *swim,* for example, although we do use the compound *nonswimmer.*)

Example

Negative	Noun	Verb	Adjective	Adverb
unhappy	happiness	(to be happy)	happy	happily

	Negative	Noun	Verb	Adjective	Adverb
1.	inadvisable	*Advice*	*Advise*	*Advisable*	*Advisedly*
2.	_____	beauty	*Beautify*	*Beautiful*	*Beautifully*
3.	*Unimportant*	*Importance*	to import	*Important*	*Importantly*
4.	*Impower*	*Power*	*Power*	powerful	*Powerfully*
5.	_____	*Swimming*	*Swem*	*Swimming*	swimmingly
6.	*Careless*	*Carefulness*	*cared*	careful	*carefully*
7.	*Sleepless*	*sleep*	to sleep	*sleepless*	*sleeplessly*
8.	*Unfriendly*	friend	*befriend*	*Friendless*	*Friendly*
9.	illogic	*Logic*	_____	*logical*	*Illogically*
10.	*ilman*	man	*manned*	_____	*manly*
11.	*Hopeless*	*hoping*	to hope	*hopeful*	*hopefully*
12.	uncritical	*criticism*	*criticize*	critical	*critically*
13.	_____	*slowness*	*Slowly*	*slow*	slowly
14.	*dreamless*	*dream*	*dreamed*	dreamy	*dreamly*
15.	_____	*ugliness*	*uglify*	ugly	*uglily*

Vocabulary Practice (Meaning Changes)

Directions: Many words may be used as different parts of speech without the addition of a prefix or a suffix. Write sentences using the following five words as different parts of speech.

Example

1. I have a clever *dog.* (*noun*)
2. The policeman *dogged* my footsteps. (*verb*)
3. Soldiers wear *dog* tags. (*adjective*)

1. Use *well* as a noun, verb, adverb, adjective, and exclamation.
2. Use *mine* as a noun, verb, adjective, and pronoun.

3. Use *hand* as a noun, verb, and adjective.

4. Use *near* as a verb, adverb, adjective, and preposition.

5. Use *down* as a verb, adverb, adjective, and preposition.

You should have twenty sentences.

Section Two

The English Sentence

Section Two

Knowing the names and classes of words in English is useful only to help understand the sentence. To classify a word as a noun, a coordinating conjunction, or a past participle is of no value in helping you to communicate your ideas and emotions to another person. Communication is the purpose of language. Although it is possible to communicate a little by using single words, most speech and writing is done by using sentences.

Single Words	*Real Meaning* (in Sentence Form)
Help!	Will you help me?
Stop!	Stop doing what you are doing.
Who?	Who is that? Who did it?

Actually, a word by itself has no grammatical meaning. Although a dictionary might classify *mother* as a noun, it could be a verb, an adjective, or another part of speech. A word like *since* is used as a conjunction, a preposition, and an adverb. It is within sentences that words "have grammar."

Grammar of the Sentence

Grammar is the method by which speakers (and writers) of a language string words together to make meaning. Native speakers know the grammar of their own language by the time they are about three years old. What makes it hard to learn another language is that the sentence patterns are different. The words are placed in a different order to give meaning.

Examples

ENGLISH: I broke my pen.

SPANISH: Rompí mi pluma. (*I broke* [past tense, one word] *my pen.*)

GERMAN: Ich habe meinen Kuli kaput gemacht. (*I have my pen broken made.*)

JAPANESE: Wata-ku-shi-wa ma-nen-pit-su-wo ko-wa-shi ma-shi-ta. (*I pen broke.*)

(*Wa* indicates the subject of the sentence; *wo* indicates the object of the sentence; *ma-shi-ta* indicates past tense.)

Here is another sentence in standard English word order.

Someone studies Korean in school.

In Korean (using English letters) it looks like this:

Hakkyo so Hanguk mal ul kongbu hamnida. (*At school Korean studying someone does.*)

The syllables *so* and *ul* indicate the subject and the object. Korean uses a different alphabet, too.

Many languages do not have different forms for singular and plural. To continue with the example of Korean, the word *ch'aek* may mean "a book," "some books," "any books," or "the books," depending on the way it is used in a sentence. In addition, several languages have different forms for speaking to men, to women, to older people, and to younger people.

The grammar of the sentence is different in different languages. You are learning English grammar and sentence structure. The position of the word in a sentence tells whether the word is the subject, the verb, the object, or the complement. The position is important because English words can shift from class to class (see page 260 for examples). The main parts of the English sentence are the *subject,* the *predicate,* the *object,* and the *complement.*

Definition

A sentence may be defined in several ways. A large standard dictionary might define it as

a grammatical unit of a word or group of words that is separate from any other grammatical construction, usually consists of at least one subject with its predicate, and contains a finite verb or verb phrase; for example "The moon is yellow" and "People eat food" are sentences.

Some grammar books define a sentence as "a group of words expressing a complete thought." Others say, "A sentence is a group of words containing a subject and a verb." The following is a functional definition: "A sentence is a group of words requiring an action, an answer, or an agreement."

Action: Please shut the door.
             Meet me in the library at three o'clock.

Answer: How are you?
             What time did you arrive?

Agreement (or disagreement):
             She is a beautiful woman.
             Unemployment is at an all-time high.

To write good, mature English sentences, you need to know the names and functions of the four parts of the sentence and the ways in which they work together to make meaning. Your teacher will use these terms to talk to you about your writing and about how to improve it.

Basic Parts of the English Sentence:

1. Subject
2. Predicate
3. Object
4. Complement

These four parts in different combinations make *all* of the possible sentences in English.

The Subject

The *subject* of the sentence is a noun or noun substitute about which something is stated or asked by the verb. It tells whom or what the sentence is about and names the person or thing that performs the action of the sentence. It may be thought of as the *actor.*

 Examples

Ahmed goes to the store. (*proper noun as subject*)

Grass is green. (*common noun as subject*)

The ugly cat ran away again. (*noun* phrase *as subject*)

To escape was his wish. (*infinitive as subject*)

Running is his favorite sport. (*present participle as subject*) (*When a present participle is used as a noun, it is called a* gerund.)

Catching that cat is my goal. (*gerund phrase as subject*)

That he will run away again is probably true. (*noun clause as subject*)

He is a bad cat. (*pronoun as subject*)

Note

More about phrases and clauses later on page 272.

The Predicate

The predicate of a sentence is the part that tells what is said about the subject. It describes the action or the state of being of the subject. It tells what the person or thing (the subject) does. It *always* contains a verb and may have some auxiliaries or modifiers. Just the main verb and its auxiliaries are called a *simple predicate*. If complements and modifiers are included, the predicate is called a *complete predicate*.

Examples

The stars *shine*. (*simple verb as predicate*)

The stars *are shining brightly*. (*auxiliary and participle with modifier as a complete predicate*)

Everyone *had gone* home. (*auxiliary and verb as simple predicate*)

The Object

The *object* of a sentence is a noun or a noun substitute that tells *what* or *who* is affected by a transitive verb. (See page 210 for verbs.) When the verb is an active transitive verb, the object is called a *direct* object.

Examples

Carlos watched the *stars*. (*noun as direct object; tells* what *he watched*)

He watched *them* carefully. (*pronoun as direct object*)

He saw *that they were disappearing*. (*noun clause as direct object*)

The other kind of object is called an *indirect* object. It states *to whom, for whom, to what*, or *for what* something is done.

Examples

Carlos told *Hamid* the story. (*Noun as indirect object:* The story was told *to* Hamid.)

Hamid handed *him* the telescope. (*Pronoun as indirect object:* The telescope was handed *to* him.)

I asked them to give *me* the telescope. (*Pronoun as indirect object.*)

If you have difficulty with indirect objects, you can rewrite the sentence and use a prepositional phrase such as *to* _____ or *for* _____ .

The prepositional phrase (see page 254) means exactly the same but uses more words.

 Examples

Carlos told the story *to Hamid.*

Hamid handed a telescope *to him.*

I asked them to give the telescope *to me.*

The Complement

The *complement* is the part of a sentence used to complete the sense of the verb. Some grammars classify objects (direct and indirect) as complements, but objects are important enough to deserve a special class by themselves. There are two kinds of complements: the *subject* complement and the *object* complement. Complements are either nouns or adjectives.

Subject Complements

Subject complements are used after linking (intransitive) verbs. (See page 211.) When nouns are used as subject complements, they always refer to the *subject* of the sentence. They mean the same thing as the subject; they rename the subject.

 Examples

Carlos is a *student.* (*noun as complement*)

He is a *star watcher.* (*noun as complement*)

When adjectives are used as subject complements, they describe the subject of the sentence.

Examples

The sky became *dark*. (*adjective as complement describing the subject* the dark sky)

The stars are *important* to Carlos. (*adjective* important *describing the subject* stars)

Object Complements

The *object complement* comes directly after the direct object of the sentence and is used to modify the direct object. It is used after such verbs as *name, elect, consider, make,* and *paint.*

Examples

Hamid considers Carlos *intelligent*. (*adjective as complement*)

Carlos painted the telescope *purple*. (*adjective as complement*)

The students considered Nguyen a *leader*. (*noun as complement*)

They elected him *secretary*. (*noun as complement*)

Note

Object complements pattern as if the words *to be* were included in the sentence.

Hamid considered Carlos (*to be*) intelligent.

The students elected him (*to be*) secretary.

Sentence Practice (Subjects and Predicates)

Directions: In the following sentences, find the subject and write the letter *S* above it. Then find the predicate and write the letter *V* (for *verb*) over it. Then make a slash (/) between the complete subject and the complete predicate. The subject always names the person, place, or thing the sentence is about. The predicate always contains the verb. Remember, the verb is the word that can change to show past, present, or future.

Example

           S   V

0. The small child/ran down the street.

1. The alphabet/is one of the great human inventions.

2. It was developed over thousands of years.
3. The English alphabet has twenty-six letters.
4. Other alphabets have either more or fewer letters.
5. The Hawaiian language uses only twelve letters.
6. The Armenian language has thirty-eight letters.
7. Alphabets, of course, let people write.
8. They can write about what happened in the past.
9. Before the invention of the alphabet, all history was oral.
10. People sang songs about the past.
11. Now we can write about history.
12. Writing helps us to remember.
13. Most languages have a written form.
14. Not all languages have writing, though.
15. Many primitive people still sing about their past.

Phrases and Clauses

There are two more parts of sentences you will need to know about to make your writing more effective—*phrases* and *clauses*. Learning about them will enable you to avoid errors in sentence structure and will also help you to punctuate correctly.

Phrases

A phrase is a group of words that does not contain *both* a subject and a predicate. A phrase is used in the same way that a single word is used. It may be a subject, an object, or a complement. It may be used to modify another part of the sentence or even to modify the whole sentence. There are several kinds of phrases. *Prepositional phrases,* described on page 254, are usually used to modify other words in the sentence.

Noun phrases are made of a noun and all of the words used to modify it. They usually function as subjects, objects, or complements.

 ## Examples

an ugly cat	the old, worn-out automobile
my older sister	some interesting books
my new camera	the youngest student

Gerund phrases use the present participle or the *-ing* form of the verb. When this form of the verb is used as a noun, it is called a *gerund.* Gerunds are used as nouns in sentences.

 ## Examples

Eating too much chocolate is not healthy.

Many people enjoy *eating sweets and candy.*

Building a house can be expensive.

Verb phrases are groups of words that include a verb and its auxiliaries but no subject.

 ## Examples

All night long *they had been sleeping.*

We *would have gone,* but we *did not have* any money.

He *did not worry* about it.

Infinitive phrases are groups of words beginning with the *to* _____ form of the verb. They may be used as nouns, adjectives, or adverbs in sentences.

 ## Examples

To look at the stars is my hobby. (*noun*)

Hoang stopped studying *to eat his lunch.* (*adverb*)

Today is the day *to take a rest.* (*adjective*)

Participial phrases are similar in form to gerund phrases but are used as adjectives rather than nouns. They consist of the *-ing* or the *-ed* form of the verb.

 ## Examples

My friends *travelling across the country* are very happy.

Smiling cheerfully, Miss Tsai took the paper.

He bought a hat *called a cowboy hat.*

 ## Note

Some grammar books call infinitive, participial, gerund, and verb phrases just *verbal* phrases.

Sentence Practice (Phrases)

Directions: In the following group of sentences, underline only the prepositional phrases. There may be more than one in each sentence.

1. In the morning I will ride to Chicago on my motorcycle.
2. I always travel about the country in the summer.
3. On the road I sometimes get rain on my face and in my hair.
4. Traveling around the country with my friends on motorcycles is fun.
5. We ride singing in the rain across hills and up mountains.

In the next group, underline only the noun phrases.

6. A well-built motorcycle is necessary.
7. A strong helmet and comfortable clothing are necessary, too.
8. Every motorcycle rider needs a comfortable seat.
9. After all, people on motorcycles sit down all of the time.
10. A comfortable seat, easy-to-reach handlebars, and handy footrests make riding easier for anybody on a motorcycle.

In the next group, underline the gerund, participial, and infinitive phrases.

11. Riding a motorcycle can be a great deal of fun.
12. It is enjoyable to be speeding down the road.
13. However, to ride a motorcycle is to take a risk.
14. I might have been worried, but I know how to ride safely.
15. A good way to learn how to ride safely would be to practice every day.

Clauses

The last of the sentence parts you will need to know is the *clause*. A clause is a group of words containing both a subject and a predicate. There are two kinds of clauses: *independent* and *dependent*.

Independent Clauses: An *independent* clause can be used independently as a sentence. *Independent clause* is simply another term for a complete sentence.

Dependent Clauses: A *dependent* (sometimes called *subordinate*) clause has both a subject and a predicate but can *never* be used as a complete sentence. It is different from an independent clause in that it starts with a word that makes it *depend* on the rest of the sentence for its meaning.

Dependent clauses are used in almost exactly the same way that phrases are used. That is, they function as *nouns, adjectives,* or *adverbs.*

Noun clauses are started or introduced by question words (relative pronouns) like these:

that	whoever
what	whom
who	whomever
which	whose
why	how
when	where
whether	if

 ## Examples

SIMPLE SENTENCE: I believe many things.

NOUN CLAUSE: I believe *that tigers are dangerous animals.*

The noun clause "that tigers are dangerous animals" is used as a noun, the object of the sentence.

SIMPLE SENTENCE: He is either brave or foolish.

NOUN CLAUSE: *Whoever doubts my belief* is either brave or foolish.

The noun clause "whoever doubts my belief" is used as a noun, the subject of the sentence.

SIMPLE SENTENCE: I do not know anything.

NOUN CLAUSE: I do not know *where tigers live.*

The noun clause "where tigers live" is used as the direct object of the sentence.

SIMPLE SENTENCE: Send the tiger cubs to the zoo.

NOUN CLAUSE: Send the tiger cubs to *whoever can feed them best.*

The noun clause "whoever can feed them best" is used as the object of the preposition *to.*

The noun clauses cannot be used as complete sentences. Even though they have both subjects and predicates, the introductory word makes the *meaning* incomplete.

That tigers are dangerous (*incomplete sentence*)

Whoever doubts my belief (*incomplete sentence*)

Where tigers live (*incomplete sentence*)

Whoever can feed them (*incomplete sentence*)

Adjective clauses are started or introduced by relative pronouns and a few question words.

who	whose	whom	which
that	where	when	some of
many of	each of	one of	none of

Adjective clauses nearly always follow the words they modify. They may be just added to a sentence.

 ### Examples

SIMPLE SENTENCE: Mario has never watched a tiger eat.

ADJECTIVE CLAUSE ADDED: Mario, *who doubts that tigers are dangerous,* has never watched one eat.

The adjective clause "who doubts that tigers are dangerous" follows and modifies the proper noun *Mario.*

SIMPLE SENTENCE: I once met a man.

ADJECTIVE CLAUSE ADDED: I once met a man *whose cow had been eaten by a tiger.*

The adjective clause modifies *cow.*

SIMPLE SENTENCE: I heard the story.

ADJECTIVE CLAUSE ADDED: I heard the story, *which made me nervous.*

The adjective clause modifies *story.*

Adverb clauses may be used to modify a verb, an adjective, an adverb, a gerund, a participle, or the entire sentence in which it is used. Adverb clauses are usually introduced by subordinating conjunctions and can be placed at different positions in the sentence. Here are some of the many words that introduce adverb clauses.

Showing Time	*Showing Condition*	*Showing Cause and Effect*	*Showing Opposition*
after	because	if	even though
before	since	unless	whereas
when	now that	only if	although
while	as	even if	though
since	as long as	whether	while

Examples

SIMPLE SENTENCE: There I saw a white tiger.

ADVERB CLAUSE ADDED: *When we were in San Diego,* I saw a white tiger.

I saw a white tiger *when we were in San Diego.*

The adverb clause modifies the verb. If the adverb clause is placed at the beginning of the sentence, you will need a comma. If it is placed at the end of the sentence, you will not need a comma.

SIMPLE SENTENCE: He acted like a big kitten.

ADVERB CLAUSE ADDED: *Because he was playful,* he acted like a big kitten.

He acted like a big kitten *because he was playful.*

The adverb clause "because he was playful" modifies the whole sentence.

SIMPLE SENTENCE: I went away later.

ADVERB CLAUSE ADDED: *Before he became angry,* I went away.

I went away *before he became angry.*

The adverb clause modifies the verb, telling when.

✓ **Check:** Avoid writing and punctuating clauses as complete sentences! It is a very common mistake and is called an *inc* (for "incomplete sentence") or a *frag* (for "sentence fragment"). There is a simple way to check for incomplete or fragmentary sentences. *Without removing any words, change it to a yes or no sentence.* If it is a complete sentence, it will make sense. If it is an incomplete sentence, it will not.

 ## Examples

Incomplete sentences

1. Because we ran away.
2. Since it was a long way from home.
3. Although it was raining and snowing.

Changed to yes or no questions:

1. Did because we ran away?
2. Was since it a long way from home?   — NONSENSE
3. Was although it raining and snowing?

Complete sentences

1. We ran away.

2. It was a long way from home.

3. It was raining and snowing.

Changed to yes or no questions:

1. Did we run away?

2. Was it a long way from home?   ⎤

3. Was it raining and snowing?   ⎦   GOOD SENSE

It is always a good idea to check to see if your sentences are complete (independent or main clauses) or incomplete (dependent or subordinate clauses).

Sentence Practice (Clauses)

Directions: Read the following sentences carefully. If the sentence contains a dependent clause, underline that clause.

Adj 1. Dr. Hubris was a young doctor who had just opened his office.

N 2. That he was just starting was clear.

N 3. Whenever a doctor starts, it takes time to get patients.

Adj 4. It was a fact that he had no patients the first few days.

N 5. When Friday came, someone knocked on his door.

N 6. What he thought was "At last I have a patient."

Adv 7. Every doctor needs patients who come for help.

_____ 8. Sometimes the patients have to sit in the waiting room.

Adj 9. A doctor sees first whoever comes in first.

Adv 10. Dr. Hubris did not want his first patient to know that he had no other patients.

_____ 11. He picked up the telephone and spoke so that he could be clearly heard.

Adj 12. He pretended that he was talking to another patient.

N 13. When the man came in, the doctor looked up from the phone.

_____ 14. He asked the man if there was anything wrong.

_____ 15. The man smiled and answered that he had just come to connect the telephone.

Sentence Practice (Clauses)

Directions: If the clause that you have underlined is a *noun* clause, write *N* in the space in front of the sentence. If it is an *adjective* clause write *ADJ.* If it is an *adverb* clause, write *ADV.* If there is no dependent clause, leave the space blank.

Sentence Patterns

How do you make an English sentence? You take the parts and arrange them according to the rules of English grammar.

Sentence Parts:

1. Subject (a noun or noun substitute)
2. Predicate (always has a verb)
3. Object (direct and indirect; nouns, adjectives)
4. Complement (follow linking verbs, nouns, adjectives)

Larger Elements:

1. Phrases (groups of words; act like single words)
2. Clauses (independent, dependent)

The position of a word in an English sentence pattern makes it function as a noun or as an adjective, as the subject or as the object. This way of working makes it difficult to translate word for word from one language to another.

Example

Yo me pongo mi sombrero blanco. (*Spanish*)

I on me I put my hat white. (*word-for-word translation into English*)

The translation is *not* an acceptable English sentence.

Example

The birds eat the worms. (birds *the subject*)

The worms eat the birds. (birds *the object*)

Changing the position of *birds* from first to last changes the meaning completely (and suggests that the birds must be dead).

Example

The eat birds the worms.

Birds worms eat.

These patterns make no sense in English, although in Polynesian either might be clearly understood.

The following are the five basic sentence patterns found in English:

1. Subject + predicate
2. Subject + predicate + direct object
3. Subject + predicate + indirect object + direct object
4. Subject + predicate + subject complement
5. Subject + predicate + direct object + object complement

Subject + Predicate

Pattern 1 is a subject plus a predicate that contains an intransitive verb.

 Examples

Plants grow. (*intransitive verb needing no object*)

Plants and animals grow. (*same pattern, compound subject*)

Plants grow and thrive. (*same pattern, compound predicate*)

Plants and animals grow and thrive. (*same pattern, both subject and predicate compound*)

This basic sentence pattern does not have to be childish. By adding a few modifying phrases, it can become mature and informative.

The beautiful green plants and the lively animals that feed upon them grow and thrive in wilderness areas and forests.

Subject + Predicate + Direct Object

Pattern 2 has a subject, a predicate with a transitive verb (needing an object), and an object. As in the first pattern, any of the parts may be compound.

 Examples

Alexander wears shoes. (*transitive verb needing a direct object* to complete the meaning)

The dog bites the mailman.

Children throw rocks.

Any pattern 2 sentence can be expanded by the use of modifying words, phrases, or clauses.

Alexander, who lives in the mountains, wears heavy shoes with knobs on them to climb around on the rocks.

Subject + Predicate + Indirect Object + Direct Object

Pattern 3 has a subject, a predicate with a transitive verb, an indirect object, and a direct object. Remember that the *indirect object* tells *to* or *for whom* or *what* the action of the verb is intended.

 ### Examples

Alexander threw me the ball. (He threw it *to* me.)

Mother baked Carlos a pie. (She baked it *for* Carlos.)

We gave the baby his dinner. (We gave it *to* the baby.)

This last sentence can be expanded into a sentence like the following:

Because it was late, we quickly gave the baby his dinner to make him stop crying.

Subject + Predicate (Linking Verb) + Subject Complement

Pattern 4 uses a different kind of verb, a linking verb (see page 211). There is a subject, a linking verb, and a *subject complement*. The subject complement patterns in the same place as an object but may be an adjective as well as a noun. The subject complement either describes or renames the subject.

 ### Examples

Alexander is happy. (Happy, *an adjective, describes the subject,* Alexander.)

Nedjat looks sorrowful. (Sorrowful, *an adjective, describes Nedjat.*)

Compare:

Nedjat looks *sorrowfully* at me. (*This sentence uses the adverb form to describe the action of the verb, the way Nedjat looks.*)

Either an adjective or an adverb may be used after such verbs as *look, feel, smell, taste,* or *sound.* Use an adverb to refer to the action of the verb and an adjective (called a subject complement or *predicate adjective*) to modify the subject.

 Examples

Adjectives	*Adverbs*
She felt happy.	She happily felt the wind on her cheeks.
Sam looked angry.	Sam looked angrily at the robber.

 Example

Alexander was a leader. (*The noun* leader *is used to identify the subject,* Alexander. *It renames the subject.*)

Maria is my aunt. (Aunt *identifies and renames* Maria.)

The first sentence may be expanded in the following way:

Alexander the Great, who lived in ancient Greece, was a leader of men and a conqueror of the known world.

Subject + Predicate + Direct Object + Object Complement

Pattern 5 is not as common as the other four. It uses a subject, a predicate containing a transitive verb, a direct object, *and* a complement that modifies the direct object.

 Examples

Alexander considered his mother happy. (Happy *modifies* mother.)

I believe myself lucky.

We elected Habib chairman. (*The noun* chairman *is used to modify or rename the direct object* Habib.)

Fred named his uncle president of the company.

These are the basic patterns of sentences in English. The position of the words tells your reader exactly what you mean. As shown in the preceding examples, you will probably use adverbs and adjectives (either words, phrases, or clauses) to make your sentences more mature, informative, and interesting.

Sentence Pattern Variations

The basic patterns have shown the kinds of sentences that make statements or assertions. They *declare* something and are called *declarative* sentences. (*classification by meaning*) Three other kinds of sentences classified by meaning are variations on the *basic* patterns.

Interrogative Sentences

Interrogative sentences ask a question. These sentences pattern with auxiliaries to make yes or no questions.

 ### Examples

Tarzan was raised in the jungle. (*declarative*)

Was Tarzan raised in the jungle? (*interrogative*)

He lived with a tribe of apes. (*declarative*)

Did he live with a tribe of apes? (*interrogative*)

Interrogative sentences also pattern with the interrogative pronouns.

 ### Examples

Who was the man who lived with the apes?

Which tribe took care of him?

What did he eat?

Interrogative sentences also pattern with certain adverbs.

 ### Examples

How was he able to live?

Where did he live?

When did he leave the jungle?

Imperative Sentences

Imperative sentences give a command or make a request. If the subject is clear to both the writer and the reader, it is often not written.

Examples

Jorge, come here!

Please open your books to page 251. (*You* open your books.)

Give me some more food! (*You* give it to me.)

Exclamatory Sentences

Exclamatory sentences show strong emotion. They are formed by putting the object before the verb and usually start with an adverb.

Examples

How ugly that is!

What a mess he made in the kitchen!

How happy I have become!

The other two variations are not classified by meaning but by form. One is called the *passive sentence* (or *passive voice,* to distinguish it from the form of the declarative sentence called *active voice*); the other is called the *expletive.*

Passive Sentences

The usual *subject* + *predicate* + *object* order can be changed with no change in the meaning of the sentence.

Example

Active voice: The dog chased the ball.

Passive voice: The ball was chased by the dog.

Active voice: The barbarians conquered Rome.

Passive voice: Rome was conquered by the barbarians.

Subject + *predicate* + *object* is changed to *object* + (*form of the verb* to be) + *predicate* (*past participle*) + (by) *subject.* When this change is made, the object becomes more important to the meaning of the sentence than the subject. The following are examples of the basic passive sentence patterns:

1. Marie is helped by Jacques.
2. Marie was helped by Jacques.
3. Marie was being helped by Jacques.
4. Marie had been helped by Jacques.

5. Marie will be helped by Jacques.

6. Marie is going to be helped by Jacques.

7. Marie will have been helped by Jacques.

Another pattern leaves out the "*by* + subject" phrase.

 ### Example

The building was built in 1457.

The money was stolen.

The glass was broken.

This pattern is used when it is not important or not known who did the building. It is also used when the writer does not want to tell who said the senator was dishonest or who broke the glass.

Effective writers use the passive pattern only when they want to make the object seem more important than the subject, when it is not important who performed the action, or when they wish to keep the identity of the subject hidden. It should be used sparingly.

The Expletive

The *expletive* with a delayed subject is commonly used in English. The two words most often used as expletives are *it* and *there*. When you begin a sentence with *it* or *there,* you place the subject later in the sentence.

 ### Examples

It is time to go.

It is still early.

There is still time to get dressed.

There are flowers in the garden.

The expletive *it* is commonly used in sentences about time, weather, and distances.

 ### Examples (Time)

It is Thursday.

It is very early.

It is noon.

Examples (Weather)

It is raining.

It is sunny.

It is snowing in the mountains.

 ## Examples (Distances)

It is fifty miles to New York.

It is three blocks from my house to school.

It is a long way to China.

The expletive *there* is commonly used with phrases telling about place or time.

 ## Examples (Place)

There are two fish on my plate.

There is no water in my glass.

There will be singing and dancing at the party.

 ## Examples (Time)

There will be a party tomorrow.

There is a bus leaving at noon.

There was a snowstorm last week.

 ## Remember

It is useful to classify English sentences by meaning—

1. Declarative (declares something, makes a statement)
2. Interrogative (asks a question)
3. Imperative (makes a command or a request)
4. Exclamatory (shows strong emotion)

   —and by special form.

5. Passive
6. Expletive with subject delayed

Combining Sentences

The five basic sentence patterns and the six variations give you the ability to tell many kinds of ideas to your reader. When used with modifiers, these patterns can express mature, interesting thoughts. However, as you read, you will notice that there are more complicated patterns. The way writers make their ideas clearer and their sentences more effective is to combine the basic sentence patterns in three ways. In addition to classifying sentences by *meaning,* we also classify them by *form,* into *simple, compound,* and *complex* sentences.

Simple Sentences

The simple sentence is a sentence that has only one subject and one predicate (although either or both may be compound). Any of the five basic patterns can be written as a simple sentence. You can always check to see if you have written a complete sentence by using the yes or no question method (see page 277).

 Examples

In the United States, baseball is popular.

In Argentina, soccer is the favorite sport.

Compound Sentences

If two or more simple sentences refer to a similar topic or idea, you can *compound* them into one sentence. They are made compound in much the same way as subjects or predicates are made compound.

 Examples

In the United States, baseball is popular , **but** in Argentina soccer is the favorite sport.

Or:

In Argentina, soccer is the favorite sport , **but** in the United States, baseball is popular.

Two simple sentences may be joined by using a comma and a coordinating conjunction (see page 252). *Always* use a comma when you join two or more simple sentences with a coordinating conjunction.

Examples

I am taking English , **and** I will study hard.

I am taking English , **but** I do not need to study.

I am studying English , **for** I do not speak it well.

I will not go to class today , **nor** will I go tomorrow.

Today I might go to class , **or** I might go to a movie.

I am studying English , **and** I will study very hard , **for** I do not know the language very well. (*three simple sentences compounded*)

1. The sentences to be joined must be complete sentences.
2. They must be similar in meaning.

To join sentences that are not similar in meaning would be silly.

 ## Silly Example

Baseball is popular in America , **and** I painted my house green.

The other method of combining two or more simple sentences into a compound sentence is to use a semicolon. The semicolon is used in place of the comma and the coordinating conjunction, but it has no meaning as the conjunctions do. It simply links the two ideas.

 ## Examples

Chess is a hard game ; checkers is an easy one.

I play chess ; my brother plays checkers ; my little sister plays with dolls.

Complex Sentences

The complex sentence is a complete sentence (independent clause) joined to a dependent clause. A dependent clause has both a subject and a predicate but starts with a *subordinating conjunction*. (See the section on clauses, page 274.) When a clause starts with a subordinating conjunction, it becomes *dependent* and cannot be used as a sentence alone. The *subordinator* makes the clause dependent on the rest of the sentence for meaning.

 ## Examples

We left Shanghai. (*independent clause, complete sentence*)

Since we left Shanghai (*dependent clause,* frag)

Although we left Shanghai (*dependent clause,* frag)

When we left Shanghai (*dependent clause,* frag)

To make these dependent clauses into complete sentences, you will need to join them to independent clauses. A dependent clause joined to an independent clause is called a *complex sentence.*

 ### Examples

Since we left Shanghai, we have traveled much. (*complex sentence*)

Although we left Shanghai, we plan to return. (*complex sentence*)

When we left Shanghai, we went to Brazil. (*complex sentence*)

When the dependent clause is placed at the beginning of a complex sentence, it needs a comma to separate it from the independent clause. If the dependent clause is placed after the independent clause, it does not need a comma.

 ### Examples

We have traveled much *since* we left Shanghai.

We plan to return *although* we left Shanghai.

We went to Brazil *when* we left Shanghai.

Here are some of the more common subordinating conjunctions with examples of what they mean and how they are used.

TO SHOW PLACE: *where, wherever*

> *Wherever* I go, my little sister follows me.

TO SHOW TIME: *after, as, before, while, when, whenever, until*

> I will be finished *before* you arrive.

TO SHOW REASON OR CAUSE: *as, because, since*

> Abdul is fat *because* he eats too much falafel.

TO SHOW A CONDITION: *if, provided that, unless*

> *Unless* he stops eating so much, he will need bigger clothes.

TO SHOW SIMILARITY OR MANNER: *as, as if, though*

> Leah walks *as if* she had a broken foot.

TO SHOW PURPOSE: *in order that, so that, as though*

> *So that* he may walk better, I will lend him my cane.

TO SHOW EXCEPTION: *although, even if, except for, in spite of, though*

> Kamilla is hungry, *although* she had a big breakfast.

Compound-Complex Sentences

The compound-complex sentence uses one or more compound sentences joined with one or more subordinate clauses.

 ### Examples

Someday we may land on the planet Mars , **and** we must be very careful (*compound sentence*), *since* we do not know what we may find there (*subordinate clause*).

Until I become rich, I will work hard; I will save my money, **and** I will put it in the bank.

By compounding the 5 basic patterns, it is possible to make 120 different combinations. By using the methods to make compound-complex sentences, you can write 360 different sentence patterns.

Section Three

Guide to Punctuation

Section Three

Why do you need to punctuate? The only reason is to make your writing clear to the reader. In English there are twelve punctuation marks; their use has become standardized.

When we speak, we can raise or lower our voices; we can shout or whisper; we can speak slowly or swiftly. When we write, we have to use punctuation to help make our meaning clear. So we use the standard punctuation marks. These marks can roughly be classed as *sentence enders, interrupters, joiners,* and *special marks.*

Sentence Enders

1. Period (.)
2. Question mark (?)
3. Exclamation point (!)

Joiners

4. Comma (,)
5. Colon (:)
6. Semicolon (;)
7. Apostrophe (')

Interrupters

8. Parentheses (such as these)
9. Dash (—)
10. Brackets [like square parentheses]

Special Marks:

11. Slash (/)—used to show either/or options

12. Quotation marks, single (') and double (")—used to show who is speaking

Other Common Marks (not properly called punctuation)

13. Asterisk (*)

14. Section mark (§)

15. Paragraph symbol (¶)

Sentence Enders

The Period [.]

The period has three main uses.

1. Use a period to end any declarative sentence, indirect question, or unemphatic request.
   a. Ngao takes the bus to school.
   b. He asked how long it took.
   c. Please lift your left foot.

2. The period is used with most abbreviations.
   a. Mr. Mrs. Ms. Dr.
   b. B.A. M.A. Ph.D.
   c. U.S.A. M.I.T. m.p.g. (miles per gallon)

Today many abbreviations do not use the period for names of organizations and for names of things that make up a pronounceable word.

   d. radar ASCAP IRS USAF USSR

When in doubt, look it up in your dictionary.

3. The period is used in a series of three, called an *ellipsis,* to show that some words have been left out of a quotation or to show a deliberate pause.
   a. ORIGINAL: This movie, with its original screenplay and superb acting, is one of the best of the year.
   WITH ELLIPSIS: This movie . . . is one of the best of the year.
   b. When the tiger opened its jaws . . .

Punctuation Practice (The Period)

Directions: Some of the periods in the following paragraph are misplaced, and some are left out. Rewrite the paragraph, putting the periods in their correct places.

The three motion pictures. Called the "Star Wars", movies have been the most successful of the last ten years. Part of their success. In earning millions of dollars, has been due to the interesting characters.there are normal human beings like Luke Skywalker, the Princess, and Han Solo. There are people who have strange powers, Like Obi Wan Kenobi, Darth Vader, and the Emperor. There are robots and androids, Like C3PO and R2D2. But most interesting are the creatures from other worlds, like Chewbacca, Jabba the Hutt, the Ewoks, and a dozen others.the last one, Of the series called "The Return of the Jedi.", Brings the story to a conclusion. That satisfies most people.

The Question Mark [?]

The question mark has only one function. It shows the end of a direct question.

How are you today?

What time is it?

Why did you decide to go to college?

In addition to being used as an independent sentence, a direct question may be used in several other ways: A question may be included

1. in a declarative statement.
    a. "How are you today?" he asked. (*no comma after the question mark*)
    b. He asked, "How are you today?" (*no period after the question mark*)
2. A declarative sentence may be used as a question by adding the question mark instead of the period.
    a. Pietro is going back to school?
    b. He earned a thousand dollars last year?

Punctuation Practice (The Question Mark)

Directions: In the following paragraph some question marks are used incorrectly, and others are left out. Add them where they are necessary, and remove them if they do not belong.

I wonder why people like science fiction? Do you ever wonder about it.? Movies like "Star Wars" and the rest are popular. My friend Pietro asked me if

I liked it? He said, "Why do you go see such silly things?" I questioned him about why he did not? He answered, "I like reality. Isn't that stuff all make-believe?" I agreed, but told him that it was just for entertainment and fun. "That's fun?" he said? "Does anybody really believe in strange creatures like robots and androids and fuzzy little men."? "Isn't it exciting to pretend to fly around the stars?" I wanted to know? He did not agree.

The Exclamation Point [!]

The exclamation point is used to show emotion on the part of the writer. You should use it if the statement, if said aloud, would be shouted. Use it to show great surprise or disbelief.

 ### Examples

Help! I am stuck under the car and can't get out!

Vote! Everybody's vote is important!

Wow! That was a hard exam!

What? Everybody failed it!

Be careful not to overuse the exclamation point. It is never a substitute for using the exact word. Also, do not use more than one. "Help!!!" is no more emphatic than "Help!" It is also incorrect.

 ### Punctuation Practice (Sentence Enders)

Directions: Write an original sentence showing how punctuation marks are used at the end of each of the following kinds of sentences.

1. A simple statement
2. A direct quotation
3. An exclamation
4. A declarative sentence containing a direct quotation
5. A statement that uses the ellipsis mark
6. A mildly imperative sentence
7. A quoted direct question
8. A declarative sentence
9. A strong two-sentence exclamation that has two exclamation points (not together)
10. A direct quotation that shows strong emotion

Sentence Joiners

The Comma [,]

The comma is the cause of more problems for writers than all of the other punctuation marks combined. Commas have eight separate uses in English.

1. Commas always go between *main clauses*—in front of the coordinating conjunctions *and, but, or, for,* and *nor* and before the two words *so* and *yet* when they are used as connectives.
    a. Sam Lee is young, and he is healthy.
    b. Sam Lee is young, but he is tired.
    c. Paula is coming, or she is going.
    d. Paula is late, for she missed her ride.
    e. Rahmin is not coming, nor does he want to.
    f. He is running, so he will be here on time.
    g. I arrived on time, yet everyone else was late.

2. Commas are used to separate a list of items in a series. They separate single words, phrases, or clauses.
    a. All we had to eat was beans, bread, bananas, and beef.
    b. The coyote is an animal with keen eyes, strong legs, and a curious mind.
    c. Nadya got up early, washed her car, cleaned the house, and got to school on time.

3. Commas are used to set off a word, phrase, or clause that introduces the main idea of a sentence (introductory elements).
    a. Yes, English punctuation is confusing.
    b. Waiting for his monthly check, Jose checked the mail daily.
    c. Obviously, he has no money until it comes.

4. Commas are used to set off sentence elements that interrupt the main idea of the sentence without adding necessary information.
    a. Will you, Demetrios, bring me another cola?
    b. Alexander Hamilton, who was born in the West Indies, became the first Secretary of the Treasury.
    c. He was an American citizen, naturally.

5. Commas are used to separate a quotation from the rest of the sentence when the quotation is part of that sentence. Commas go outside opening quotation marks and inside closing quotation marks.
    a. "I want to study economics," he announced.
    b. Someone asked, "Why study that dismal science?"
    c. He replied, "I think it is exciting."

6. Commas are used to set off phrases that are in contrast to the main idea of the sentence in which they occur. Such phrases usually begin with a word showing contrast, such as *not* or *but*.
   a. It is history, not economics, that is exciting.
   b. History is easier than economics, but more valuable.
   c. It is history, rather than economics, that teaches the story of human-kind.

7. Commas are used to set off the parts of dates, addresses, and large numbers.
   a. Grandmother Han was born on September 16, 1899.
   b. She is one of the 1,234,567 people over eighty years old.
   c. Mrs. Han lives at 4321 Elm Street, Albany, New York.

8. Commas are used to help the reader understand the sentence if there might be some confusion. There is no set rule for this use.
   a. The day before she reached her eighty-fifth birthday. (*As punctuated, the sentence seems incomplete.*)
      The day before, she reached her eighty-fifth birthday.
   b. Like Grandmother Grandfather is very old.
      (*confusing sentence*)
      Like Grandmother, Grandfather is very old.
   c. When eating the grandparents sit down first.
      (*Is someone eating the grandparents?*)
      When eating, the grandparents sit down first.

Punctuation Practice (The Comma)

Directions: In the following sentences, put in the needed commas and cross out the ones that are not needed.

1. There has been according to reports, a decrease in crime rates.
2. To many people, crime is an evil that can be avoided.
3. Very few people, really want to commit crimes.
4. Crime is caused, largely, by poverty, hunger, and want.
5. There is a saying, "Love of money is the cause of evil."
6. "Lack of money is the cause of evil", someone else said.
7. If, all people, were rich, and no one were hungry, stealing might stop.
8. Of course, crimes of violence are a different matter.
9. They are caused by emotion, for poverty does not make people kill.
10. If you want to help stop crime, write to Crime Stoppers, 9898 Belvue Road, San Fernando, California.

The Colon [:]

The colon has one main use and three minor uses. The main use is to call attention to or to explain the statement that came before it. It is used *only* after a complete sentence (main clause, or independent clause). It patterns just like a period. However, it is correct to use a structure *after* the colon that is not a main clause.

 Examples

1. Dr. Wojewski teaches three related subjects: Russian, German, and French. (*calls attention to a series*)

2. He likes one subject best: Russian. (*calls attention to a word that means the same as the object, called the* appositive)

3. He enjoys an old Russian saying: "To a man with a hammer, all problems look like nails." (*calls attention to a quotation*)

4. Only one thing is as interesting to him as an old saying: another old saying. (*calls attention to an explanation*)

 Remember

The colon must follow a main clause. A frequent mistake writers make is to put a colon in the middle of a sentence.

Incorrect: I like to write: stories, poems, and essays.

The colon also has three minor uses.

1. The colon is used to write the time of day.
   a. It is 1:30 in the morning.
   b. I am supposed to get up at 6:30 A.M.
   c. On weekends, I sleep until 8:00 A.M.

 Note

A.M. is an abbreviation for *ante meridian,* which means "before noon." P.M. is an abbreviation for *post meridian,* which means "after noon."

2. The colon is used to refer to parts of the Christian Bible. It separates the chapter from the verse.
   a. Proverbs 20:1 says, "Strong drink causes rage." (Proverbs *is the book of the Bible; the quotation is from Chapter 20, Verse 1.*)
   b. John 4:8 states, "God is love."
   c. The preacher spoke about the words from Genesis 8:2.

3. The colon is used between titles and subtitles of books, in outlines, and in business letters.
    a. We read *Moby Dick: or the Great White Whale.*
    b. EXAMPLES:
    c. Dear Sir:

The Semicolon [;]

The semicolon has two main uses.

1. The semicolon is used to join main clauses that do not have an *and* , *but* , *for* , *nor* , or *or* in them. It functions in the same way as a comma + coordinating conjunction.
    a. Sonja likes poetry; she reads it and writes her own.
    b. Some of her poetry is good; some of it is not so good.
    c. Sometimes she reads it aloud; other times she does not.

Note

When the second of two main clauses is connected to the first by a conjunctive adverb (*hence, however, therefore, thus,* and so on) or by a transitional phrase (*on the other hand, in fact,* and so on), a semicolon is required.
    d. Omar wanted to go home; however, he did not have enough money.
    e. He had no car; on the other hand, he did have a bicycle.
    f. He rode his bicycle; in this way, he reached home.

2. The semicolon is used when a series of items have internal commas. In this use it separates the larger groups.
    a. To get to the United States we went through Beirut, Lebanon; Lisbon, Portugal; and Paris, France.
    b. We traveled with Hamad, a left-handed barber; Tareg, an animal doctor; and Yasser, a retired water-carrier.

Punctuation Practice (Colons and Semicolons)

Directions: In the following sentences, colons and semicolons have been left out or misused. Put in the colons and semicolons where they are necessary, and cross out the ones that are misused.

1. In the 1700s, a Frenchman named Galland discovered an Arabian book: *The Arabian Nights.*
2. He translated it into French; and it was an immediate success.
3. During the next hundred years it was translated into several languages : Italian, Spanish, German, and English.

4. There were several English versions, however, the best one was by Jonathan Scott.

5. *The Arabian Nights—or a Thousand and One Tales* is a series of stories told by Schehera-zade, a princess, to Schah-senan, the sultan, Schah-riar, the sultan's brother, and Dinar-zade, the sister of the Schehera-zade.

6. Schehera-zade usually started telling stories at 7.00 P.M. and ended at 12.00 midnight.

7. She told stories of adventure, she told stories of love, she told stories of magic.

8. One of the favorite stories was about a sailor: it was called "Sinbad the Sailor."

9. Sinbad had many dangerous adventures, however, he always came home safely.

10. One early translator made a mistake in the title, he called it "Sin, the Bad Sailor."

The Apostrophe [']

The apostrophe's function is to show the possessive case (except for personal pronouns), to show letters omitted in contracted words and numbers, and to form special plurals.

1. The apostrophe is needed to show the possessive form of nouns.
   a. The violins of the orchestra → the orchestra's violins
   b. The violin belonging to one musician → the musician's violin
   c. The violins belonging to many musicians → the musicians' violins
   d. The violins belonging to many children → the children's violins
   e. The violin of one (indefinite pronoun) → one's violin

For compound nouns, the apostrophe is added to the last word of the group.

   f. My mother-in-law's new car
   g. The United States' policy
   h. The Queen of Sheba's dress

For compound subjects of a sentence, the apostrophe can tell the reader who possesses what.

   i. Sancho's and Pancho's motorcycles (Each has a motorcycle.)
   j. Sancho and Pancho's motorcycle. (They share a motorcycle.)

If a singular noun ends in *s* or has a *z* sound, you can add *'s* or just *'*.

   k. Carlos's book or Carlos' book
   l. Ramirez's horse or Ramirez' horse

2. An apostrophe is used to show that a letter or letters have been left out (contractions).
   a. Cannot → can't
   b. I would → I'd
   c. They are → they're

3. An apostrophe is used to show the plurals of certain words, letters, and numbers.
   a. Among them they had two M.A.'s and three Ph.D.'s.
   b. My *r*'s sound like *l*'s.
   c. Zamadin got three A's and two B's.
   d. in the early 1980's (or 1980s)

Punctuation Practice (Apostrophes)

Directions: Add the necessary apostrophes to the following sentences. Cross out any unnecessary apostrophes.

1. The man who lives next door has three dog's.
2. Its hard to understand why.
3. My neighbors dogs are always barking.
4. Ive had a small dog myself since the 1970s.
5. Its name is Buzz (spelled with two z's).
6. My neighbors name is Katz (spelled with one *k*).
7. The whole family of Katzes goes away on weekend's.
8. They go to his sister-in-laws house.
9. When they are gone, the dogs barking drives me crazy.
10. Its bad enough that they bark, but they also climb the fence's and run around the citys streets.

Sentence Interrupters

Parentheses [()]

Parentheses (singular form, *parenthesis*) are used for two main reasons: to show unimportant information added to a sentence (parenthetical expressions) and to enclose numbers and letters used within a sentence.

Nguyen came to this country (in 1975) and wanted to stay until he had finished college (in 1980).

He actually stayed until he got married (he was thirty years old).

During college he worked at many jobs: (a) as a dishwasher, (b) as a car washer, (c) as a dog washer, and (d) as a window washer.

The Dash [—]

The dash is used for clarity to show a break in the thought of a sentence, sometimes in place of a comma or a colon—never a semicolon or period. If you use a typewriter, show a dash by typing two hyphens together.

I want to explain—will you listen to me?—about mice.

Running about the house, eating up the cheese, tearing holes in the bread wrappers, making noise in the night—mice make me angry.

Field mice—often hundreds of them—sometimes come into my house.

 Note

Commas, parentheses, and dashes are all used in much the same way. Use commas when the added information is slightly interesting; use parentheses when the added information is of little interest to your reader; use dashes when the added information is of great interest.

My grandmother, who came from Bulgaria, never learned to read English.

My grandmother (a nice old lady) never learned to read English.

My grandmother—a royal princess in Bulgaria—never learned to read English.

Brackets [[ ]]

Brackets are used to show comments within a quotation or are used when it is necessary to replace parentheses within parentheses.

Marie Poche once said, "It [experience] is what you have when you are too old to get a job."

"Nothing," my father told me, "makes you remember it [an unpaid doctor's bill] like a new illness."

The Slash [/]

The slash/virgule is used to show a choice or option.

Do exercises 5 and/or 6.

I advise you to take that credit/no-credit class.

Have a nice day/week/year/forever.

Note

Formal and academic writing makes very little use of dashes, slashes, and brackets.

Quotation Marks ["] [']

Quotation marks are used to show the exact words that were written or spoken by someone other than the writer, the titles of certain works, and the special use of a word.

1. Direct quotations
   a. When asked to define *nostalgia,* Haakim said, "It's like grammar. You find the present tense and the past perfect."
   b. "My son," the father said, "never go to jail, never gamble, and never buy anything that eats."
   c. My history teacher, Dr. Proctor, told the class, "Remember the words of Abraham Lincoln. 'Most people are about as happy as they let themselves be,' and remember them well." (*Single quotation marks* ['] *used for a quotation within a quotation*)
   d. The word "fox" may refer to an animal, but many times it means a pretty woman or an attractive man.

2. To show the titles of short works: stories, songs, poems, movies, television programs, magazine articles, and chapters in a book.
   a. Have you read "The Cop and the Anthem" by O. Henry?
   b. In Vietnam we heard a Vietnamese version of the song "My Darlin' Clementine."
   c. Her favorite poem is "Mu'allaqa" of ancient Yemen.
   d. Have you seen "Jaws IV" yet?
   e. "M*A*S*H" was the most popular television show for almost eight years.
   f. We were assigned "Internal Circuit Modules," a twenty-nine-page chapter in *Understanding Computers.*

Note

To show titles of longer works, such as books, magazines, newspapers, or long poems, use *italics.* Italics are letters that are slanted *like this.* In typewriting and handwriting, you show that you want to use italics by underlining the words.

I have never understood *The Decline of the West* by Spengler.

My sister subscribes to *Time.*

Instead, I read the *Daily News.*

Punctuation Practice (Review of All Marks)

Directions: Write a sentence for each of the following items.

1. A direct quotation
2. An indirect quotation
3. A list at the end of a sentence
4. Two main clauses joined by a coordinating conjunction
5. Three or more items in a series
6. A sentence showing possession
7. A sentence with an unimportant parenthetical expression
8. A sentence with a startling expression added
9. Two main clauses joined without a coordinating conjunction
10. A quotation within a quotation
11. A statement showing options
12. A declarative sentence with a quoted question
13. An expression of time
14. A sentence with a title in it
15. A list in the middle of a sentence

Appendix I

Selected Topics for Compositions

Generally, topics for paragraphs and longer compositions are given by the teacher or are developed from class reading and discussion. Sometimes you will be asked to select your own topic. Here are some topics that you might use. Most of them call upon your personal experience or your own ideas. It will not be necessary for you to go to the library to get the specific examples needed for an effective composition. Note that these are only topics. You will need to develop your own controlling ideas.

I. Personal Experiences
   An unforgettable experience
   An embarrassing moment
   The use of leisure time
   A person who influenced me greatly
   Making an important decision
   Long-range goals in life
   A frightening time
   The value of good friends

II. The Family
   Being the oldest child
   Being the youngest child
   Being the middle child
   Problems of raising children
   Divorce
   My mother
   My father
   My grandparents
   My relatives

III. Education
   Benefits of a two-year college
   Benefits of a four-year college
   College differs from high school
   Education outside of school
   Is a local school better than a distant one?

Education in two countries (compare and contrast)
Qualities of a good teacher
How to get the most out of college

IV. Matters of Taste
What is the best (or worst)
    Television show
    Motion picture
    Book
    Sports event
    Music
Who is the best (or worst)
    Friend
    Teacher
    Writer

V. Places
(Describe one of the following places; tell why you would like to visit; or compare any two)
A zoo
A small town
A large city
A trip anywhere
The countryside
My hometown
A museum or art gallery

VI. General Topics
What the future holds
Safe driving
Too many possessions
The best form of government
Spectator sports
Drug abuse
Teenage marriages
The best kinds of jobs
Fast foods
The influence of television

Appendix II

A Guide to Spelling American English

English spelling is irregular, confusing, and difficult even for native speakers of English. Spelling in the United States (called *American spelling* in this country) differs from spelling in England.

 Examples

England	United States
centre	center
analyse	analyze
inflexion	inflection
labour	labor
theatre	theater
tyre	tire

In the United States, people have developed their own way of spelling words. Even today, when most spellings are standard, there are often several possible "correct" spellings. Both *traveler* and *traveller* are accepted. Both *grey* and *gray* are correct. Why does spelling cause such a problem?

Spelling Problems

In addition to the fact that many words have more than one acceptable spelling, there are three causes for spelling problems in American English.

1. American English is not *phonetic* (fo-net-ik). In English the same letters can be used for several sounds.

   bough—*pronounced* "ba-oo"

   cough—*pronounced* "koff"

   tough—*pronounced* "tuff"

   dough—*pronounced* "do-u"

Each of the five vowels (*a, e, i, o, u*) may be pronounced "uh."

leg*a*l—*pronounced* "lee-guhl"

cam*e*l—*pronounced* "kam-uhl"

ev*i*l—*pronounced* "ee-vuhl"

come—*pronounced* "kuhm"

usef*u*l—*pronounced* "yooss-fuhl"

The reason that English cannot be a phonetic language is that there are forty-one generally used sounds and only twenty-six letters in the alphabet. Each letter, especially the vowels, must represent more than one sound. Remember, writing is an attempt to put the sounds of speech onto paper.

2. Many English words keep the old spellings. The words contain letters that are no longer pronounced.

comb—*pronounced* "kowm"

knight—*pronounced* "ni-eet"

often—*pronounced* "awff-uhn"

3. The English language includes thousands of words taken from other languages. In some of these words, the spelling of the other language has been kept.

pizza	*Italian*
punch	*Pharsi*
pause	*Greek*
pastor	*Latin*
pack	*German*
pastrami	*Turkish*
palisade	*French*
peal	*Old English*
peccary	*American Indian*

Correct spelling is considered a sign of intelligence and education. More important, it makes written communication quick and easy. How is it possible to learn how to spell correctly? In spite of the problems built into English, you can learn. Here are ten common steps to good spelling.

1. Look at the word.

2. Copy the word correctly.

3. Remember how the word looks.

4. Listen to a native speaker say the word.

5. Pronounce the word yourself.

6. Divide the word into syllables.

7. Write the word several times.

8. Study the difficult parts of the word.

9. Write the word correctly in a sentence.

10. Learn the basic spelling rules.

English has sixteen vowel sounds. These sounds are represented by the vowels (*a, e, i, o, u,* and sometimes *y*) alone or in combination. The problem is that each sound may be spelled in several different ways. Here are the sounds and the ways they are spelled in English. There are four columns. The first gives the symbol used in the International Phonetic Alphabet (IPA); the second gives the symbol used in the recommended *New Horizon Ladder Dictionary of the English Language* (Ladder); the third gives a common word in which the sound appears; the fourth gives various ways the sound is spelled in American English.

IPA	Ladder	Key	Variations
ɑː	a	father	sergeant
			pot
			hearth
			memoir
æ	ae	am	plaid
			bad
ɛ	e	get	any
			said
			says
			dead
			heifer
			friend
			leopard
e	ey	baby	bait
			day
			gauge
			break
			obey
			veil
			bouquet
ɪ	i	in	fear
			been
			pretty
			weird

			here
			sieve
			women
			busy
			build
			nymph
i	iy	be	see
			flea
			deceive
			key
			people
			machine
			quay
			phoebe
ɔ	ɔ	all	haul
			caught
			paw
			often
			broad
o	ow	go	sew
			foe
			brooch
			shoulder
			grow
			owe
ʊ	u	put	wolf
			took
			could
u	uw	too	dilute
			suit
ə	ə	ago	item
			heard
			sir
			gallop
			does
			flood
			journal
			circus
ɝ	ər	defer	were
			err
			stir
			shirr
			liqueur

			fur
			sure
			burr
			myrrh
aʊ	aw	out	bough
			cow
aɪ	ay	aisle	height
			bible
			pie
			choir
			buy
			by
			rye
ɔi	oy	boy	avoid
iu	iy + uw	beauty	feud
			pew
			lieu
			view
			do
			you
			due
			use
			yule

The consonants (all of the rest of the letters) do not vary as much as the vowels. Here are the consonant sounds in the same columns.

IPA	Ladder	Key	Variations
b	b	bit, rub	none
tʃ	č	child	none
d	d	did	none
f	f	far	phone
			rough
g	g	go	g before a, o, u
h	h	home	none
dʒ	ǰ	edge	judge
k	k	kill	cold (c before a, o, u)
			duck (ck at end of word)
l	l	love	none
m	m	man	none
n	n	net	none
ŋ	ŋ	sing	none
p	p	part, stop	none
r	r	red	none

s	s	s<u>i</u>t	sau<u>c</u>y
ʃ	š	<u>sh</u>ip	mi<u>ss</u>ion
t	t	<u>t</u>en	none
θ	θ	<u>th</u>ink	none; spelled <u>th</u>
ð	ð	<u>th</u>at	none; spelled <u>th</u>
v	v	<u>v</u>ery	none
w	w	<u>w</u>ent	none
hw	hw	<u>wh</u>at	none
j	y	<u>y</u>es	none
z	z	<u>z</u>oo	none
ʒ	ž	vi<u>s</u>ion	mea<u>s</u>ure

 ## Note

The letter *q* is not listed here because it has the same sound as *k*. *C* has two sounds: *s* before *e* or *i* (*city, service*) and *k* before *a, o,* or *u* (*cat, cow, cup*). *G* also has two sounds: *j* before *e* or *i* (*gist, gentleman*) and *g* before *a, o,* or *u* (*gap, got, gun*)

Spelling in American English is not completely irregular. There are some rules that can help you to spell most words correctly. You will just have to learn the words that are exceptions, the ones that do not follow the rules. Writing, as you know, is an attempt to put the sounds of the spoken language onto paper. Pronouncing a word correctly is important for correct spelling. Three of the four basic spelling rules are based on the way a word is pronounced.

Pronunciation Problems

People learning English as another language have two pronunciation problems: their ears and Americans' mouths. American English has three sounds that are not found in most other languages.

1. The sound *uh* (IPA symbol [ə]): *gum* [gəm], *come* [kəm], *sun* [sən].
2. The sound *ih* (IPA symbol [ɪ]): sit [sɪt], pity [pɪti], busy [bɪzi].
3. The American *r* (IPA symbol [r]): read [rid], rice [rais], rat [ræt].

For example, people who speak a Romance language (Spanish, Italian, Portuguese, Romanian, French) *do not hear the difference* between *live* and *leaf* or *bite* and *bit* because the *ih* sound does not exist in their language. People who speak Asian languages *do not hear the difference* between the American [r] and [l] because of the difficulty of pronouncing the American *r*. To them the words *read* and *lead* or *batter* and *battle* sound alike. If you have one of these problems, the solution is for you to *read* the word as it is correctly written. Do not rely on what you *think* you hear.

The second problem is the way Americans speak their own language. Anyone learning another language is confused because native speakers seem to speak so fast. Even native speakers who try to spell words that they have only heard will spell them incorrectly.

 ## Example

Two native speakers of American English might say:

"Hi, Pete. Did you eat yet?"

"No, did you?"

"No, let's go to MacDonald's."

And it would sound something like this:

"Hi, Pete. Djeet-yet?"

"Naw, djoo?"

"Nope, less gotuh McDonald's."

The solution, again, is that you must *read* the words as they are correctly written. Speaking is an excellent way to increase vocabulary, but the best way to improve spelling (and vocabulary as well) is to read. Reading, seeing the words on paper, will also help you to tell the difference between the many words that have *similar* sounds or spellings.

 ## Examples

accept/except	advise/advice
farther/further	loose/lose
presents/presence	to/too/two
quite/quiet/quit	since/sense/cents
effect/affect	coarse/course

Spelling Rules

There are four basic spelling rules that will help you to spell many problem words. To understand these rules, you will first need to know about prefixes and suffixes. A *prefix* is a syllable added to the beginning of a word. A *suffix* is a syllable added to the end of a word.

Prefixes

A prefix is added to the base word, called the *root,* without adding or dropping any letters.

dis + appear = disappear

dis + solve = dissolve

im + possible = impossible

im + mortal = immortal

un + happy = unhappy

un + necessary = unnecessary

Spelling Practice (Prefixes)

Directions: Write the correct spelling of the root word with the prefix added. If you are not sure, use your dictionary.

1. dis + continue   *discontinue*
2. dis + satisfy   *dissatisfy*
3. mis + pronounce   *mispronounce*
4. mis + spell   *mispell*
5. re + place   *replace*
6. re + evaluate   *revalute*
7. un + noticed   *unnoticed*
8. un + willing   *unwilling*
9. il + legal   *illegal*
10. il + legible   *illegible*

Suffixes

Many suffixes—endings added to words to change form or meaning—pattern the same way that prefixes do: they are simply put on the end of the root. Common suffixes are *-al, -less, -ly, -ness,* and *-ment.*

Examples

instrument + al = instrumental

friend + less = friendless

natural + ly = naturally

kind + ness = kindness

develop + ment = development

Spelling Practice (Suffixes)

Directions: Write the correct spelling of the root word with the suffix added. If you are not sure, use your dictionary.

Add *-ly* to the following roots.

1. usual _Usualy_
2. casual _Casualy_
3. quick _Quickly_
4. sudden _Suddenly_

Add *-less* to the following roots.

5. heart _heartless_
6. help _heelpless_
7. cheer _Cheerless_
8. mind _mindless_

Add *-al* to the following roots.

9. accident _accidental_
10. environment _environmental_
11. region _regional_
12. department _departmental_

Add *-ness* to the following roots.

13. kind _Kindness_
14. swift _Swiftness_
15. cheerful _cheerfulness_
16. helpful _heelpfulness_

Add *-ment* to the following roots.

17. treat _treatment_
18. govern _government_

Combine the suffix *-al* and the suffix *-ly* and add them to the following roots.

19. basic ___*basical   basicaly*___
20. accident ___*accidental   accidentaly.*___

Problems with Suffixes

All of the words in the previous list end with a consonant, and all of the suffixes begin with a consonant. The suffix is simply added to the root. Sometimes, however, a root will end with the letter *e.*

Rule 1:   *When the suffix begins with a vowel and the root ends with an* e, *you must drop the final* e *of the root.* Common suffixes beginning with a vowel are *-ing, -ed, -ence, -ance, -able, -ous, -er,* and *-al.*

 Examples

love + ing = loving
bride + al = bridal
fame + ous = famous

 Spelling Practice (Suffixes Beginning with a Vowel)

Directions: Write the correct spelling of the following combinations.

1. arrive + al ___*arrival*___
2. force + ed ___*forced*___
3. use + age ___*usage*___
4. become + ing ___*becoming*___
5. extreme + ly ___*emte extremly*___
6. assure + ance ___*assurance*___
7. hope + ing ___*hoping*___
8. drive + er ___*driver*___
9. drive + ing ___*driving*___
10. drive + able ___*drivable*___

Exceptions: Words ending in *ce* and *ge* do *not* drop the final *e.* The reason is that the final *e* is necessary for the correct pronunciation of the word. To drop the *e* would change the way the word is said.

Examples

> notice + able = noticeable [now-tis-ə-b l]
>
> manage + able = manageable [maen-ij-ə-b l]

Without the final *e*, these words would be pronounced [now-tik-ə-b l] and [maen-i-ga-bəl].

Rule 2: The second rule is also concerned with the way words are said: *If a word has one syllable and ends with a vowel and a single consonant,* then *double the final consonant before adding a suffix beginning with a vowel.*

Why?

In American English, the sound (pronunciation) of the word usually determines the spelling. American English regularly adds a vowel to change the spoken sound of the written word.

 ## Examples

> cap [kaep] + e = cape [keyp]
>
> met [met] + e = mete [miyt]
>
> bit [bit] + e = bite [bayt]
>
> mop [map] + e = mope [mowp]
>
> cut [kət] + e = cute [kuwt]

To keep the correct vowel sound, it is necessary to double the final consonant. Otherwise, the result will be a different word.

 ## Examples

> cap + er = caper (to jump about)
>
> cap + p + er = capper (someone who puts caps on)
>
> bit + er = biter (someone who bites)
>
> bit + t + er = bitter (not sweet)
>
> mop + er = moper (someone who acts sad)
>
> mop + p + er = mopper (someone who uses a mop)
>
> cut + er = cuter (more attractive)
>
> cut + t + er = cutter (someone who cuts)

The same rule is used if the word has more than one syllable but is stressed or accented on the last syllable.

Examples

begin + ing = beginning

regret + ed = regretted

admit + ed = admitted

advise + or = advisor

If the word is not stressed on the last syllable, there is no need to double the final consonant; the sound will not change.

 Examples

benefit + ed = benefited

kidnap + ing = kidnaping

 Spelling Practice (Doubling Final Consonant)

Directions: Write the correct spelling of the word that results when the suffix is added to the root word. If you are not sure, check your dictionary.

Root Word	+ -ed	+ -ing
1. beg	*beged*	*beging*
2. stop	*stoped*	*stoping*
3. commit	*commited*	*commiting*
4. transmit	*transmited*	*transmiting*
5. excel	*exceled*	*exceling*
6. control	*controled*	*controling*
7. begin	*begined*	*begining*
8. infer	*infered*	*infering*
9. meet	*meeted*	*meeting*
10. regret	*regreted*	*regreting*
11. hop	*hoped*	*hoping*
12. mate	*mated*	*mating*
13. hope	*hopped*	*hopping*
14. equip	*equiped*	*equiping*
15. crush	*crushed*	*crushing*

Rule 3:   Rule 3 applies to those words that contain either an *ei* or an *ie*. Again, the sound is the guide. *If the sound is [iy], as in* see, *write* ei *after the letter* c *and* ie *after any other letter. When the sound is other than [iy], write* ei. *This rhyme may help you remember this rule.*

> *I* before *e* except after *c*
> or when sounded like *a*
> as in *neighbor* and *weigh*

 ## Examples

After c	After Another Letter	Sounds Like
perceive	belief	their
ceiling	achieve	eight
receive	yield	neighbor
receive	piece	weight

 ## Exceptions

If you will learn this rather strange sentence, you will remember most of the exceptions to the *ei/ie* rule: *Neither foreign financier siezed either species of weird leisure.*

 ## Spelling Practice (ei or ie)

Directions: Write the correct spelling of the words. Use your dictionary if you are not sure. If the word is one of the exceptions, write an *X* after it.

1. bel *ie* ve
2. ch *ie* f
3. w *ei* gh
4. sc *ie* nce
5. n *ei* ther
6. y *ie* ld
7. n *ei* ghbor
8. gr *ie* f
9. rel *ie* f
10. n *ei* ce
11. forf *ei* t
12. consc *ie* nce
13. dec *ie* ve
14. l *ei* sure
15. f *i* nd

Rule 4:   Rule 4 applies to all of the words that end in *y: Except for* -ing, *the final* y *after a consonant is changed to* i *before a suffix.*

 ## Examples

beauty + ful = beautiful
lovely + ness = loveliness

copy + er = copier

crafty + ness = craftiness

modify + ing = modifying

marry + ing = marrying

This rule is also used when you make a noun ending in *y* plural and when you make a verb plural. Change the *y* to *i* and add *es*.

 ## Examples

baby → babies

city → cities

fly → flies

library → libraries

bury → buries

copy → copies

Remember, if the final *y* has a vowel before it, do not change the *y* to *i*.

 ## Examples

alley → alleys

turkey → turkeys

annoy → annoyed

donkey → donkeys

 ## Exceptions

day/daily

lay/laid

pay/paid

say/said

 ## Spelling Practice (Final y)

Directions: Write the correct spelling of each word with the suffix added. If you are not sure, use your dictionary.

1. boy + s _____ *boys* _____
2. chimney + s _____ *chimneys* _____

3. say + ed __*said*__

4. lonely + ness __*lonelyness*__

5. fiery + ness __*fieryness*__

6. mercy + ful __*mercyful*__

7. mighty + ly __*mightly*__

8. easy + er __*easier*__

9. try + es __*tries*__

10. duty + ful __*dutyful*__

11. duty + ful + ly _____

12. study + es __*studies*__

13. marry + es __*marries*__

14. pay + ed __*paid*__

15. pay + ing __*paying*__

These rules will help you with many words. In American English there are always exceptions to the rules. Also, each person has certain words that cause problems. It is a good idea to keep a list of your own problem words and memorize them.

Appendix III

Correction Symbols; Exercise

Correction Symbols

sp	spelling error, check dictionary
∧	something left out, make additions noted
Agr	check for agreement: subject-verb, pronoun-noun
¶	start a new paragraph
no ¶	no paragraph
p	punctuation error
	X = omit punctuation
	O = put in correct punctuation
	, = incorrect punctuation
M̸	change to lowercase
m	change to uppercase
idiom	incorrect idiom, see suggestions on your paper
WW	wrong word form
Frag	sentence is fragmentary or incomplete
det	incorrect determiner form
gram	grammatical error
art	article needed
no art	no article needed
(x)	delete character or letter
(word)	delete word
∿	transpose letters: (e)(i) = *ie*

Name

EXERCISE

READ ALL DIRECTIONS BEFORE WRITING ANYTHING.

1. Write your name on the line at the top of this paper.

2. Draw a circle around the word *Name* at the top of this paper.

3. Draw another circle in the upper left-hand corner of the paper.

4. Draw a line under this word: LINE

5. Mark an *X* through this picture of a bird.

6. Make a line through these zeros: 0 0 0 0 0 0 0 0

7. Write today's date on this line. _____

8. Put a number under each of these candles.

9. Draw a circle around each number below the candles.

10. Make a large *X* through this picture of a fish.

11. Mark another *X* on the lower left-hand corner of this paper.

12. Put a little dot in each of these circles: ○ ○ ○

13. Draw a little circle on each of these lines: ____ ____ ____

14. Mark an *X* on the lower right-hand corner of this paper.

15. Draw a circle in this space:

16. Put a + in the circle you just drew.

17. Raise your right hand.

18. Raise your left hand.

19. Do not follow any direction except for number 1.

20. Do not tell anyone.

Appendix IV

Answers

Chapter One

Page 11

Limiting Practice:
1.	a-3	2.	a-3	3.	a-1	4.	a-1	5.	a-1
	b-2		b-4		b-3		b-3		b-2
	c-4		c-2		c-4		c-4		c-3
	d-1		d-1		d-2		d-2		d-4

Page 12

Limiting Practice: Answers will vary.

Page 13

Writing Practice: Answers will vary.

Page 13

Original Paragraph: Answers will vary.

Page 17

Writing Practice (Categorizing):

Title will vary.

    I. Food from animals
        A. From four-footed animals
            1. Pork
            2. Beef
            3. Hamburger

    B. From other animals
      1. Fish
      2. Chicken
      3. Eggs

II. Food that is harvested
    A. From trees
      1. Bananas
      2. Oranges
      3. Apples
    B. From the ground
      1. Rice
      2. Peas
      3. Celery

III. Food that must be prepared
    A. Noodles
    B. Bread
    C. Soup

Topic: Food

Controlling Idea: Sources of food (will vary)

Page 20

Writing Practice (Categorizing):

List 1. Topic: College classes

I. Mathematics
    A. Geometry
    B. Algebra
    C. Calculus

II. Languages
    A. French
    B. English
    C. Spanish

III. Sciences
    A. Physics
    B. Chemistry
    C. Geology

List 2. Topic: Fine arts

I. Visual arts
    A. Painting
    B. Drawing
    C. Sketching

II. Plastic arts
   A. Sculpting
   B. Modeling
   C. Carving

III. Music
   A. Operas
   B. Symphonies
   C. Concerts

List 3. Topic: Animals

I. Domesticated
   A. Dogs
   B. Cows
   C. Pigs

II. Man-eating animals (wild animals)
   A. Sharks
   B. Tigers
   C. Bears

III. Birds
   A. Eagles
   B. Crows
   C. Sparrows

List 4. Topic: Countries

I. Spanish-speaking
   A. El Salvador
   B. Mexico
   C. Peru

II. European (Near Eastern)
   A. Iran
   B. Iraq
   C. Turkey

III. Oriental (Far Eastern)
   A. China
   B. Viet Nam
   C. Korea

Chapter Two

Page 27

Writing Practice (Sentence Combining):

Answers will vary, but the basic skill is to make sentences as short as possible without leaving out any of the information. Sentence combining allows practice in many different patterns and in the use of conjunctions and transitions.

Suggested answers:

1. Sally and Sarah are twelve-year-old identical twins.
2. They wear similar clothes and hairstyles and identical necklaces.
3. They look, walk, and talk very much alike.
4. Teachers and strangers cannot tell one from the other; even their mother sometimes has trouble.
5. However, Sally likes to read and study math, whereas Sarah likes games and sports.
6. Both like boys, but Sally is shy, and Sarah is not.
7. They look and dress alike, but they do not act alike, for each is an individual.

Page 30

Correct order:

1. Sentence 2	4. Sentence 7	7. Sentence 6
2. Sentence 5	5. Sentence 9	8. Sentence 4
3. Sentence 1	6. Sentence 8	9. Sentence 3

Answers to other Writing Practice exercises in this chapter will vary.

Chapter Three

Page 40

Definition: Answers will vary

Page 42

Sentence Combining (possible answers):

1. It was about noon when the snow began to fall.
2. At first it came down slowly in tiny white flakes.
3. The gentle wind became stronger and stronger.
4. The snow in the air became thicker and thicker.
5. It was impossible to see more than a few meters in any direction.
6. The snow swirled around the trees and bushes.
7. The wind blew the snow into cracks in old houses.

8. In addition, it began to cover the road and pile up on the edges.

9. The wind blew even stronger, and the snow increased.

10. Finally, as the sun went down, the world was covered with white.

Page 43

Correct order:

1. Sentence 5   4. Sentence 3   7. Sentence 7
2. Sentence 6   5. Sentence 2
3. Sentence 4   6. Sentence 1

For practice, write these sentences in paragraph form.

The answers for the other Writing Practice exercises will vary.

Page 45

Paragraphs will vary in content.

Page 46

Paragraphs will vary.

Page 48

Paragraphs will vary.

Chapter Five

Page 60

Sentence Combining (suggested answers):
At this time it would be a good idea to start to shift sentence elements about within the sentence. For example, the first sentence *could* be written:

1. Most inventions have developed in a series of steps that were slow.

Change the sequence of the sentences. Make 1b a single word:

1. The development of most inventions has been a slow series of steps.

2. For example, the common wheel has changed gradually over many years.

3. The first rough, uneven, wheellike devices, logs, were then smoothed to roll more easily.

4. The next step was a solid wheel cut from a section of a tree trunk.

5. *Omit.*

6. Finally, after centuries, the lighter, faster, spoked wheel was developed.

7. The rims still wore out, until someone had the simple idea to make metal "tires" for them.

8. *Omit.*

9. The wheel with metal hub and axle has been used for a long time and is still in use today.

10. *Omit.*

Page 62

Correct order:

1. Sentence 3

2. Sentence 7

3. Sentence 9

4. Sentence 4

5. Sentence 1

6. Sentence 6

7. Sentence 11

8. Sentence 2

9. Sentence 8

Off the topic: Sentences 5, 10, 12

The answers for the rest of the Writing Practice exercises in this chapter will vary.

Chapter Six

Page 72

Correct order: Paragraphs will vary.

Page 75

Controlled Writing: Answers will vary.

Page 76

Guided Writing: Answers will vary.

Page 80

Guided Writing: Answers will vary.

Page 81

Free Writing: Answers will vary.

Page 83

Free Writing: Answers will vary.

Chapter Seven

Page 87

Sentence Combining: Check to make sure that there are no unnecessary repetitions; use pronouns. Omit sentence 10.

Page 92

Controlled Writing: Answers will vary. Check for pattern of model. The rest of the exercises in this chapter will vary in form.

Chapter Eight

Page 99

Sentence Combining:

1. Sentences 5 and 12
2. Sentence 16
3. Sentences 4 and 13
4. Sentence 14
5. Sentence 11
6. Sentence 3
7. Sentence 8
8. Sentence 10
9. Sentence 7
10. Sentence 2
11. Sentence 1
12. Sentence 15
13. Sentence 6
14. Sentence 9

Combine carefully to avoid repeating. Most sentences can be easily combined for a more effective, mature style.

Pages 100, 101, 103, and 104

Answers will vary.

Page 111

Sentence Combining (suggested answers):

1. Both astrologers and astronomers study the positions of the stars and planets.

2. While astrologers claim to tell the future of people on earth, astronomers claim (only) to tell the future positions of the planets.

3. Although a great many people believe in astrology, many others believe it is superstition; (4) astronomy, though, is a true science.

5. Astronomers know that Pluto is 3,664,000,000 miles from earth, so they laugh and ask the question, (6) "If Pluto is so far away, how can it affect people here on earth?"

Page 112

Sentence Combining (suggested order):

1. Sentence 5   6. Sentence 7

2. Sentence 4   7. Sentence 1

3. Sentence 6   8. Sentence 10

4. Sentence 8   9. Sentence 3

5. Sentence 2

Sentence 9 could be left out or placed after sentence 4.

Pages 112 and 113

Paragraphs will vary.

Chapter Nine

Page 117

Kinds of Propositions:

1. Correct (can be argued; define *healthy*)

2. Vague terms (needs definition, explanation)

3. Fact

4. Vague (needs definition of all terms)

5. Vague (may be *C* when *better buy* is defined)

6. Taste

7. Vague (define *highly*)

8. Taste

9. Fact by definition (can be explained, not argued)

10. Vague (all terms)

Page 118

Revise propositions according to the explanations given in the preceding exercise.

Page 120

Fact and Opinion:
1. Fact (can be checked in a newspaper)
2. Opinion (define *lots of* to make an argument)
3. Fact (can be checked on map)
4. Opinion (define *overweight*)
5. Fact by definition
6. Fact (use statistics to verify)
7. Fact by definition (use a calendar to check)
8. Opinion (a matter of personal experience; will vary)
9. Fact (can be checked with FBI statistics)
10. Fact (can be checked with AMA statistics)

Page 120

Thinking Practice: Use information in preceding exercise for answers.

Page 123

Writing Practice: Answers (paragraphs) will vary.

Page 124

Definitions: Answers will vary. Students should discuss different answers and try to reach agreement.

Page 125

Writing Practice: Answers (paragraphs) will vary.

Page 126

Free Writing: Answers (paragraphs) will vary.

Page 129

Sentence Combining: Sentences are best combined following the Suggestion on page 27. Students should include all necessary information and leave out repetitions.

Page 130

Writing Practice: Answers (paragraphs) will vary.

Page 132

Writing Practice: Although answers (paragraphs) will vary, it is necessary to redefine the vague words so that the reader can agree to the definition.

Page 133

Reasoning Practice:

1. Probably a true statement, judging by the evidence.
2. Perhaps true; the woman could be another relative, a nurse, or a friend.
3. Perhaps true; it could be during vacation or on a weekend.
4. There is no way to know from the illustration.
5. Probably false, judging by the size of the bed.
6. There is no way to know from the illustration.
7. There is no way to know.
8. There is no way to know; probably not, judging by the evidence.
9. Perhaps; it could be milk, water, or juice.
10. There is no way to get into the woman's mind to find out.

Many of these statements *may* be true, but many of our inferences are hard to check without further evidence.

Page 134

Writing Practice: Answers (paragraphs) will vary. The general conclusion is that situation comedies have the best chance of being popular.

Page 136

Writing Practice: Answers (paragraphs) will vary.

Page 137

Writing Practice: The obvious inductive conclusion is that men in America wear different kinds of hats for (1) social occasions and (2) occupations. The deductive conclusion is that the man *might* be a cowboy.

Page 137

Writing Practice: Answers (paragraphs) will vary.

Chapters Ten, Eleven, and Twelve

All of the Writing Practice exercises in these chapters will have varying answers and responses.

HANDBOOK: Section One, Basic Grammar

Page 197

Meaning Practice:

1. *Well:* a hole in the ground for water or oil; a natural spring; in good health; good or pleasing.
2. *Read:* to get meaning from written words; to say written words.
3. *Frog:* an amphibious animal; part of railroad track; a flower-holding device.
4. *Bat:* a flying mammal; a stick for hitting a ball (baseball, cricket); potter's clay; an old brick; a board (various uses).
5. *Clip:* to hit; to cut short; a tool for cutting; a device for holding things together.
6. *Close:* to shut, as a door; near in time or space.
7. *Cold:* not warm; a common illness.
8. *Fast:* not slow; tied tightly; not to eat.
9. *Felt:* past tense of *to feel;* a kind of cloth made from wool.
10. *Graze:* to come very near; to eat grass, as animals do.

Page 198

Meaning Practice:

HAND [haend] *n.* (*plural,* hands [haendz])   1. The part of the arm below the wrist. Each hand has four fingers and a thumb.   2. A pointer that moves around a circular dial, as on a clock or gauge.   3. A style of writing: *She* *writes a fine hand.*   4. Help or physical assistance: *Give me a hand with this ladder.*   5. *Often plural:* Control over: *The robber is in the hands of the police.*   6. A person who works: *a farm hand; a hired hand.*   7. Showing appreciation for something by clapping the hands together; applause: *Let's give the musician a big hand.*   9. A unit of length equal to four inches used to measure the height of a horse.   10. The cards dealt to a player in a card game.   *Verb:*   1. To give or pass with the hand: *Hand me that book.*   2. To pass along from person to person: *Old stories are handed down from father to son.*   *Adjective:*   1. Made to be carried in the hand: *a hand tool.*   2. Made with the hands rather than by a machine: *hand-made toys.*   *Idioms with hand:*   1. *At hand:* close by, near.   2. *In hand:* under control.   3. *Out of hand:* out of control.   4. *On the other hand:* preface to another point of view.   5. *Hands down:* easily.   6. *Hand down*   a. to give a decision, as a judge or a court of law.   b. to give as an inheritance.

Here are over twenty differing meanings for the simple word *hand.* A very large library dictionary would have at least ten more, including some slang terms.

Pages 199–200

Answers:

Add *s.*

If noun ends in *ch, x, ss, sh,* add *es.*

If noun ends in *y,* change *y* to *ie* and add *s.*

Page 203

Noun Practice (Singular to Plural):

1. Goats are important animals in the Middle East.
2. Goats can eat weeds or shrubs and still be healthy.
3. Farmers are happy to have goats.
4. They can get fine products from the animals.
5. The meat is cooked on spits with tomatoes and onions.
6. The hides make soft leather easily cut with knives.
7. Milk from goats is more healthful than milk from cows.
8. The females are called nannies.
9. The males are called billies.
10. The babies are called kids.

Page 203

Noun Practice (Singular to Plural):

1. cities	6. churches	11. busses (*or* buses)
2. cliffs	7. wives	12. copies
3. replies	8. valleys	13. radios
4. bushes	9. foxes	14. baths
5. women	10. businesses	15. industries

Page 204

Noun Practice (Possessive):

1. animal's hair	6. desert's ponds
2. goat's milk, cow's milk	7. ponds' water, desert's sands
3. goats' feet	8. these animals' diet
4. area's climate	9. weeds' tops, shrubs' leaves
5. farmer's fields	10. farmer's friend

Page 204

Noun Practice:

1. boys' school	9. fox's box
2. year's pay	10. class' (class's) noise
3. Sam's car	11. mother's voice
4. Maria's dress	12. child's shoes
5. Pete's bad habits	13. Bess' (Bess's) paragraph
6. goat's smell	14. classes' noise
7. Lee's house	15. dog's bark
8. teacher's directions	

Page 205

Noun Practice (Count and Noncount Nouns):

1. little furniture	6. few friends
2. few ideas	7. little wind
3. few animals	8. few cities
4. little snow	9. few books
5. little music	10. little money

Note: Few is used with plural nouns. It is possible to say *little animal* (singular), but that changes the idea from *amount* to *size*.

Page 205

Noun Practice (Count and Noncount Nouns):

1. much furniture
2. many ideas
3. many animals
4. much snow
5. much music
6. many friends
7. much wind
8. many cities
9. many books
10. much money

Page 209

Pronoun Practice (Case Changes):

1. I
2. I
3. We
4. us, her and me
5. whom
6. our
7. who
8. his (*before a gerund*)
9. he
10. Whoever

Page 210

Pronoun Practice (Demonstrative and Possessive Pronouns):

1. This, my
2. Those, mine
3. That, hers
4. These (*or* Those), her
5. These, theirs

Page 212

Verb Practice (Kinds of Verbs)

1. I
2. T
3. L
4. L, T
5. T, T
6. L
7. L
8. T
9. I
10. I

Page 224

Verb Practice (Tense Changes):

1. Yes, I went to school.
2. Yes, we have had a test.
3. Yes, I have passed.
4. Yes, I went to the party.
5. Yes, I have gone to the next one.
6. Yes, they have gone.
7. Yes, I broke something.
8. Yes, I have eaten something.
9. Yes, she asked that.
10. Yes, they surprised me.
11. Yes, there has been some extra food.
12. Yes, they froze it.
13. Yes, he has got (gotten) some.
14. Yes, I wanted more to eat.
15. Yes, I have got (gotten) fat.

Page 225

Verb Practice (Tense Changes):

1. landed
2. was
3. was
4. had
5. changed
6. gave
7. was, did
8. said, loved
9. stayed
10. built, sailed

Page 236

Verb Practice (Subject-Verb Agreement):

1. is
2. watches
3. is
4. is (Rule 3)
5. offer
6. are
7. sees
8. follow
9. interest
10. are
11. buys
12. spends
13. finds
14. makes
15. enjoys

Page 236

Verb Practice (Subject-Verb Agreement):

1. are
2. is
3. is
4. ride
5. race
6. organize
7. decide
8. starts
9. waits
10. are

Page 245

Modifier Practice (Adjectives to Adverbs, Adverbs to Adjectives):

1. to change suddenly
2. to cause possibly
3. to result probably
4. to journey safely
5. to welcome cheerfully
6. a quick departure
7. an angry fight
8. an effortless run
9. a perfect fit
10. an intent look

Page 246

Modifier Practice (Adjective and Adverb Placement):

1. bright shining sea
2. large towels, hot sand
3. a new bathing
4. his old, ragged
5. The yellow sun
6. had red arms and sunburned legs
7. had ever been (*or* time ever she, *or* beach ever)
8. badly sunburned *or* sunburned badly
9. leave quickly
10. Suddenly Hrand *or* saw suddenly
11. Quickly they *or* They quickly *or* towels quickly
12. Hurriedly they *or* They hurriedly *or* car hurriedly
13. looked in his pockets *or* In his pockets Hrand *or* car in his pockets
14. only once
15. them in the sand
16. new bathing, too small
17. old trousers, too ragged
18. Suddenly he *or* He suddenly *or* missing keys
19. Swiftly he *or* he swiftly *or* old car
20. Happily they *or* They happily *or* drove happily *or* home happily

Page 247

Modifier Practice (Misused Forms):

1. surely
2. rainier (*no* more)
3. happy
4. dark

5. really	8. rapidly
6. closer and closer	9. well
7. soaking	10. quickly

Page 248

Modifier Practice (Sentence Combining):

Answers will vary. These are suggestions.

1. I took off my wet clothes and dried myself thoroughly.
2. I put on warm, dry jeans and a warm, dry shirt.
3. I hurried to the front-room window.
4. I watched the fierce rain pour down.
5. The old house across the street suddenly shook.
6. The heavy rain was washing away the old foundation.
7. The left front corner of the house gradually sank.
8. The corner was dipping lower and lower toward the street.
9. The old house moved toward the rain-filled street.
10. The house floated gently down the street to the river.

Page 251

Structure Word Practice (Articles):

A (The) man who makes his own brick wall or barbecue often finds it necessary to clean (the) cement or (the) dirt from the wall that he has just built. Hydrochloric acid will do the job. It works by dissolving a thin layer of (the) mortar or (the) dirt. To use it, mix one part of acid with ten parts of water in a glass container. Always add the acid to the water. Adding the water to the acid will cause it to boil. Always wear rubber gloves, and do not get any of the acid on (the) skin or (the) clothes. It will make a hole in them. When finished, wash the bricks with water.

Articles in parentheses may be used or not.

Page 251

Structure Word Practice (Determiners):

The following are just some of the many possible answers.

1. The (a), the (a)	4. an, a, some
2. a	5. the (his, some) a (the)
3. the (some?)	6. The (Some), his

7. a, his

8. the, a, a

9. the (some), the

10. a (the)

11. the

Page 257

Structure Word Practice (Coordinating Conjunctions):

The Young Chemist

A student had just started to study chemistry. He had learned a little but not very much. He liked the laboratory and studied hard, but he did not like the math or (and) the lectures. All the time it was either study math or listen to lectures. It was not too bad, but he would rather work in the lab. One day he got some bottles, flasks, and test tubes, for he was going to experiment. Another student watched him and asked, "What are you doing?" "I am going to mix water with phosphate or maybe acid, or maybe this green stuff," he replied. His friend asked, "Do that and what will you make?" The student said, "It will be a universal solvent." "What is a universal solvent?" asked the friend. "Well," answered the student, "it is a liquid that will dissolve everything." The friend thought for a minute and then asked, "But what will you keep it in?"

Page 258

Structure Word Practice (Prepositions and Adverbial Particles):

Smart Food

Nadya was having trouble in (with) college. She was going to give up. Thinking about her problems, she decided to ask the smartest man she knew what made him smart. The man, with the name of Mr. Schultz, sold fish at (in) the market on (at, down at) the corner. He said, "I can figure out your problem. You don't eat enough fish heads." Nadya did not check into (look into) his statement but asked, "Will you sell me some of them?" "Sure," said Schultz, "at a cost of only fifty cents each." So Nadya ate one of them on Monday, two of them on Wednesday, and three of them on Friday. She did not feel any smarter and was about to call off the attempt.

"You need to eat more heads of (from) these fish," said Schultz. Nadya reached into (for) her purse, took money out of it, and bought twenty fish heads. "That should last me until next week," she thought. The next week she pointed out to Schultz that he was selling fish heads to her for (at) fifty cents each, but he sold the whole fish for thirty cents. "See," he replied, "when you think over the matter, you are finally starting to get smart."

Page 263

Vocabulary Practice (Class Shifting):

Here are some of the many possible answers. If there is no such form in English, the word *none* is used.

	Negative	*Noun*	*Verb*	*Adjective*	*Adverb*
1.	inadvisable	advice	advise	advisory	advisedly
2.	(*none*)	beauty beautician beautifulness	beautify	beautiful beauteous	beautifully
3.	unimportable	importation importer importing	import	importable imported	Ø
4.	powerless	power	power empower	powerful	powerfully
5.	(*none*)	swimmer (a) swim	swim	swimming	swimmingly
6.	careless uncaring	care carefulness	care	careful caring	carefully
7.	sleepless	sleep	sleep	sleepy	sleepily
8.	unfriendly friendless	friend friendship	befriend	friendly	friendly
9.	illogic	logic logician	Ø (be logical)	logical	logically
10.	unman	man	to man	manlike mannish	manly mannishly
11.	hopeless	hope	hope	hopeful	hopefully
12.	uncritical	criticism critic	criticize	critical	critically
13.	Ø	slowness	slow	slow	slowly
14.	dreamless dreamlessness	dream dreamer	dream	dreamy dreamlike	dreamily dreamy
15.	Ø	ugliness	uglify (*rare*)	ugly	ugly

You may have used the *-ing* form of the verb as a noun (gerund). You may have written the verb in the infinitive form (*to care*). From 15 random words you have developed over 100.

Page 263

Vocabulary Practice (Meaning Changes):
Answers will vary.

Page 271

Sentence Practice (Subjects and Predicates):

      S   V
1. The alphabet/is one of the great human inventions.

     S   V
2. It/was developed over thousands of years.

              S   V
3. The English alphabet/has twenty-six letters.

         S   V
4. Other alphabets/have either more or fewer letters.

            S   V
5. The Hawaiian language/uses only twelve letters.

            S   V
6. The Armenian language/has thirty-eight letters.

     S   V
7. Alphabets, of course,/let people write.

     S   V
8. They/can write about what happened in the past.

                 S   V
9. Before the invention of the alphabet, all history/was oral.

     S   V
10. People/sang songs about the past.

        S   V
11. Now we/can write about history.

     S   V
12. Writing/helps us to remember.

        S   V
13. Most languages/have a written form.

        S   V
14. Not all languages/have writing, though.

        S   V
15. Many primitive people/still sing about their past.

Page 274

Sentence Practice (Phrases):

1. in the morning, to Chicago, on my motorcycle
2. about the country, in the summer
3. on the road, on my face, in my hair
4. around the country, with my friends, on motorcycles
5. in the rain, across hills, up mountains
6. A well-built motorcycle
7. A strong helmet, comfortable clothing
8. every motorcycle rider, a comfortable seat
9. people on motorcycles
10. A comfortable seat, easy-to-reach handlebars, handy footrest, anybody on a motorcycle
11. riding a motorcycle
12. to be (speeding down the road)
13. to ride a motorcycle, to take a risk
14. to ride safely
15. to learn how to ride, to practice every day

Page 278

Sentence Practice (Clauses):

1. who had just opened his office (*ADJ*)
2. that he was just starting (*N*)
3. Whenever a doctor starts (*ADV*)
4. that he had no patients the first few days (*N*)
5. When Friday came (*ADV*)
6. What he thought (*N*)
7. who will come for help (*ADJ*)
8. *no clause*
9. whoever came in first (*N*)
10. that he had no other patients (*N*)
11. so that he could be clearly heard (*ADV*)
12. that he was talking to another patient (*ADJ*)

13. When the man came in (*ADV*)
14. if there was anything wrong (*ADV*)
15. that he had just come to connect the telephone (*ADV*)

Page 294

Punctuation Practice (The Period):

The three motion pictures called the "Star Wars" movies have been the most successful of the last ten years. Part of their success, in earning millions of dollars, has been due to the interesting characters. There are normal human beings like Luke Skywalker, the Princess, and Han Solo. There are people who have strange powers, like Obie Wan Kenobie, Darth Vader, and the Emperor. There are robots or androids like C3PO and R2D2. But most interesting are the creatures from other worlds, like Chewbacca, Jabba the Hut, the Ewocks, and a dozen others. The last one of the series, called "The Return of the Jedi," brings the story to a conclusion that satisfies most people.

Page 294

Punctuation Practice (The Question Mark)

I wonder why people like science fiction. Do you ever wonder about it? Movies like "Star Wars" and the rest are popular. My friend, Pietro, asked me if I like it. He said, "Why do you go to see such silly things?" I questioned him about why he did not go. He answered, "I like reality. Isn't that stuff all make-believe?" I agreed but told him that it was just for entertainment and fun. "That's fun?" he said. "Does anybody really believe in strange creatures like robots and androids and fuzzy little men?" "Isn't it the excitement of pretending to fly around the stars?" I wanted to know. He did not agree.

Page 295

Punctuation Practice (Sentence Enders):
Answers will vary

Page 297

Punctuation Practice (The Comma):
1. There has been, according to crime reports, a decrease in crime rates.
2. To many people, crime is an evil that can be avoided.
3. Very few people really want to commit crimes.
4. *Correct.*
5. There is a saying, "Love of money is the cause of evil."

6. "Lack of money is the cause of evil," someone else said.

7. If all people were rich(,) and no one were hungry, stealing might stop.

8. Of course, crimes of violence are a different matter.

9. They are caused by emotion, for poverty does not make people kill.

10. If you want to help stop crime, write to Crime Stoppers, 9898 Belvue Road, San Fernando, California.

Page 299

Punctuation Practice (Colons and Semicolons):

1. book:	6. 7:00 . . . 12:00
2. French, and	7. adventure; . . . love;
3. languages:	8. sailor;
4. versions:	9. adventures;
5. sultan; . . . brother;	10. title;

Page 301

Punctuation Practice (Apostrophes):

1. dogs	6. neighbor's
2. It's	7. weekends
3. neighbor's	8. sister-in-law's
4. I've	9. dog's
5. two *z*'s	10. It's . . . fences . . . city's

Page 304

Punctuation Practice (Review of All Marks):

Answers will vary.

Index